The World's Number One, Flat-Out, All-Time Great, Stock Car Racing Book

Jerry
Bledsoe

Down Home Press, Asheboro, N.C.

ISBN 1-878086-36-7

THE RACER'S PRAYER by Bro. Bill Frazier
Copyright 1971 by Bro. Bill
Reprinted by permission of the author

Library of Congress Cataloging in Publication Data
Bledsoe, Jerry. The world's number one, flat-out, all-time
great, stock car racing book.
1. Automobile racing - United States - Miscellanea. 2.
Darlington Stock Car Race. I. Title. II. Title: Stock car racing
book.
GV1033.B53   796.7'2'0973

Cover Design: Tim Rickard

For Linda and Erik

Dome Home Press
P.O. Box 4126
Asheboro, North Carolina 27204

Contents

Introduction
to Anniversary
Edition

This book first appeared in time for the big race at Daytona in February of 1975. I was there, of course, brimming with excitement. It was my first book, and knowing nothing about the book business, I was sure that it was going to make me rich and famous.

Playboy was going to review it, I'd been told, and the *New York Times* had excerpted a section of it in their Sunday sports section. When I got to Daytona, I looked up Ken Squier, the CBS announcer whom I'd gotten to know while researching the book, and he interviewed me on a national radio show broadcast from a hotel bar on the beach.

I was not content, though, to wait for my book to leap off the shelves of bookstores. I had driven to Daytona in my Volkswagen camper, which was packed with thousands of handbills that I'd had printed. Two friends, Bill Lee and Macon Short, had come with me, and during the days before the race, we put those handbills in the lobbies of almost every hotel on the beach. On race day, wearing t-shirts on which a boardwalk artist had attempted to repli-cate the book's cover, we spread out through the parking lot of the race track, affixing handbills to every car windshield. During the race, we handed them out in the infield and taped long rows of them above the urinal troughs in the men's rooms.

An order form appeared at the bottom of each handbill, and I could barely contain my excitement when I returned to one men's room to check on the supply and saw that the order form had been carefully torn from one.

My excitement diminished daily, however, after I returned home and discovered that only a few orders were trickling in. The grand total turned out to be 11, not enough to even begin to pay for the handbills. That was not the worst of my surprises, however. I had worked out a deal with the track at Rockingham, North Carolina, to allow me to sell my books at the third race of the season. The track provided me a tent, tables and chairs. We were to split the profits. There I sat for two full days without selling a single copy. So much for my dreams of riches and fame.

In the end, the book brought in almost enough money (primarily, I suspect, from library sales) to pay for the expenses I incurred during the year and a half that I spent on the racing circuit researching it. The two and a half years of work that I'd put into it were for nought.

I used to say that writing this book was not one of the smarter things I'd ever done. "What I realized too late," I'd tell audiences to an appreciative chuckle, "was that people who are interested in stock car racing don't read, and people who read aren't interested in stock car racing."

So why, you may be wondering, have I bothered to bring this book back 20 years after its dismal first appearance?

Well, it was well received by critics, several of whom said that it lived up to its title. A couple called it a classic work on the subject, and to be a classic, it has to stay around, right?

For another thing, after I had written other books, some of which even sold enough copies to make writing them profitable, people kept asking where they could get my first book. I had to tell them that I didn't know. I only had a couple of copies myself.

Now and then, a letter would arrive from a rare book dealer saying that he had a customer willing to pay as much as $50 for a copy. The day that a fellow appeared at an autographing with a copy for me to sign an i said that he'd bought it at a bargain -- only $85, nearly 10 times its original price -- I realized that I'd made a mistake in not buying a few hundred copies to keep when I'd had the chance.

People willing to pay exaggerated prices for a book are collectors, of course, usually more interested in the book itself than its contents. But some of the people who asked about the book were readers who were curious about stock car racing, or at least willing to read about it, and many were serious race fans who had heard about the book some way or another and wanted to read it.

When I set out to learn about stock car racing in the week before Labor Day, 1972, Darrell Waltrip was preparing to run for rookie of the year. Kyle Petty and the late Davey Allison were kids hanging around the pits with their famous fathers. Dale Earnhardt was working for an insulation company and only dreaming of racing.

Stock car racing has become far more competitive and sophisticated since then, its audience spreading not only throughout our culture but throughout the world on satellite TV. A huge market has grown for racing collectibles. And a great many race fans now buy and read books about racing.

But why should they want to read a book about racing that first appeared 20 years ago?

I could use the old argument that we can't appreciate the present without understanding the past, of course, and while that certainly is true, it isn't the only justification.

Despite all the changes in stock car racing in the past 20

years, its heart and soul - the spectacle; the speed; the raw nerve, the skill, the courage required of the drivers; the love of cars that inspires it all - have remained constant, and that is what I set out to capture in this book, hoping to make it as valid tomorrow as today. Whether or not I succeeded, I leave to you.

Jerry Bledsoe
Asheboro, N.C.
January, 1995

Foreword

Cruising the Milky Way

For us it was the Milky Way. That sounds a little high-flown, I know. The Milky Way was just a drive-in out on the edge of town. It had always been there on the National Highway, as far as I knew, occupying a couple of different buildings as I was growing up. At first it was a place where my parents would sometimes take my brothers and me for an ice cream cone on a Sunday afternoon. But by the time I had entered my teens, it was another thing altogether, a far more important thing. By then the Milky Way was in a big new brick building with plate-glass windows, and it sat in the corner of a big parking lot that had been tarred and graveled and somehow still managed to stay full of potholes.

That parking lot was the center of our social life. Thomasville was like all other little towns; it just happened to be in North Carolina. There wasn't much to do. Oh, Bill Price ran a skating rink out on the Lexington Highway where we would sometimes check by to see if there were any good-looking girls in those scanty skating skirts, but skating seemed childish. And Spud Stoker had a dank, ratty theater uptown where we had gone as kids to watch Saturday cowboy movies and Flash Gordon serials, but nobody went there any more. There was a drive-in theater out on the High Point Road called the Midway, it being halfway to High Point; but it was more often

called the "Passion Pit," although I certainly had never found
any passion there, nor to my knowledge had any of my friends,
despite our mighty straining to make everybody believe that we
had known some nights of glory at the Midway.

No, none of those places really had anything to do with our
lives. Our place was the Milky Way, and we spent most of our
idle hours there, sitting in cars in the parking lot, or riding
slowly through, circling the Milky Way maybe fifteen or twenty
times in a night, cruising, checking to see who was there and
what was going on. If you had a car that was any good at all,
and there weren't any cops in attendance, you were expected
to announce your departure each time by "layin' rubber," or
"gittin' one," or "scratchin' off"—all of which were one and
the same and simply meant making the rear tires squeal on
takeoff—and if you did it properly, you usually could expect the
feat to be acclaimed by a shout of "GIT ON IT!" from the
parking lot, and you could smile a smile of genuine accom-
plishment and satisfaction.

Those were the years that the golden-oldie deejays now call
the "Fabulous Fifties" and pine about a lot. We wore penny
loafers with white socks, pegged pants with scalloped pockets,
and shirts with the collars turned up. We coated our hair with
oily tonic and combed it into a "duck's ass," which we called a
"DA" in polite company. We carried in our billfolds a package
of two-for-a-quarter rubbers (this being double optimism) pur-
chased in the Milky Way john from a machine that had a little
decal on it that said, "Sold only for the prevention of disease,"
a message that had been altered by some wit with a ball-point
pen who had marked through "disease" and scribbled "babies"
above it. We talked a lot about a certain waitress in town who
was supposed to "do it" with just about anybody. The girls
wore calf-length skirts and bobby socks, and they all creamed
over Elvis. Unfortunately, they never "did it," at least to my
knowledge.

The most important thing in our lives then was the car. We
lived for the day when we would turn sixteen and could get our

driver licenses. Then we lived for the day when we could get our own cars. We were probably the first generation of youth to know the full joy and freedom of owning our own cars, and we were convinced that the only reason people lived and worked was to be able to have a nice car to ride around in.

Any car would do in the beginning, of course, but everybody wanted a "nice" car. That meant a car that looked good and ran fast. We spent a lot of time on those cars, always washing, waxing, tinkering, doing little things to fix them up, make them "sharp." Sharp cars were equipped with four-barrel carburetors and "Hollywood" mufflers. They had a lot of chrome and were further decorated with "STP" and "Wynn's Friction Proofing" racing decals on rear side windows. The little shelf under the rear window was for plastic-covered pillows, two-toned, like the cars, and with "Ford" or "Chevrolet" or "Plymouth" printed across them. Front bumpers sported custom-painted license plates bearing nicknames or girls' names. Fender skirts were required, and if you had real class you put little blue lights beneath them to reflect off the whitewalls. But ornate hood ornaments; Continental kits; jeweled mud flaps; red, white, and blue foxtails flying from radio antennae—these were scorned as "niggerish."

We sat at the Milky Way in those beautiful cars, and we talked, talked about girls who "did it" and about . . . cars! Fast cars. Racing cars. Stock car racing was becoming a big thing by then, and we spent hours debating the relative merits of Fords, Chevrolets, Plymouths, Oldsmobiles, and the driving styles of Fireball Roberts and Buck Baker and Lee Petty, who lived just over the road. And even if you were like me and had no real interest in such matters, you feigned it, and worried that maybe something was seriously wrong with you because of it.

And even if, like me, the fastest car you'd ever owned was a '53 Plymouth ("Why in hell don't you git rid of that goddamn Mayflower, Bledsoe, and git something that'll run?") that coughed and wheezed and suffered a total nervous collapse every time it was nudged beyond the city limits, shimmying until it rattled your teeth if you tried to push it past forty, you still were expected to prove yourself. . . .

Out on the super! Down on the Cunningham Brick Yard road! Just like Buck Baker! Fireball Roberts! Lee Petty! Running hard with . . . Larry Deaton! He was tall and skinny with bad teeth and a bad complexion, and his '55 black-and-white Ford would really run. "That ol' boy's got a lead foot," they all said of Larry Deaton. And Doug Dunning! He was a wild man with his daddy's new Dodges. Everybody said he'd get himself killed before he was twenty (he fooled them by a few years). Wild! Lord, yes! Wild! Careening through the night in the back seat of Doug Dunning's Dodge, four or five of us sometimes, all feeling the fear and exhilaration of running some ol' boys from down Denton who'd had the gall to cruise through the Milky Way and challenge Doug Dunning. *Goddamn! RED LIGHTS!!!!! The law! Get the fuck out of here! Oh, shit! Fleeing down the super with the state cops closing in, watching that speedometer . . . ninety-five . . . one hundred . . . goddamn! one hundred and ten! Skidding onto back roads, tires squealing, running with the lights off. . . . Goddamn, Doug, you're goina kill us all!*

And sometimes it happened, of course. Somebody would miss a curve and crash. The night would be rent with sirens and flashing red lights, and crowds would materialize from nowhere to gawk at blood and broken glass in flashlight rays. The kid who sat next to me in junior-year homeroom got it that way one Friday night.

The car was towed into town to the Studebaker place at Slimey Corner, where all the bad wrecks were taken, and parked out back under the trees, set apart from the rusting hulks of past wrecks, because for a time this one would be an attraction. I went to see it with a few of my buddies the morning after it happened. A little clump of people was standing around it. A kid who looked to be about eleven was eagerly pointing out the bloodstains to new arrivals.

"That right there's part of his brains," the kid said.

"Busted his head open like a punkin," a man told us.

"Really wracked it up, didn't he?" said one of my friends. "He must've really been movin'."

"They said he wudn't doin' but about ninety," somebody said.

"Who was he runnin'?"

"They ain't sure. Somebody said they thought it was one of them boys from down Silver Valley. They ain't caught nobody."

Thomasville hasn't changed much since then. Some cosmetic changes, of course. But the heart and soul are the same. The reigning Finch family has sold its furniture dynasty to some big conglomerate. There's a new hospital and an underpass finally for the mainline railroad tracks that divide the town. Big furniture showrooms are spreading over my old neighborhood. The Studebaker place has been long out of business, and the bad wrecks are taken someplace else now; I don't know where. The Milky Way no longer exists. The building stood vacant for a long time after it went out of business, then served a stint as a paint store. It is Wahoo's Fine Foods now, and there is no curb service and it is not open at nights, so the kids must gather at some other place. They try to gather at a new hamburger joint in the center of town that does not welcome their company. Sometimes they sit around in the parking lot of the big new shopping center south of town, but the cops harass them there.

The kids don't seem to have changed much either. They have nicer and newer cars than we did, in fresh fruit colors, and they look a lot like racing cars. They have racing stripes, air scoops on the hood with the engine sizes written on them, and "spoilers" on the back. Brand names are spelled out in big letters on rear fenders. They have exhaust pipes that come out the side, super-light wheels, and wide racing tires. The rear ends are jacked up so that the cars resemble baboons walking. And on the rear side windows they have decals that say "STP" and "Wynn's Friction Proofing."

And in the country, where I live now, I hear those cars late at night, the powerful engines roaring, winding out in every gear, as the young men (and women) inside race toward adulthood.

I bring all of this up for one reason: It is on this foundation that stock car racing is built.

Prologue

Welcome to Darlington

THE HEAT was becoming more oppressive by the minute. By noon the temperature had already swept past ninety, and it showed no sign of stopping short of a hundred. Not that it wasn't expected. It was always this hot in early September in the South Carolina lowlands, and people who came to the race knew it, for most of them had been before. That was part of it, the heat, the glaring sun, the sweating, the overwhelming need to replace lost liquids. It wouldn't be Darlington without it.

Darlington! The name is almost sacred to people who love stock car racing. It is spoken reverently throughout the South. Darlington was the first "superspeedway" for stock cars, and its Southern 500 was the first of the big stock car races. Sportswriters always call it the "granddaddy of them all." Before the racetrack came and made it famous, Darlington was just a small farmtown surrounded by long flat fields of cotton, corn, and peanuts. And racing wasn't allowed on Sunday, which was why the Southern 500 was always held on Labor Day. Except on this one weekend a year, Darlington remained much the same as it had always been, but on Labor Day weekend it became much more, a celebration of . . . what? Of American life as it had evolved in the 1970s?

Axlegrease! Why was I thinking such crap? The heat probably. I couldn't help myself. There is a tendency to look for

some significance amid all this senselessness. I should have been
at Myrtle Beach, just seventy-five miles away, sitting in the
shade watching bikinis. But this—here it was a full twenty-four
hours before the race, and there were thousands and thousands
of people crowded around the Darlington Raceway, wandering
idly in the sun, looking for some way to escape the boredom
while they waited to get inside, where the sun would be just as
hot and there would be even less to do. Outside, at least, there
was a country band playing for tips under the scraggly trees behind the grandstand, and the armed forces had set up recruiting
exhibits, and if that was not your idea of entertainment, there
were the souvenir stands, and a Winston Cup car stood available for inspection. And, of course, there was the Little Joe
Weatherly Stock Car Museum, entry to which I was waiting for
somewhat impatiently in a very long line under the very hot
sun. Not that I was so eager to get inside to see Little Joe's '64
Mercury, or Buck Baker's '50 Olds, or Herb Thomas's '51 Hudson, or Junior Johnson's famed No. 3 Chevrolet that all of those
factory-backed Fords chased with so much frustration back in
'63. But the place was *air-conditioned*. And outside the beer
kept getting hot, you see. That was the problem. You could
take a beer out of the cooler, pop the top, and before you could
get down a couple of good swallows, it would be hot already. I
can't stand hot beer, and I couldn't see how life could be sus-
tained in this heat without beer. A fellow to whom I was con-
fiding this problem a short time earlier had told me that at the
souvenir stand in the museum, I could buy a Styrofoam beer-can
cup that would keep a can of beer cold in hell. That seemed as
close to fulfilling my immediate requirements as could reason-
ably be expected, so I was waiting in the line.

    The line moved agonizingly slowly. A guard had been posted
at the door, and he would only allow a person to enter after another had left. Once in the air conditioning, of course, nobody
was in any great hurry to leave. But I had determined to wait
until I got in—or was carried away with heat stroke. I was that
desperate.

"What'd you do with *that?*" somebody said in the line behind me.

It was a guy who looked to be in his twenties, barefoot and shirtless, drinking a Blue Ribbon from the can. He was talking to a buddy, a young man in a state of attire similar to his own, and they were both grinning and leering at a racetrack queen, a Winston Cup girl, who was standing on the pavement a few feet away smiling politely and trying valiantly, despite the heat, to keep up a good company image. "Now, just what would you do with *that?*"

"Shit fire, what *wouldn't* I do?"

They both laughed uproariously.

The Winston Cup girl pretended not to notice. She was tall and blond and had a long, angular, and very pretty face. She was wearing hot pants and a floppy hat with "Winston" printed all over it. Tight white boots stretched almost to the knees of her long brown legs. She was fortunate not to be representing a deodorant company, for there were big sweat rings under the arms of her bright red body suit.

"A woman't sweats like 'at's bound to be hot," said the guy with the Blue Ribbon, and he and his buddy laughed again.

The girl's assignment was to stand beside the Winston Cup car, a Chevrolet Monte Carlo built by Junior Johnson, a one-time driver who is usually called "the legendary Junior Johnson" in stock car racing circles, or sometimes, "the lead-footed chicken farmer from Rhonda," Rhonda being the little community in Wilkes County, North Carolina, where Junior was from. After cigarette advertising was banned on television, the R. J. Reynolds Tobacco Company started pumping a lot of money into stock car racing so that anytime stock car racing was on TV or radio or written about in newspapers and magazines, people would see and hear and read about Winston cigarettes. This car with its leggy blond companion was just another way of selling cigarettes. The car was painted red and white, the Winston colors, and it was sitting on a trailer with its hood up. The car's vital statistics were painted on the side: "427 C.I., 600 H.P., 850 series carburetor, CM High Riser Intake, Bore

4.750, Stroke 3.760, Compression 12.5 to 1, 200 M.P.H. plus."
The car was attracting a steady flow of people, who stood brooding and nodding and whispering over it, seemingly understanding all of that gibberish on the side. I had inspected the car myself a short time before.

"Look at that," some guy had said to me, laughing, pointing at the little sign on the air breather that said, "Made in Rhonda." "Made in Rhonda. Ain't that somethin'?"

Four people had come out of the museum, grudgingly, looking as if they had been pushed, and the line moved forward a few paces. The man ahead of me in line was wearing a blue service-station suit, no doubt to impress people that he was a man knowledgeable about cars and racing. His name, Ed, was stitched above his shirt pocket in red thread. His teeth were yellow, and his deeply wrinkled, leathery skin lay in rolls on the back of his neck. He was talking to a man with a big belly who had a pack of Lucky Strikes showing through the pocket of his white sport shirt. They were talking about Junior Johnson.

"What year was it he won the pole?" Big Belly was asking.

"Sixty-five, wudn't it?" said Yellow Teeth. "It was the race where Buren Skeen got killed."

"Yeah, I believe you right. Who won that year?"

"Ned Jarrett, I believe."

"You know, I wisht ol' Junior hada won that 500 one time."

"He won the 300 'at year."

After what seemed to be an interminable period of this, I finally made it into the museum, where I browsed through the exhibits, enjoying the coolness with some excited fans ("Look, mama, it's Richard's car!). The souvenir stand was jammed with customers thumbing through the colorful striped racing jackets (no true fan is without one); the eight-by-ten color photos of Buddy Baker, Richard Petty, and Bobby Allison; postcards featuring favorite cars; T-shirts with the likenesses of popular drivers and their cars pressed into the fabric; records about Fireball Roberts and Little Joe Weatherly; books and magazines about racing; ashtrays with "Souvenir of Darlington" printed on them; Confederate flags, and all the other junk. I finally got my beer cup and headed reluctantly back out into the heat.

My Volkswagen van was already inside the track, parked in the infield with press privilege, and that was where I headed. The beer was there. Except for a very few cars belonging to people employed at the track, the infield was empty. But within a few hours it would be transformed into a gypsy city of more than thirty-five thousand people and thousands of vehicles. The gates were to open shortly, at one o'clock, nearly a full day before the start of the race. This happened at no other track, but at Darlington it was tradition, dating from the early days when thousands of people would arrive a day early for the race. There being no place to house them in the small town, the track had allowed them to camp in the infield. It had evolved into an annual party, the biggest, wildest, whoopingest, holleringest, drinkingest, gamblingest, carousingest, knock-down, fall-out blowout held in the South. A lot of people came to Darlington more for the infield party than for the race, as was always evident on race day, when they would be stretched out somewhere sleeping as the cars roared around the track.

The notoriety of the Darlington infield had spread far, and people who had never spent a night there could tell you stories about it.

"If you want to get you a little," one fellow had whispered to me confidentially, "look for a hearse. The whores always set up in hearses."

I had heard the whore hearse story several times. Also the one about the ol' gal who pulled a Lady Godiva act on a motorcycle, making several turns through the infield, with her husband, several cops, and a gaggle of admirers in pursuit, before she whipped out onto the track for a lap, then disappeared through the gate, never to be seen again.

Many of these stories had come from the fertile mind of Bob Colvin, a humorous, imaginative man, who until his death promoted the races at Darlington. He spread the stories with the help of sportswriters, and the stories were told over and over each year. People seemed to need to believe them.

There were stories told about the infield that were true, of course, stories of fights, brawls, cuttings, although these, too, were usually exaggerated. Still, the potential for violence always lurked about the infield, and the sense of danger was part of its appeal.

"I wouldn't spend a night in that infield for a thousand dollars."

I must have heard that line twenty times or more when I had mentioned my intention to do just that.

"I just want to see what it's like," I'd reply.

One guy, a sportswriter, shrugged and said, "Well, it's your ass."

They were believing their own stories now.

All of this caused a delicious air of anticipation, a sense of embarking on an exciting adventure among the crowds waiting now to get inside the track. Some of them had established their positions at the gate nearly two days earlier, and the long wait added to the anticipation. They had come, lugging all the accouterments of middle-America life, in cars with tents strapped on top, or pulling trailers; in pickup trucks with makeshift covers and expensive campers on the back; on motorcycles; in twenty-thousand-dollar "motor homes"; and in big U-rent trucks, with full-size beds, dining room tables, sofas, and easy chairs in the back. And now they were ready for the party to start.

I took a quick, refreshing gulp of cold beer before I plopped it into my newly acquired beer-can cooler, which had pictures of race cars printed on it in red and blue. Thus replenished, I walked across the infield and through the tunnel under the second turn to check on the crowds on the back side of the track. I dutifully noted that the cars and trucks were lined up two abreast at the gate, the first two in line being pickup trucks, one an old black Chevrolet with a homemade cover on the bed, the other a new green-and-white Ford with a plywood viewing platform on the back. The vehicles were empty, the people having sought shade under nearby trees, where they rested on blankets and folding lawn-chairs. A Charley Pride song blared loudly from somebody's stereo tape player.

"Hot enough for ye?" said the gate guard. He was standing just inside the locked gates, drinking ice water from a jar he had just taken from a plastic ice chest in the trunk of his car.

"Sure is."

Some kids were throwing paper planes outside the fence, and one of the kids came over and called out to the guard.

"You goina open the gate, mister?"

"'Bout to," he said, wiping the water from his mouth and placing the jar back in the ice chest. "Won't be long now."

I went back across the infield to the pit row gate near the first turn. In a nearby corner of the infield, a large group of cops, probably more than a hundred, had gathered in the sun, sweltering in their uniforms, getting final instructions before the wild hordes outside the gates descended on them. They had been recruited from police departments and sheriffs' offices in nearby towns and counties, and they were being paid by the track to represent law and order in the infield for the next thirty hours. Their main job would be to insure that full-scale rioting didn't break out, but they would spend a lot of time wrestling with unruly drunks and breaking up fights.

I slipped into the sliver of shade on one side of a little white cement block building where a fat boy had pressed himself tightly against the wall in an effort to avoid the sun. The building where we were seeking refuge, I was to learn later, had been constructed as a jail for the infield crowd but had been largely unsuccessful for this purpose due to a tendency among some of the detainees to express their displeasure about the accommodations by tearing out the windows and even bashing out the block walls so that they might go to find facilities more to their liking. Eventually the building was converted to storage. The fat boy was sweating profusely. He had red hair, his fair skin was freckled, and his T-shirt was wet with sweat. He worked at a service station in Hartsville, and each year he volunteered to work at the track so that he could see the race for free and hang out with racing people. His job was to stand at the pit row gate

and insure that once the wild horde was safely inside the infield, nobody escaped, or tore down the fences, or made off with
any race cars. He would have help with this assignment, but his
help had not yet reported for duty.

"Not much shade, is it?" I ventured.

"Better'n nothin'," he said. "I can't take 'at sun. I git blistered."

"Noxzemer's good for that," offered a maintenance man who
had just come to the little building to pick up some equipment
and was taking a break in the shade.

"Don't help me none."

"That your car?" I said to the fat boy, nodding toward a new
Dodge Charger, apple red and glistening with fresh polish, that
was parked by the gate.

"Mine'n the bank's."

"Nice-looking car. What'll she do?"

"I ain't had 'er but a hunnerd'n ten. She'll do more'n 'at."

I whistled.

"Who you pulling for?" I asked.

"In the race?"

"Yeah."

"Isaac."

Bobby Isaac, one of the superstars, would be starting his red
Dodge in seventh position.

I nodded.

"I'd sure like to see a Dodge git it," the fat boy said.

His help had arrived now, a short little guy in horn-rimmed
glasses with narrow shoulders and hairy arms. His auxiliary deputy sheriff's uniform—khaki shirt, and green trousers with a
stripe down the side—looked new and was a little too large. He
was loud and obviously impressed with the authority the uniform gave him, and he reminded me of Barney Fife on the old
Andy Griffith TV show. He exchanged greetings with the fat
boy, and the fat boy asked him, "You git to talk to Ellie Mae?"

He was talking about Ellie Mae Clampett of the old "Beverly
Hillbillies" TV show, who is in real life Donna Douglas, a blond
actress from Louisiana. She was the race celebrity this year, and

the day before had ridden in the big Southern 500 parade and taken part in the Miss Southern 500 beauty pageant at the track that night.

"Yeah," said Barney Fife, hitching up his belt. "I got to talk to 'er last night."

The fat boy grinned. "She give ye any sugar?"

"Naw. She had a husband wouldn't git three feet away from 'er. I don't keer where she went, he'd be right there. Well, I don't blame 'im. He's prob'ly heard about these *southern* gentlemen." They laughed.

The subject turned to the people waiting to get inside, and I let it be known that I was planning to spend the night in the infield.

"I wouldn't stay out there tonight if they give me this racetrack," said Barney Fife.

"What goes on out there?" I asked.

"I don't mean to be smart, but what you ought to ask me is what *don't* go on out there."

"Okay, what don't go on?"

"Nothin'. They ain't nothin' don't go on out there. Shoot, I tell you, they ain't no way I'd bring my wife and kids out here in this infield the way some of these people do. No way. You take Labor Day '70, we had a bunch of Indians from up Pembroke down here. They'd just come up and cut you and leave you standin' there. Cut sixteen. One ol' boy, they had to take a hunderd and sixty-four stitches in 'im."

"Well," I said, "I guess I'll just have to see what happens."

"If you keerful, if you watch yourself, if you don't go lookin' for no trouble, you'll prob'ly be all right, but if you lookin' for a fight, you won't have to look far."

"I'm not looking for a fight," I said. "I just want to see what happens."

He grinned.

"Some ol' boy might git to feelin' good and shoot up in the air a few times," he said. "Don't pay no 'tention to that."

Then he seemed to grow reflective for a moment.

"You know," he said, "these ain't roughnecks, or gangsters,

or rebel rousers, most of 'em. They just ordinary American people. But you git 'em out here like this and about half of 'em drunk and you better watch out."

The gates had opened. The first vehicle to come bouncing across the bank of the track, headed for the infield, was an old bread truck, painted white, that had been converted to a camper. Inside were several young men, shirts off, drinking beer, feet propped up, and as the truck neared the gate where we were standing, one of the young men let loose with a wild, curdling "rebel" yell that must have startled birds in the adjoining county. A beer can sailed out of the back of the truck and clattered across the track.

"Well, boys," said Barney Fife, "she's on."

The truck raced across the infield and parked. The young men got out, and the first thing they did was to erect a thirty-foot pole and hoist a big Confederate flag.

The
Southernization
of America

IF THIS BOOK were unfolding as planned, we would now be getting on with the big race at Darlington. This was supposed to be a simple book, you see. It just isn't going to be as simple as I thought. I do have reasons for this interruption, though. I'm sure you will understand.

I think that what I had better do is tell you a little about how this book came about in the first place. The truth is that until I started working on it, I'd never given any thought to writing it—or any other book, for that matter. Well, that isn't exactly true. I *had* entertained the *idea* of writing books, of being an *author* and getting on the "Tonight Show" and making lots of money and being pursued by beautiful women and having all of my old friends say, "And I never thought he'd amount to a hill of beans," and that sort of thing. But the actual writing of a book was another thing altogether.

So then one day I am just sitting around doing nothing in particular when the telephone rings and there is this book editor on the line, and he is asking me—*me*—if I have any ideas for books. Now, if there is any thing that any writer, or aspiring writer, or person who has deluded himself into thinking he is a writer, wants to avoid, it is being caught without a well-rounded set of ideas, of subjects that he is just itching to write about given the proper opportunity. So here I am with a real live book editor from New York on the line—my big break, as it were—and my head is as empty as a Nixon pronouncement on morality. Totally blank.

"Uh," I said, as my mind darted into dark, closed-off hallways, frantically feeling for light switches.

"I, uh . . ."

And suddenly I heard this total stranger speaking in my voice:

"Well, I always wanted to write a book about stock car racing."

Stock car racing! Ridiculous. An absolute lie. I never wanted to do any such thing. In my whole life I had been to but four stock car races, once in high school just to be going along with the crowd, another time when my cousin Charles risked his fool neck by entering a jalopy in one of the amateur Saturday night races at Bowman Gray Stadium, and twice on newspaper assignments (although one of those was rained out). I simply had no interest in such doings, despite having grown up in a southern car culture in which any male over the age of fourteen who did not have an intimate relationship with the workings of the internal-combustion engine was considered at least a touch queer, if not a total fruit. To me a car was just a means of getting from one place to another, nothing more. That people would want to put them on tracks to see which would go fastest and last longest was a waste of time and resources, not to mention dangerous.

So why had I blurted out that lie? Was it that I was so eager to be able to say that I was "working on a book" that I would say anything? But why *this* subject? Why not something appealing, like hootchie-kootchie dancing? Of course, stock car racing *is* a "southern" subject, and I was aware that a writer who lives in the South is more apt to be considered favorably by New York editors if he picks southern subjects, probably because past southern writers had been so successful in creating in the minds of Yankee editors an image of the South as a mysterious and exotic land apart, which it may have been. Anyway, southern writers were set apart (when I was first becoming acquainted with a few New York editors, one of the first questions I was asked was, "Do you consider yourself a southern writer?," and I really didn't know what to say), and all of them were expected to have something important to say about their sultry homeland. I had a definite problem in this area, as I didn't have anything much that I really wanted to say about the South —although I will admit to a long-harbored secret desire to write something about it that didn't contain the term "good ole boy."

There was one thing, I guess, that I wanted to say, hardly profound, though, a thing that I had noticed in recent years while so many southern intellectuals were running around wringing their hands and holding one seminar after another to fret about how the South was "losing its identity." It had seemed to me, in traveling around the country, that while the South certainly was changing, homogenizing with the rest of the country, it was not so much that the South was becoming like the rest as that in the important thing—the soul—the rest of the country was becoming more South-like. Or maybe it had really been that way all along. I had thought about this in terms of maybe an article called "The Southernization of America," a title that I thought had a nice ring to it, which I never got around to writing.

This wasn't an easy thing to pin down, of course, more a feeling than anything else, but there seemed to be ample evidence to support it. All those Yankees howling to the heavens when they had to integrate *their* schools and bus *their* kids. Hell, nobody wanted the blacks around, not too close anyway, not unless they were willing to be niggers. And look at the rise to national respectability of the old racist, George Wallace. As a leader, who did we have but Richard Nixon with his "southern strategy," and what were his politics but the mean and corrupt politics of the Old South? In matters spiritual, we had the ascension of Billy Graham, a lacquered and polished old-time southern tent show evangelist, to the exalted position of America's foremost religious leader. It seemed the South had launched an all-out invasion of the nation's culture. Consider the remarkable rise nationwide in the popularity of country music, southern-bred—all those twangy-voiced ol' boys and girls singing about cheatin' and honky-tonkin' and hard times and truck driving and people getting killed in car wrecks. That stuff was being played twenty-four hours a day on radio stations all across the country (nearly a thousand all-country stations in 1974), and you could get regular fixes on prime time TV.

I suppose you could even point to stock car racing, the only big-time sport to come out of the South, as part of the evidence. You could see a Saturday night stock car race in almost any state in the country now, and those old lead-footed country boys from North Carolina and Tennessee and other points south who had made the big time were going to Michigan and California and Texas to race on new "superspeedways" that had been built for them (they were even holding "Richard Petty Day" in places like Rochester, New York, for godsakes), and all the big races could be seen now live on network TV. (To digress for a moment here, it should be pointed out that stock car racing and country music had a lot in common. They had been created out of isolation and rejection by southern working-class whites—rednecks, as the intellectuals had tagged them. This sport, this music provided not only entertainment and a means of expression, but a dream as well. Vast numbers of southern boys dreamed of going off to Nashville to be on the "Grand Ole Opry" and drive Cadillacs and wear sequined suits, or of driving at Darlington and Daytona and knowing the joy of victory and getting the kisses from the bosomy, leggy race track queens. In this there was hope. You could be poor and uneducated and scorned by society, but if you could learn to pick a guitar or drive a car, you just might luck out and find that glory, that pot of gold at Darlington or Nashville. David Pearson had done it. So had Johnny Cash. Maybe anybody could.)

As I said, hardly profound. Maybe even wrong. Hell, I don't know. It isn't important. The thing is that it wouldn't make a lot of sense to go to all the trouble of writing a whole book on stock car racing just to say a little thing like that, which shouldn't even be in a stock car racing book to begin with.

No, I don't know why I said I wanted to write a book about

stock car racing. I doubt that I'll ever know, and it's probably best now that I don't find out. I said it. That's it. And this editor said he thought it sounded like a very good idea, and would I sit down and write out a proposal, a plan for the book? So I did it that afternoon, wrote everything I thought I knew about stock car racing, which turned out to be a page of misinformation mostly.

But they bought the damned thing.

So the first thing I knew, I was wandering around the Darlington Raceway feeling conspicuously ignorant and out of place. I couldn't even understand half the language being spoken in the garage, and the part I did catch would have been quickly erased by a gigantic transistorized fully-automatic expletive deleter if it had been spoken in the White House.

It did not take me long to see that I was going to have trouble. The plan for the book was very simple. I was going to tell "the story" of stock car racing through one race, the most colorful race of them all: the Southern 500.

I knew, of course, that I couldn't just spend a week at Darlington and write a book. Nothing is that easy. It would take research, follow-up interviews, that sort of thing. I figured three months would do it. That first week, though, was enough to give me some idea of how much I didn't know, which was considerable, and I thought the best thing for me to do was to go to more races, which I did. The season ended, a new one began, and I kept going to races. First thing I knew I was back at Darlington at the Southern 500 again. This year of traipsing around the country behind race cars, of hanging around tracks, watching and listening, talking to drivers, mechanics, fans, race queens, sportswriters, racing officials, promoters, hangers-on, and assorted other track characters convinced me that the simple plan for my book was shot. It would be impossible for me to tell all I wanted to tell about stock car racing through one race. There was just too much to tell. It was too big. It had surprised me in the beginning to learn that automobile racing, in all its forms, was second only to horse racing as the most popular spectator sport in the nation. It had surprised me to learn that more than forty million tickets to stock car races were sold every year in this country, 80 per cent of those at small tracks in little towns where local boys run. Stock car racing had replaced baseball as the sport of the people. I wanted to write about that, to write about some of the characters I had bumped into, about the past and some of the old-timers. I wanted to write about the danger, about the pain of losing a husband, father, son to stock car racing, about all sorts of things that I couldn't do by writing about just one race.

So that is why I am not writing the short and simple book I planned. We will get back to Darlington, but I simply *have* to stuff all this other stuff in somewhere, and this seems as good a place to start stuffing as any.

Stuffings, Part 1

The Rough and Rowdy Past

Moonshine Heritage

It HAD BEEN nearly a decade since superjournalist Tom Wolfe had discovered stock car racing and Junior Johnson and done them up in grand style for *Esquire* in an article entitled "The Last American Hero Is Junior Johnson. Yes!" And here now in the late spring of 1973 was the result of it.

Junior Johnson stood outside a theater in Charlotte, North Carolina, with his wife Flossie, she elegantly gowned, and Junior himself turned out in a stunning, flowery Hollywood-style outfit that would be certain to turn heads back at home in Wilkes County, and people kept coming up to Junior and saying, "That was good, Junior, I really enjoyed that."

"I enjoyed it more this time than I did the first time I seen it," Junior said. "I tell you, if you'd knowed my daddy, that couldn't've been no more like 'im. Now he had his ways, but that was just the way he was."

The occasion was the first public showing—the worldwide premier, as it were—of a new movie called *The Last American Hero*, which made the claim of having been based on Wolfe's excellent article, although the connection, except for the title, is indeed hard to find. The movie is about a North Carolina mountain boy who quit hauling his daddy's moonshine likker to become a hard-charging stock car racer. That was Junior Johnson's story essentially. But the movie people had changed things around considerably, as they are so apt to do, fictionalizing Junior's life. The hero of the movie is renamed Junior Jackson, and the action is set in the present. Junior Jackson's daddy took great pride in the likker he made, and Junior hauled it in his new black Mustang, which he tinkered with a lot so that it would go fast. When Junior's daddy got caught and went off to jail, telling his boys to get out of the likker business, Junior went racing. He drove in demolition derbies, and in no time at all he was a top-running stock car driver.

Well, people in the South who knew anything about racing and moonshining knew it just didn't happen that way. Moonshining had all but vanished as a family trade in the hills; certainly nobody took any pride in making what is now called "sellin' likker" any more. And all those old mountain boys who might have been hauling likker twenty or thirty years ago were now busy building condominiums for the tourists, or else they had gone off seeking bright lights and excitement in Detroit, or Los Angeles, or someplace. They didn't even hold demolition derbies in the South—that being a savage peculiarity of the North and of Southern California, wherein drivers in old jalopies battered one another until only one was left—and no aspiring or self-respecting stock car racer would ever be caught near one. And everybody knew, too, that nobody starts into stock car racing and goes right to the top. It takes a lot of time, effort, and money. The movie didn't do particularly well in the South, where the company had obviously been hoping to make a bundle. Many of those who went to see it came away talking about how Hollywood had once again missed a chance to make a realistic movie about stock car racing, this being just another in a long line of hokey movies that Hollywood had churned out on the subject. But a few months later, a funny thing happened. The New York movie critics in their little fantasyland cocoons discovered *The Last American Hero*, and the way they started going on about it, you'd have thought that ultimate truth had at last been located. They gushed over the "realism" of it and expounded with great joy about having at last found something real in "this plastic world." The film was hailed as "a contemporary American classic" and made its way onto ten-best-of-the-year lists. And in the South some people shook their heads and said, "Oh, well . . ." and talked of the perils of overeducation.

Anyway, on the night of the first showing, Junior and Flossie left the theater and walked across the street to the Ramada Inn, where the movie company was putting on a big bash in their honor. The movie's stars were there along with some local bigshots, a lot of Junior's racing friends, a few sportswriters, and a passel of theater managers and entertainment writers that the studio had hauled in on junket from here and there around the South. After all the introductions, picture-taking, autograph-signing, and the like had been gotten out of the way, and the party settled down to serious drinking, Junior, who is reserved, a somewhat shy man despite his heroic exploits, found himself being hotly pursued by a tall and somewhat tipsy blond theater manager. She talked and laughed loudly and clung to Junior to his obvious dismay.

Finally, Junior managed to slip away and retreated into a corner where he stood talking quietly with a few sportswriters about the old days when he was still racing and outrunning everybody on the track. He had quit driving in 1966, but stayed in racing as a car builder and owner. The year before, his Chevrolet, driven by Bobby Allison, had won more money than any other car. Among the sportswriters Junior is usually known as a man who doesn't have much to say, but on this night he was talking openly and easily, seeming to take pleasure in reminiscing about his father and the likker-making and -hauling days ("I've never seen Junior open up like that before," one of the sportswriters would say later.). After a while one of the writers said, "Junior, what'd you think about that feller that come down and wrote you up for *Esquire?*"

"I liked 'im a whole lot."

"Wudn't he a little funny? I mean, he was right much of a dandy, wudn't he?"

"Well," said Junior, grinning, "he was a *little* weird."

"What y'all doin' hoggin' Junior?"

It was the blonde again, pushing into the circle. Junior winced slightly. She had a silly grin, and she moved very close to Junior, looking straight into his eyes. "I got a message for you," she said with a wink.

Junior looked around quickly, nervously.

"Wait a minute," he said. "Where's my wife?"

The next morning, the entertainment writers, several of them nursing severe hangovers, were herded into one of the lounges in the VIP tower at Charlotte Motor Speedway, where they were to interview Jeff Bridges and Valerie Perrine, the stars of the movie. And there in the front of the booth, looking fresh and chipper, sat Junior Johnson. It was the first day of qualifying for the World 600 to be held a few days hence, and as Junior sat looking over the track, a twin-engined plane buzzed the tower, and he grinned.

"That's Cale, ain't it?" somebody said, meaning Cale Yarborough, one of the top drivers, who was driving Junior's Chevrolet this season.

"Yeah, Junior," said a track official, "your driver's checkin' in."

"I hope he don't fall," said Junior. "I'd have to drive that thing myself."

The entertainment writers asked a few perfunctory questions of the movie stars, and then they turned to Junior. They wanted to know all about that moonshining business, and Junior told them, told about how his daddy had made the likker, good likker, too, copper still likker, not like this stuff that the fast-buck operators run off hurriedly through car radiators nowadays, and about how he and his brother had done the hauling, running out of the mountains in the dead of night in those '40 Fords with Cadillac engines, cases of likker-filled half-gallon fruit jars stacked where the back seat should be, keeping a close eye out for the tax agents, deputy sheriffs, and highway patrolmen who itched to catch them.

Did they ever get caught? somebody wanted to know.

"My daddy was sent off three times, or four. He pulled four or five years."

Junior got caught only once, received a sentence of two years, and pulled almost a year of it at the federal penitentiary in Chillicothe, Ohio, before he was paroled. He was already becoming well known as a stock car racer at the time, and he hadn't been "messin'" in the whisky business for a good while, he says.

"I got caught at the still," he said. "I never got caught on the road. They never outrun me."

One thing he wanted everybody to understand: The Johnsons didn't think there was anything wrong with what they were doing, despite what the government's laws said.

"We thought it was just a law made to take away your right to do what you wanted to do and to make a livin'," he said. "We thought we was as much justified doin' what we were doin' as the guy who was sellin' the sugar, the containers, stuff like that.

"In our section that was just a way of life. Hit was just a business."

"Do you still remember how to make it?" somebody asked.

Junior grinned.

"Yeah."

Wilkes County, North Carolina, where Junior was born and still lived, where he kept his cattle and his ninety thousand chickens, was once dubbed the "Moonshine Capital of the World," and it could have been so. Certainly a lot of home-distilled whisky had moved out of its hollows and coves to the towns and cities of the Piedmont, but whisky-making was widespread throughout the hills of Appalachia from Pennsylvania to Alabama—and not only in the hills, for many a still was concealed in a Carolina or Georgia swamp, or in a stand of flatland pines. The mountain settlers, however, were largely of Scotch-Irish descent, rugged individualists, and they in particular had brought with them a tradition of whisky-making. The land they settled was rugged, had a low crop yield, and the problems of transporting the meager crops to lowland markets made it simply not worth the effort. But a mountaineer could grow a little corn and grain, make it into whisky, haul it to the lowlands, and turn a nice profit. There was only one major obstacle: the federal government. From the earliest days of its existence, the government had assessed a large tax on whisky. To make whisky without the proper licenses and supervision—without cutting in the government—was illegal. The mountaineers, for many of whom whisky-making was simply a matter of survival, held that it was their inherent right to make and sell whisky without government interference. The government considered them mere lawbreakers, however, and sent its agents to stop them. Thus were born the tales of the moonshiners and revenuers, from Snuffy Smith to *Thunder Road* to Junior Johnson. Yes.

Moonshining was usually a family affair, and it was hard work. The elders presided at the still, while the young men did the heavy work—and the driving. The men who drove the likker had to have cars fast enough to get them away from the lawmen, and they spent a lot of time working on the cars, becoming expert mechanics as they employed all the tricks for squeezing out speed. And, like Junior, they all took great pride in not getting caught on the road, not being outrun. Their heyday was from the thirties until the late fifties, when pressure from the relentless tax agents—too many mountain boys and men being carted off to federal penitentiaries—began breaking up the family bootleg industry. But when they were going strong, it was really something. Legends grew around whisky runners like Junior Johnson and Curtis Turner. Men sat at country stores and filling stations and chewed tobacco and swapped stories of their exploits, laughed about how they would outrun and outwit the lawmen with their own red lights and si-reens, and . . . the "bootleg turn"! . . . both Junior and Curtis were expert at that—they'd come up on a roadblock, cock their wheels, and be throwing up dirt going the other way before the lawmen knew what was happening.

The pride that the whisky runners took in their fast cars and driving abilities led naturally to competition among themselves.

Sometimes they would race one another on their runs. Sometimes on Sundays they would get together in pastures outside Mount Airy, or Atlanta, or Spartanburg, get drunk, and race and bet big money.

Luckily for the whisky runners, stock car racing was beginning to grow as the moonshine business was breaking up, and they moved easily and quickly to it. They had everything that stock car racing required: guts, driving ability, and they knew how to build fast cars. Most of them would have raced for the hell of it (and often did in the early days), and they soon dominated stock car racing. Most of the best drivers of the early days were ex-bootleggers, wild men in cars, and the fans came to see them because of that.

Some of those old whisky runners are still around racing in one way or another, although only a couple still attempt to drive. Today's drivers are a new breed (although one of the current young independent drivers, Buddy Arrington, was caught running a load in the mountains of Virginia in 1971), and stock car racing, which once capitalized heavily on the bootleg image, is now big business, respectable, if you will. Like the whore who married the mayor, it looks on its moonshine past with disdain.

Coming of Age

ORGANIZED stock car racing of a sort was beginning to get under way in the South by the late thirties. Inspired by the moonshiners, a few promoters, seeing the promise of a fast buck, started staging races, usually at old fairgrounds horse tracks. Whisky runners and "shade tree" mechanics turned out to race their souped-up cars. They were a rowdy bunch, and the whole thing was very disorganized and makeshift.

In 1936, a fellow named Sig Haughdahl, whose family had come from Norway to settle in Minnesota, organized a stock car race at Daytona Beach, Florida. Daytona Beach had been a favorite speed spot almost from the time cars were invented. The beach was long, wide, flat, and hard, a perfect place for racing. Henry Ford had come there to make speed runs in 1905, and Barney Oldfield set records on the beach in 1910. Almost every speedster who wanted to set a new record came to Daytona Beach to do it. That was why Sig Haughdahl had come. He had started out working in a machine shop, moved into motorcycle and car racing, and he wanted to set a speed record. He did it on the beach in 1922, running his aircraft-engine-powered *Wisconsin Special* at 180 miles per hour, although his feat was never officially recorded. In 1935, Daytona Beach, which had taken to calling itself the "World Capital of Speed," found itself in the embarrassing position of having no tourist-attracting

speed activity at all, and the city fathers prevailed on Sig
Haughdahl, who still had a shop there, to organize a beach
race. Until that time, most of the racing on the beach had been
in a straight line, sometimes for as far as twenty miles. For
longer races, posts were stuck in the sand at two points on the
beach, and the cars raced back and forth around the posts. This
had the dangerous and undesirable feature of having cars running on the beach in two directions at the same time. Haughdahl's idea was to form an oval beach-road course at an isolated
section of the beach by cutting two passes through the dunes,
connecting the beach to the adjoining roadway.

The race was fraught with problems from the beginning,
however. The city put up a five-thousand-dollar purse over the
objections of some of the city fathers, and the whole thing
quickly became bogged down in politics, with one city father
supposedly seizing the purse and another hiding the tickets before the race.

Nevertheless, the race was run in March of 1936, and although
it had attracted some of the top racing people of the day, it was
a total flop. Cars got stuck in the deep sand of the turns, and
the race was mercifully brought to an end short of its scheduled
250 miles with nobody really quite sure of who was running
where.

One of the drivers in that first stock car race at Daytona Beach
was a young man named Bill France, age twenty-seven. France
was born in Horse Pasture, Virginia, and grew up in Washington, D.C. He was a tall, lean man who had played basketball
in high school. He had given up bank clerking to become a
mechanic. In 1935, France had loaded his wife, Anne, their
year-old son, and all the family belongings into the car and
headed to Florida to seek his fortune. The story is that he
settled in Daytona Beach because that was where his car broke
down. He went to work as a house painter at first, landed a
better job as a mechanic at the Buick place, and finally opened
his own Pure Oil service station on Main Street. France had been
interested in racing since his teen years. He recalls that he
drove his first car race at the age of eighteen in a Model T Ford

at Pikeville, Maryland, winning twelve dollars for his effort. His racing interest continued after coming to Florida, and despite the fiasco of that first stock car race on the beach-road course, France saw potential for the sport. Two years later he was promoting races on the course himself.

The bootleggers of Atlanta discovered the Daytona Beach races and took to them with relish. Oftentimes the best race wouldn't be the one on the beach but the one that the bootleggers would run from Atlanta to Daytona Beach. Those races began at Red Voght's garage, and the money that was bet on them was far more than any driver could hope to win at Daytona. Red Voght put together some of the fastest cars that the Atlanta bootleggers had, and he later became one of the best builders of early-day stock car racers.

World War II brought most track racing to a temporary halt, but at war's end stock car racing came back stronger than ever, and all the old crowd was there, as rough and rowdy as ever. Bill France, who had sat out the war working in a boatyard, was again promoting races (and sometimes driving in his own races), not only at the beach but at other little tracks around the South. Old tracks reopened, and new ones began springing up—in the North as well as the South. Still, stock car racing was a disorganized, slipshod, every-man-for-himself affair with few rules and no way to enforce those that existed. Promoters were often shady characters who made off with the gate receipts before the races even started, leaving the drivers to run for nothing or face the wrath of the crowd. Clearly the thing that was needed was order, some organization. Bill France was one of many who saw that, but one of few to try to do something about it.

In 1947, Bill Tuthill, who lived in New Rochelle, New York, was a small-time promoter of motorcycle and midget car races in Connecticut. He promoted a stock car race in Rhode Island that year, and Bill France brought up a group of the southern drivers for it. Tuthill had once attempted to organize the midget-track operators, but that had failed, and with stock car racing now growing in popularity, he thought an attempt to organize it would work. Bill France had been thinking along the same lines, and the two decided to call a meeting of some other promoters to discuss the idea. The meeting was held in December in a bar atop the old Streamline Hotel in Daytona Beach. It broke up after a day-long discussion with nothing really accomplished. But France and Tuthill didn't give up, and within the next two months they put together a plan for an organization that would be called the National Association for Stock Car Auto Racing (NASCAR). The name was a little redundant, but it made a nice acronym. It had been suggested by Red Voght, who had attended the December meeting. The only thing that France and Tuthill needed now was a lawyer to put their plan in lawful form, somebody who could also help out with any legal problems that might develop, and Bill France knew one, Louis Ossinsky, a former college football star who had come to Daytona Beach as a high school coach and had his law office just across the street from France's service station, where he was a cash customer.

NASCAR was incorporated on February 21, 1948, with one hundred shares of stock: fifty owned by France, forty by Tuthill, and ten by Ossinsky. The first race to be sanctioned by the organization was one that France promoted on the 3.2-mile beach-road course that same month. Red Byron won the race in a Ford coupe that Red Voght had built, taking one thousand dollars of the three-thousand-dollar purse.

As France and Tuthill had conceived it, NASCAR would bring legitimacy to stock car racing. It would set rules and enforce them, with France, who had been named president, as the final judge. It would insure that promoters paid the posted purses, establish a point fund to pay bonuses to top drivers at the end of the year, and, it was hoped, get some insurance for drivers. But NASCAR didn't exactly get off to a rip-roaring start. It sanctioned only nine races in its first year, most of them promoted by France.

In 1949, however, Bill France came up with the idea that would make him rich. He decided to hold a "new car" race. Until that time, stock car racing had been confined to "modified" cars, usually small, light cars, with big, refined engines, beat-up, nondescript things that weren't anything like the cars that people drove every day. For this new race, the cars would come right out of the showrooms. Regular cars. Fords, Mercurys, Lincolns, Chevrolets, Pontiacs, Oldsmobiles, Buicks, Cadillacs, Plymouths, Dodges, Chryslers, Henry Js, Nashes, Hudsons (the Hudson Hornet would become one of the top cars of the early days), Studebakers, and Packards. At last people would really be able to tell which cars were the best and the fastest.

The race was held on June 19 at a three-quarter-mile dirt track off Wilkinson Boulevard in Charlotte, North Carolina, and hours before the start, the roads were blocked for miles with cars trying to get there. More than thirteen thousand people paid to get in, and a lot more slipped in free. A fellow named Jim Roper, from Kansas, won it in a Lincoln. Thus was born NASCAR's Grand National Division, which would eventually make stock car racing a big-time sport.

Not long before that race was held, a man named Harold Brasington went to Indiana to see the Indianapolis 500. The Indianapolis Raceway was the only decent auto track in the country at the time. Brasington was from Darlington, South Carolina, where he did construction work and owned some earth-moving equipment. He liked racing. He had been to a lot of dirt-track stock car races. Brasington returned from Indianapolis fired up with a crazy scheme to build an Indianapolis-type track for stock cars—right there at Darlington. A lot of people who heard about his plan thought that old Harold had flipped out. But there was one thing about Brasington: When he set his mind to something, he went at it with great enthusiasm and ceaseless energy. He was a good salesman, too, for he had soon talked a lot of local businessmen into investing in his scheme. They would, he promised, make their money back after the first race. One businessman exchanged seventy acres of farmland on the western edge of town for stock, and Brasington set about building his racetrack. He finished it in the summer of 1950, and the wild old boys who ran stock cars had never seen anything like it. It was oval-shaped, a mile and a quarter around, with banked turns—and it was paved! Brasington and his stockholders announced a five-hundred-mile race to bear the glorious name of the Southern 500. Such a thing had never been attempted with stock cars before, and nobody was even sure that they would hold together for that distance. And Bill France—who agreed to sanction the race after another organization that had at first agreed to do it came up with no entries —wasn't sure that a track in a little out-of-the-way place like Darlington would draw enough people to bother with bringing the drivers there. He was wrong.

Twenty thousand people showed up to see seventy-five drivers prove that stock cars could race for five hundred miles (the average speed for Johnny Mantz's winning Plymouth was only seventy-six miles per hour). They came back year after year, too, in ever-growing numbers, and the Darlington Raceway was quickly out of debt and very profitable, paying an average dividend of 10 per cent every year (in 1958, a 100 per cent dividend was paid). Most of the stock has remained in the hands of the original owners or their families, but Harold Brasington sold his stock not long after the track was completed and never really profited from his vision.

A lot of people were surprised that such a big crowd would show up for that first race at Darlington, for it had received little notice in southern newspapers. If they used one at all, most of the larger papers carried only a brief story after the race, tucked away under the baseball scores on a back sports page with a small one-column headline. Baseball was the thing then, and it grabbed all the attention. Almost every small town in the South had a professional or semiprofessional team. "Respectable" people didn't think much of stock car racing at the time. Stock car racers were looked down on much as motorcycle gang members are today. Roughnecks. A wild bunch banging around on those dirt tracks, drinking, gambling, fighting—always fighting. "I think they liked to fight about as good as race," says Junior Johnson. "Just as soon fight as drive. They fought all the time. They'd stop the race and fight."

A lot of people loved it. The wilder the better. That was why they came to races. They wanted drivers to be hard-charging and hard-living. Wild. On the track and off. Somebody they could swap stories about.

Curtis Turner!

Now, there was one. More stories were told about Curtis Turner than any stock car racer who ever lived—and there was probably as much truth as fiction in them. Turner always tried his best to live up to the stories, at any rate, and he was the epitome of the wild, rough, and rowdy early-day stock car racer.

Ask anybody who knew him what Curtis Turner was like, and they are apt to shake their heads and say, "They'll never be another'n like 'im."

"Anything you heard about 'im, just add a little bit to it," says a friend of his later years, Horace Crowe.

Turner had worked in his daddy's saw mills and run moonshine out of the mountains of Virginia before he ran his first stock car race at Mount Airy, North Carolina, in 1946. He was probably the greatest dirt track racer who ever lived, and it is estimated that he won more than 360 races in his lifetime (in the early days, nobody bothered to keep records). He was tall, good-looking, and swashbuckling. He appealed to women and took advantage of it. He liked to party and to drink as much as he liked to race, and he would sometimes party all night, come to the track, catch a nap on the hood of his car before the race, then get up and win it. Because he had trouble remembering names, he called everybody Pops, and he was called that in return. His best friend was another colorful driver from Virginia, Joe Weatherly, usually called Little Joe. Weatherly was almost as wild as Turner—and loved as much by the fans. He was short, squat, and frizzy-haired, with a mischievous grin. He wore black-and-white saddle-back oxfords and a gaudy Darlington Raceway shirt most of the time. He was always making wisecracks and pulling practical jokes, and the sportswriters called him the Clown Prince of Stock Car Racing. He once filled the water bottle that Turner carried in his racer with gin. Turner didn't like that much. He preferred Canadian Club. With 7-Up. Curtis and Little Joe kept an apartment at Daytona Beach where they

would stay when races were held there. The party started at the
apartment a week before the race and continued twenty-four
hours a day until the race was over. Little Joe, the story goes,
served drinks in flower vases from a fire extinguisher. "That way
you don't have to make so many pit stops," he said. On the
track, Turner and Weatherly were fierce competitors who took
great joy in banging one another around. Not just on the track,
either. There are stories of how, after a party, they would take
rental cars out on back roads to race, banging them together
just as they did on the track, and it is often told of how Little
Joe left one of these cars steaming in a motel swimming pool
one night.

Little Joe died in January of 1964 when he slammed his Mercury into the wall in the sixth turn of the Riverside Raceway in
California. A sportswriter called Turner to get his reaction. "Ol'
Joe was about to quit racing," Turner said. "He told me so.
But he never thought he'd go the way he did. . . . Naaw, you
don't ever think about death. You're not even aware of it. You
just don't think about it in racing. Damn, there's four hundred
ways that little sonofabitch Joe could've made a rich livin', but
I don't guess he'd been happy doin' anything else."

Turner was often called the "millionaire lumberman" by
sportswriters and track announcers. It began as a joke when
Turner was deeply in debt and it stuck, but it could have been
true at one time or another. He did make a lot of money in the
lumber business. People who knew him well say that he made
—and lost—several fortunes. He was a wheeler-dealer of the first
order, and he always had a deal of some sort working. One of
his schemes that failed was to bring legal betting to stock car
racing. He also built his own superspeedway at Charlotte, then
went bankrupt and lost it.

"Curtis was quite a promoter and really a kind of con man,"
says Richard Howard, the president of the speedway that
Turner built. "I don't want to say much about a dead man.
They wasn't but one. He was a man that lived on the fat of the
land, parties, race drivin', loved people, conned a lot of money

out of a lot of people. . . . I guess he died owing more money than anybody in the world."

Somebody who didn't know him well might have guessed that Turner would die, as had his friend Little Joe, on a racetrack, but if his closest friends had been asked to predict how he would have gone, they would have been more apt to point to . . . that damn airplane. Turner was one of the first drivers to get an airplane when stock car racers eventually started making big money. It was a sign of status for a long time with the big-name drivers (as well as a nice tax writeoff), and a few top drivers still fly their own planes to the races. Turner was as wild in the air as on the track. Tim Flock, one of the top drivers of the early days, who was one of Turner's best friends, says he has never known fear such as he knew in Turner's plane. He recalls flying with Turner into tree-lined fields much too small to accommodate the twin-engined Aero Commander. When Turner ran out of runway, Flock says, Turner would kill one engine, gun the other, and put the plane into a spin. On takeoff, Turner would rev both engines until Flock thought they were going to rip away from the wings, then shoot almost straight into the air.

"In flyin' airplanes, there wudn't nothin' he couldn't do," says Flock. "I believe he could land on a tin barn—that twin-engine."

Once Turner was flying with a friend over Easley, South Carolina, when they ran out of liquor. Turner's friend, who lived in the town, said he knew where they could get a bottle, so Turner set the plane down near the supply source, although there was no airport there, and taxied into a church yard. It was Sunday morning, the church was packed, and some of the churchgoers took offense at the intrusion and called the cops. Turner made his takeoff on the highway, flying under a traffic signal, as the cops raced to stop him. Federal Aviation Agency officials were waiting when he landed at Charlotte, however, and he lost his license for that one.

At the Charlotte speedway, he would sometimes fly in for races after all-night parties at his home in Roanoke, Virginia, and land on the backstretch. He always kept a well-stocked bar

on the plane, which some who flew with him say was quite
necessary.

Turner took his last flight in the fall of 1970. His plane suddenly went into a tailspin shortly after taking off from the
Dubois-Jefferson Airport near Dubois, Pennsylvania. Turner
was killed along with a friend, Clarence King, a golf pro from
Roanoke. They had just given a lift home to another friend.
PLANE CRASH BRINGS END TO LIVING LEGEND, read the headline
in one big southern newspaper. Some of his friends have
guessed at what might have caused that crash.

"He had a bad habit of when he got the plane up, he'd just
say, 'Here you fly it,' and he'd git back there and lay down and
go to sleep," says Tim Flock. "Didn't matter if you'd never been
in a plane before."

Turner died only a few days before he was to attempt a racing
comeback at the Charlotte speedway that he'd built and lost.

Turner and the other drivers of his kind never failed to put
on a real show, and they attracted thousands of people to the
racetracks in the late forties and early fifties. But it wasn't just
those wild country boys bringing the people out. It was the
whole car phenomenon. The war had brought new prosperity,
and with that money, people were buying cars first thing. That
was particularly true in the South. For the South, cars meant
an end to isolation. Any country boy could get himself a car, a
big, powerful, fast car, and he could *be somebody!* The car was
power. The car was . . .

Well, in the wake of Watergate and the "energy crisis," James
Reston was complaining in the New York *Times* about how
much more riled folks in this country got about gasoline being
in short supply than they did about Watergate. You could tam-
per with an American's freedom, he concluded, but don't dare
mess with his car. And there was Reston missing the whole
point. Freedom wasn't some abstract thing being watched over
off in Washington. Hell, freedom *was* the car. A car wasn't abstract. You could get in a car and go anywhere you wanted anytime you wanted . . . a car . . . man, a car could open up all

kinds of possibilities, a whole new life. With a car you could know what freedom really meant. And that was never truer than it was in the South after the Second World War, when for the first time it was possible for even poor country people to have cars. So when they went off to stock car races, it was a form of . . . well, there's no other word . . . worship. Precisely. Worship of new-found power—and freedom.

Up in Detroit, the executives of Ford and Chrysler and General Motors and all the others started looking at this wild thing that was going on down South. Proportionately, they were selling more cars in the South than anywhere else, and somebody noticed that if, say, a Plymouth won a big stock car race, sales of Plymouths would soar the next week. Naturally, that gave them some ideas, and by 1955 the car manufacturers—or "the factories," as they came to be called around the tracks—began slipping into stock car racing. The first thing you knew, Detroit had all these old moonshine runners signed to high-paying contracts, and the stock car tracks were overrun with Detroit engineers and PR men, and nobody had ever seen anything like it. Stock car racing was a completely new thing. And rich.

Detroit brought a lot of money and new respectability to stock car racing. Sportswriters and a lot of other people who had previously turned up their noses at the stock car crowd began looking at them in a new light. Competition became keener than ever, if less colorful, and more and more people began coming to the races. The factories stayed for a few years, then pulled out to look things over, and by the midsixties, were back in force. By then there were new and much faster tracks to draw the fans' attention. Bill France had opened the 2½-mile Daytona International Speedway, bringing stock car racers to incredible new speeds. And in 1961, two other high-banked speedways, both 1½-mile tracks, opened at Charlotte and Atlanta.

Status, power, speed, excitement, and, of course, sex (*oh, those thrusting pistons!*), these were Detroit's selling points, always had been, and stock car racing highlighted them all. Through the midsixties, the activity was almost as feverish in the engineering departments in Detroit as it was at the race-tracks. Each year, the manufacturers came out with new and bigger engines, new gimmicks to push speeds higher and higher.

And Bill France was caught in the middle. It was he who had to decide whether each factory's new development fit within the rules, and it was not an easy time for him, or for NASCAR, both remaining embroiled in controversy most of the time. When in 1965, France ruled that Chrysler couldn't run its new "hemi" engine, Chrysler pouted and pulled its cars and drivers out. That cut attendance and hurt promoters, who, in turn, sent up a howl at France. The next year, when France allowed the hemis to run, it was Ford's turn to pout and pull out. It continued that way, back and forth, with things staying in a constant state of upheaval.

By this time, NASCAR was essentially a one-man operation. France had been gradually tightening his control over the organization. In 1950, when NASCAR was struggling to bring new tracks into the fold in order to keep alive (it had sanctioned only eighty-five races in its second year), Bill Tuthill had turned over half of his forty shares to Ed Otto, one of the biggest race promoters in the Northeast, so that he would let NASCAR sanction his races. It was a big break for NASCAR, because it moved its influence out of the South for the first time. Otto was soon helping to bring in other tracks from other states outside the South, notably California. In 1954, France and Tuthill had a falling-out, and Otto and France bought Tuthill's shares and made them treasury stock (Tuthill still lives near Daytona Beach, where he operates the Museum of Speed and writes racing articles). France and Otto never had a close relationship either, however, and it broke apart in 1963, with France buying Otto's shares. That left only the ten shares owned by the lawyer Louis Ossinsky, and France eventually got those after Ossinsky's death in 1971.

France was becoming richer and richer as stock car racing grew, and some of those old country boys who had raced with and for him in the early days began thinking that they ought to be getting a little bigger cut of the action. One who tried to do something about it was Curtis Turner.

"Bill was gittin' to be a millionaire and we was still eatin' cornbread and buttermilk," says Tim Flock. "That's the whole story. . . ."

It was 1961, the factories were not involved for the most part, and things weren't going as well for some of the factory drivers who were now operating on their own.

"Curtis got it in his mind that the promoters weren't paying the drivers enough money," Flock says. "He always believed we ought to git 40 per cent of whatever they took in at the race-track, and the promoters said they wudn't no way they could do it. So he got with Jimmy Hoffa. He was goina back us any amount we wanted. The Teamsters was goina have a union for race drivers called the Professional Athletes' Association.

"We had every name driver and had 'em signed up and we was really goina fix these promoters, you know. So one by one, we lost every one of 'em. France called 'em up and told 'em he was goina close all of his racetracks all over the United States and they goina starve to death, and if we listened to Jimmy Hoffa, he was goina bar 'em if they didn't come back. So he skeered 'em to death. One by one, he got 'em back. So finally it left Turner and me, so I stayed with 'im all the way."

The union was another of Turner's schemes. He had turned to the Teamsters after getting into financial troubles with the speedway he had built in Charlotte, and Hoffa had promised him a big loan for unionizing the drivers. France knew, too, that if Turner were successful, he might organize his own sanction-ing body and snatch stock car racing from his firm grasp. He responded by banning Turner and Flock from NASCAR races for life.

Backed by Teamster lawyers, Turner and Flock sued. "Had me on the witness stand for four hours," Flock recalls, "Turner up there for six." They lost the case, however, and the ban re-mained in effect. Turner still attempted to organize his own little racing group, but it was a feeble attempt and quickly failed. Turner still raced some at small tracks not affiliated with

NASCAR, but in 1965, when attendance was suffering because
of the Chrysler pullout, one of the things that France did to
bring the fans back was to reinstate the old warhorse. Turner
came back and won his first race, the inaugural race at the new
one-mile North Carolina Motor Speedway at Rockingham. And
when Turner was killed, France served as a pallbearer at his
funeral.

Turner and Flock had learned a lot in their attempt to organize the drivers. The drivers had always been independent,
competitive (so much so that they would sometimes resort to
sabotage), and afflicted with suspicions and petty jealousies.

"There's no way in the world," says Tim Flock, "no man
livin' other than God could git the drivers together and stick
'em together. These guys, they don't mess around together."

Richard Petty was one who learned this the hard way several
years later. In the summer of 1969, a group of drivers held a
secret meeting and organized the Professional Drivers Association, hiring to represent them the New York lawyer who also
represented the National Basketball Association players' organization. Petty, the winningest stock car racer of all time, was
named president of the new organization. The drivers wanted a
"greater voice in the direction of racing," according to Petty.
They wanted a pension plan, better insurance, better working
and safety conditions, and more money from the promoters.
Petty was quoted as calling France a czar who wielded absolute
control over stock car racing.

France, as might be expected, saw the new organization as a
threat and an affront to his authority. He spoke of conspira-
torial "sources . . . detrimental to the sport" behind the drivers. It was clear that France and the drivers would have a
head-on confrontation sooner or later, and it came just three
weeks after the drivers organized.

France had built a big new six-million-dollar speedway, the
biggest and fastest stock car racing track of them all, in a big
flat field near Talladega, Alabama, not far from Birmingham.
The track was 2⅔ miles long and had the highest banked turns

of any track (stock cars would break the 200-mile-per-hour barrier on this track).

When the drivers showed up for the first race, however, they found that at the new high speeds, the track's surface chewed tires to shreds after only a few laps. Goodyear engineers worked frantically to develop new compounds that would hold together on the track. The drivers charged that the track was unsafe and began to talk of pulling out of the race.

France saw this as a move by the drivers to break him, and although none of the drivers has ever admitted it publicly, they plainly did see it as their chance to win concessions from France. But France held firm. He claimed that the tires were being cut by "foreign matter" on the track and that the track was safe at "racing speed," which he said was about 175 miles per hour.

"Who is to say what the racing speed would be on this or any other track?" asked Petty. "To win it might require us to race at 190 or 195 miles per hour, and all of us are here to race to win. We contend that the track is not safe at the speed we would be required to run."

"We will have a 500-mile race here tomorrow and the prize money that has been posted will be paid," France told the drivers. "Whether you run for it will be up to you to decide. But whatever you decide, there will be no hard feelings, no recriminations. We will welcome you back at our next race."

Throughout the day before the race, France huddled with small groups in the garage and pits trying to quell the rebellion, but at seven o'clock that night, Richard Petty left the track for home, and he was followed by twenty-one other drivers and their cars, including almost all of the big names. Infuriated, France went on the public-address system.

"Let the garage area be cleared!" he announced. "Cars that will not run in tomorrow's race must be taken from their stalls immediately and removed from the raceway."

For the fans, many of whom had already bought tickets, France promised that he would put on a race, and that they could use their tickets to see this race and another one at either

Daytona or Talladega. A few drivers remained to run, and France went to work to line up a field for his race, calling in unknown drivers and cars from other divisions. One of the regular drivers who remained was Richard Brickhouse, a little-known driver from eastern North Carolina. He was a member of the drivers association, but he stayed behind because he saw "a golden opportunity to win a race and that is what I've always wanted." He got what he wanted. He won at an average speed of 153 miles per hour, using 40 tires. France, who believes in rewarding loyalty, provided Brickhouse with a car and financial backing for future races, but he received a cold reception from his fellow drivers and soon quit big-time racing.

The boycott by the top drivers cost France a lot of money, and despite his promise of no hard feelings or recriminations, some changes were made.

"Winners never quit and quitters never win," France told reporters after the race. "As far as I'm concerned, those boys quit. The boys who raced today saved Talladega, and the boys who didn't, owe their futures to those who did race. . . . They won't run for me again without posting substantial bond. How can you depend on them?"

"We didn't want to put on a show," replied Petty. "We wanted to put on a race. He cheated the public Sunday. They put on a good show instead of a good race."

For future races, France required drivers to post their cars as bonds to insure that they ran. And to insure a field of drivers, the track promoters got together and agreed to pay five hundred dollars' appearance money to each of the drivers finishing in the top twenty-five positions in the previous year's point standings.

Although the drivers scored a minor victory, it was France who once again emerged on top with a stronger hand than ever. Under pressure from France, the Professional Drivers Association slowly disintegrated, and finally died in 1973, when Petty resigned as president.

"Me and Bobby [Allison] put a lot of money in that thing," Petty says, "and we didn't have that much to gain. The other drivers had more to gain than we did, but they just won't stick together."

By the end of 1971, the car manufacturers had pulled out of racing again, and this time it looked to be for good. A lot of people were happy to see them go.

"Factory participation was okay as long as they didn't try to control the sport," Bill France said. "The trouble was that each factory was unhappy unless it won every race. And somebody had to win and somebody had to lose."

The factories had grown weary of the perpetual game of one-upmanship and squabbling with NASCAR, but to some it seemed that the main reason they left was because they had milked racing for all that they could get out of it. When speeds had reached 200 miles per hour, a clamor had been raised about safety, and NASCAR moved to restrict power and cut speeds, leaving little reason for the manufacturers to stay and continue to develop still bigger and faster engines. In the years that they had been in racing, the manufacturers had exploited and helped create a public taste for speed and power, and they had put hundreds of thousands of superpowered cars on America's highways, thus abetting, for profit, a mass slaughter of a magnitude that has seldom been seen. NASCAR is sensitive to criticism that racing glamorizes and encourages speeding and racing on the highways (and the inevitable deaths that come from it), and it goes out of its way to get drivers involved in highway safety programs and have them make speeches saying that racing is for the track and not the highway, although many drivers have terrible records of highway traffic violations (one sportswriter who dared check into drivers' highway records got decked by a driver for his efforts).

There was a lot of talk at the time the factories withdrew about how racing had now come back to where it had started, meaning individual car owners and drivers fending for themselves. But this was hardly the case, for stock car racing in the seventies bore little resemblance to the rough and rowdy sport of the forties and early fifties, when most of the drivers drove for the sheer hell of it. Stock car racing had become big—and very serious—business, losing much of its color and character in the process.

Even to call it stock car racing was a misnomer, for the cars that were being raced now were not at all like the genuine stock cars that were raced at the beginning. A real stock car, just out of the showroom, would fall apart after a few laps at top speed around a track like Daytona, and no driver would be fool enough to drive it. No, stock cars were now sophisticated and expensive racing machines, and the country boys who drove them talked of aerodynamics and magnafluxing and other complicated engineering matters. A top-running car could cost as much as forty thousand dollars to build, and it was built like a tank, weighing thirty-eight hundred pounds, powered by a six hundred horsepower engine. These cars were built from the ground up in racing shops, the sleek, air-tight, superthin sheet metal bodies encasing a cage of heavy steel protection bars, all the parts reinforced, balanced, and polished to precision. The cars have no doors, no side windows, no headlights or heavy bumpers. The insides are gutted except for the driver's seat, which looks like something out of a spaceship, molded to fit the individual driver so as to give his right side maximum support against the force of constant left-hand turns.

Most of the changes in the cars came gradually and for reasons of safety. At first, NASCAR turned its back as the drivers made modifications to beef up their cars for strength and speed, and everybody cheated in order to keep up with the competition. Rules were later modified to accommodate the changes, and such things as seat belts and harnesses, firewalls, roll bars, and other safety features were required. Unfortunately, some changes were spurred by driver deaths.

The fuel cell that is now required in all Grand National cars (a foam-rubber-filled rubber bladder within the gas tank to prevent ruptures and keep the fuel stable) was developed by Firestone after Fireball Roberts was killed. Roberts was one of the best and most popular drivers in stock car racing. Born in Florida, he picked up his nickname as a semipro baseball pitcher, and later studied engineering at college before he gave it up to race. His car was involved in a wreck with Junior Johnson and Ned Jarrett in the World 600 at Charlotte in 1964, and the gas tank ruptured and caught fire. Roberts' driving suit was ablaze when he was pulled from his car, and he was seriously burned. He remained hospitalized for six weeks before an infection killed him. His death also pointedly showed how far stock car racing had grown in popularity in a few years, bringing banner page-one headlines in southern newspapers; and while he lay injured, so many calls came to the hospital asking about his condition that an appeal had to be issued to stop them because they were tying up all the hospital's lines. But the development of the fuel cell spurred by Roberts' death greatly decreased the risk of fire, which had been the racers' greatest dread.

Better tires also lessened the risk of death and injury. Tires were a problem from the beginning. In the early days, all the cars ran on regular tires, but as speeds increased, tires became a real problem, and many a driver was sent through a fence or flipping down the track from a blowout. In the late fifties, Goodyear decided to develop a safer tire for racing. Experiments and tests were undertaken (a couple of drivers, ironically, would die making test runs), and the result was the Blue Streak Stock Car Racing Special. At first there was only one tire for all kinds of stock car racing, but as the new, bigger, and faster tracks were built, it became apparent that one tire wouldn't do. Each track required its own special tire, and the Goodyear engineers were kept busy testing and refining many different stock car racing tires. The Blue Streak Special is essentially a wide, squat tire, thin and light, with a concave surface and very little tread. Probably the greatest development in racing tires came in 1965, when Goodyear brought out its safety "inner liner." To simplify it, this was a tire within a tire, the inner tire being under great pressure, so that if the outer tire is cut or blows out, the inner tire expands and enables the driver to keep control. Some drivers have gone several laps on the inner liner before stopping to change tires. The inner liner has without doubt saved many drivers from injuries and death —not to mention a lot of torn-up cars. At the speeds the drivers now run, the slightest debris on the track will cut a tire and cause a blowout. And there was always debris. If parts weren't falling off the cars, the fans would sometimes throw bottles or beer cans to cause wrecks or try to take out a driver they didn't like (most of this has been stopped by erecting high wire fences between grandstands and tracks and by offering large rewards for fingering debris throwers).

The development of such safety features has made NASCAR stock cars the safest of all racing cars. Drivers have survived without serious injury crashes so spectacular that it would seem impossible for anybody to come through alive. But drivers are still killed occasionally, and they are all aware of this possibility, although none will admit giving any real thought to it.

"I think probably the biggest problem that we have in stock car racing now is sudden stops," Bill France has been quoted as saying. "Or if a car is sitting sideways and somebody would drive at high speed directly into the driver's door. It's bad if you get hit right at the door beside or opposite the driver. If your car is standing still and somebody runs into you, it's a sudden jolt. But we have had excellent experiences as far as drivers not getting seriously injured if a car does not stop too suddenly."

The withdrawal of the car manufacturers from racing really didn't change things very much. The "hot dogs," as the top drivers are called, remained hot dogs—Richard Petty, David Pearson, Bobby Allison, Cale Yarborough, Buddy Baker, Bobby Isaac—and the same car owners who had always produced the winning cars (which the hot dogs drove) still had the winning cars. Most of the hot dogs were hired guns, driving for a percentage, not having to worry about building or working on the cars. Only Richard Petty had always driven his own car, although in 1973, Bobby Allison started driving his own cars. The hot dogs, of course, win all the races (there have been freakish times when other drivers have won, however). The factory pullout sent the owners of the top cars scurrying for sponsorships to take up the slack. It can cost well over two hundred thousand dollars to keep a competitive car racing for one season, and not even the best driver can win that much every year. So the car owners searched for companies interested in selling something to racing fans, and once they found them, both car and driver became spokesmen for the company. Top sponsorships may range upward to $250,000 or more a year, but these are rare. Nevertheless, the pits and garages are once again filled with PR men, most of them wearing gaudy outfits with the names of their products written all over them, stumbling over one another as they maneuver to get in camera range every time a picture is taken or to crowd behind a driver who is being interviewed for TV. The drivers themselves are walking billboards, and any young man who yearns to become a stock car racing superstar nowadays not only needs to learn how to drive well, but he also must be good-looking and personable and present a good image on TV.

"These companies want sharp young men, somebody who can stand up and talk for 'em, give 'em a good image," says an official of the Darlington Raceway.

Most drivers are not superstars, of course. They don't drive top cars, and they don't get big sponsorships. These are the so-called independents. They have been there all the time, plugging along at the back, making their hard and lonely way even when the factories were in racing. They struggle along in second- and third-rate equipment with little money and sometimes, if they are lucky, their cars may sport advertisements for a mobile home lot or a hometown cafe whose owner slips them a few bucks to help out in order to be able to say that he is in racing. The independent drivers usually start out at small local tracks, become hotshots, and move up through the ranks, dreaming of making the big time. Finally, they build a Grand National car, take what money they've saved and all they can borrow, and set out on the circuit. They learn very quickly that it isn't easy or glamorous. Some go broke quickly and fall out, and there are always others ready to move in and take their places. Some struggle along for years, doing all the work on their cars as well as driving, getting along with inexperienced and makeshift pit crews, grumbling about the ever-increasing costs of racing and the low return that the promoters pay, knowing that no matter how hard they try, they will never win a race unless something drastic happens. Sometimes it will cost them more for tires to run a race than they will win. When an independent goes looking for a sponsor, he will likely be told that the company might consider helping him when he can show them something, but he can't show them anything until he gets the money to be able to do it.

"Really, it's just hard for them to compete," Richard Howard says of the independents. Howard is a top car owner, and well knows the cost of racing.

"If a man walked up to you and said, 'Here's a brand-new car, you gotta run it in six races,' you better sure give it back to him if you ain't got a bunch of money."

Howard says he sometimes tries to dissuade new, independent drivers from going into big-time racing. "I bring 'em in here and set 'em down and try to talk 'em out of it, and I can't. It's just like tellin' a man, 'Don't git married, don't smoke, don't chew, don't drink,' you know. It's aidin' 'im on."

There are two classes among the independents, however. The upper class, smaller than the other, is made up of drivers who can make a living racing. In order to do this, they make every race (even running when they're sick), run hard to finish as high behind the top runners as possible, plow most of the money they win back into their equipment, and depend on finishing high in the year-end point standings in order to make a profit. The point fund was one thing that worked to the advantage of the independents. Points were awarded on the basis of races entered and laps run as well as finishing position. In a few recent years, some of the top drivers didn't do well in the point race because they only entered the biggest races. In fact, one of the top independents, Benny Parsons, won the national championship in 1973. But in 1974, NASCAR changed the point system so that the drivers who win the most money would get the most points, and thus pick up the bulk of the bonus point fund. Racing is like everything else in America: All the money filters to the top, and if through some freakish circumstance it doesn't, then the law is changed to make it work out that way. And nobody knows that better than the racing independents.

Most of the independents suffer along, driving conservatively to save their equipment, finishing at the back, taking bottom money, getting no help, praying that an engine doesn't blow or that they don't get involved in a wreck that will tear up the car and mean financial disaster, knowing that behind their backs, the top drivers, the sportswriters, and the fans are calling them "strokers," a derogatory term in racing. It's a hard and perilous existence. Independents are the backbone of racing, but that doesn't seem to mean much to anybody. Whenever an independent thinks he might be able to get a little ahead, something or somebody almost always comes along to slap him back down.

"It's like having a slave in the old days, see," says independent Frank Warren. "They don't want him to die, but they don't want him to get too prosperous either."

Some of the older independent drivers who have been around racing for a long time stay on even when they lose money, working in the winter to be able to race in the summer.

You can ask any stock car driver why he races, and you will not likely get a satisfactory answer. Most drivers are not particularly articulate in the first place, and on top of that they are generally reserved and close-mouthed. What they are likely to say is, "Well, it's what I like." Or they will talk about how racing gets in your blood.

They are seldom likely to go deeper into motivations. "You go messin' around in your head like that," said one driver when pressed for a better answer, "and you liable to go crazy."

There is something to that business of racing getting in the blood. For a lot of men who race, it is very difficult to let it go. They often continue racing far past their primes simply because they just can't stand to quit. Those drivers who make it to the big time and do well for a while will attempt comebacks, or they will stay on, building or working on the cars, just to be near racing, or they may go back to the small tracks and race on into old age. Speedy Thompson, one of the great early-day drivers, died recently from a heart attack while racing on a little dirt track in North Carolina.

Bill France stepped down as president of NASCAR in 1972, turning the job over to his son, Bill, Jr., who was thirty-nine at the time. In the twenty-four years that he had run it, France had seen NASCAR grow into one of the biggest racing organizations in the world, the biggest by far in stock car racing. In his last year in office, NASCAR sanctioned more than sixteen hundred races at ninety tracks in thirty-four states, and was even sanctioning stock car races in West Germany. Several other organizations sanction stock car races, including the United States Auto Club (USAC), the Automobile Racing Club of America (ARCA), and International Motor Contest Association (IMCA), mostly in the Midwest and Northeast, but none could approach NASCAR for the number of races run and purses paid, and none has anything to compare with NASCAR's Grand National Division, with its average of thirty annual races, two thirds of them at the big, fast superspeedways.

Under Bill France, Jr., NASCAR didn't change much, but the younger France, a more personable and moderate man than his father, was better liked by many of the drivers and others in racing. Nevertheless, NASCAR remained a strong-handed outfit. It brooked no insubordination and little criticism—at least from lesser-name drivers—and it was not hesitant to crack down on those who deviated from expected behavior. When in 1973 some independent drivers began complaining too loudly about the increasing costs and the hard life of the independents, some were called in for talks, and they quickly got the message: Shut up or start looking for someplace else to race.

In such circumstances, drivers have little recourse. They all know that if they want to stay in big-time racing, NASCAR is the only game in town.

The handbook that is given to rookie drivers tells them what is expected of them both on the track and off, and tells them what they should say to interviewers and at public appearances. "Remember," says the book, "NASCAR is your sanctioning body, too, and its welfare is *your* welfare. Hurt NASCAR and you are hurting yourself and your earning potential."

One rookie found in 1973 just what can happen if NASCAR thinks a driver is saying things that are out of line. Darrell Waltrip was one of the best young drivers who had come along in years, and he seemed a shoo-in for the Rookie of the Year award. He had a good car and he ran hard and well. At the spring race in Atlanta, constant rain washed out qualifying runs, and NASCAR decided to have a drawing for starting positions. It was decided that the faster cars would be lumped in one group to draw for the first positions, with the slower cars drawing for the back spots. Seventeen cars were included in the group of faster cars. Waltrip should have been among that group, but he was put with the other. He was understandably upset about it.

After the drawing, Lin Kuchler, NASCAR's executive vice president, was standing in the garage area talking with a group of sportswriters, when Waltrip came up to ask why he hadn't been included in the first group.

"You were overlooked and I apologize," said Kuchler.

"I get overlooked more than anybody I know," Waltrip replied.

"Where you starting?" a sportswriter asked.

"Thirty-ninth, where I can get it tore up," Waltrip said bitterly.

"Listen," said Kuchler, bristling. "I respect you, but I'm going to tell you this. For a man who's running for Rookie of the Year, you've got the wrong attitude. You've been quoted more than any other rookie. You've got a bad attitude, and frankly I don't care whether you run with us or not."

Humiliated, Waltrip got the message and began apologizing. He did not become Rookie of the Year.

No matter how hard it tries to stifle criticism from within the ranks, however, NASCAR is not always successful. The top drivers and car owners usually are not hesitant to speak out, knowing that NASCAR would not likely risk the ire of the fans and promoters (as well as the big-money sponsors) by taking action against them. In the fall of 1973, Bobby Allison proved that it was not only possible to get away with severe criticism of NASCAR, but that it could even be profitable.

In the garages and pits there is always grousing about how NASCAR is letting this driver or that get through inspection with illegal equipment, or how NASCAR is making secret payments to certain drivers, and things of that nature, and that is to be expected. But at the National 500 in Charlotte in October of 1973, the whole thing burst into the open, as it often had in the early days, and NASCAR came away looking very bad. It was a hectic race from the beginning. At the start, Charlie Glotzbach, who had won the pole position, got kicked to the back for having an illegal carburetor. In the middle of the race, Buddy Baker's car owner, angry over NASCAR rules, pulled his car out, charging that NASCAR had been badgering his team. The race was won by Cale Yarborough, driving a car owned by Richard Howard, who also operates the Charlotte speedway. The first-place money was more than forty-three thousand dollars, very big money for stock car racing. Richard Petty finished second, and Bobby Allison third. Allison, however, protested the first two cars, claiming that they were illegal, and that he was the rightful winner. NASCAR officials impounded all three cars and began breaking them down for inspection. The inspection dragged on for six hours while a lot of people fumed.

"You can't show me a race driver who doesn't cheat," Richard Howard angrily told a reporter as he waited for a decision. He was upset not only because his car had been challenged, but because the uproar would give his track a bad name. "I'll admit we cheat, and I'll take it to court to prove that all forty cars here were illegal. Why does it always happen here? Why not at Daytona?"

NASCAR did not make a decision on Allison's challenge until the following day, when it acknowledged "borderline infractions" in Yarborough's and Petty's cars, but let the race results stand. Reporters found sources who told them that Petty's engine was slightly oversized, but that Yarborough's was grossly larger than allowed.

Allison responded by threatening to quit racing and sue NASCAR. "I feel like a man who has just been cheated out of forty-four thousand dollars," he told reporters. "When NASCAR says there were only small infractions, that is an out-and-out lie.

"There was no question but that the cars were illegal. What took so long was deciding how NASCAR was going to lie out of the situation. . . . I simply cannot participate in a sport where the important thing is who can cheat the most."

The year before, Allison had driven Richard Howard's Chevrolet, having a fantastic season. Asked about that, he said he assumed that the car was legal when he was driving it.

Allison was soon called to a meeting with top NASCAR officials in Daytona Beach, and he emerged from the meeting smiling and talking of conciliation, to announce that he would continue racing and drop any action that he might have considered against NASCAR. The word around the tracks was that NASCAR had given Allison a substantial sum for his kindnesses.

When he retired, Bill France, or Big Bill, as he is called by associates to distinguish him from his son, told a reporter, "If I've been a czar or a dictator, I've been the most benevolent one in racing."

That one caused some chuckles among those who knew of France's solitary, iron-handed rule of stock car racing.

"He's a demandin' guy," says Tim Flock, who had felt France's "benevolence." "His way or no way. . . . He had to be roughshod over everybody to accumulate the money he did.

. . . He's demandin', yeah, but he's a real smart businessman.
To come from a Pure Oil fillin' station settin' on Main Street in
Daytona . . . you gotta give him credit for hard work and
knowin' what he's doin'."

Even France's most severe critics give him this grudging respect for his accomplishments. He made stock car racing into
a big-league national sport, and he made a lot of money doing
it. He did not leave racing after his retirement. He remained
at the helm of his International Raceway Corporation, which
operates the highly profitable Daytona and Talladega tracks (the
Daytona 500 in February is the biggest stock car race of all,
drawing more spectators than any other race except the
Indianapolis 500). France owns control of the corporation, but
his chief partner is Union Oil Company, the same company for
which he had started pumping gas shortly after arriving in
Daytona Beach.

France is a big, shambling man, who does not seek the lime-
light. He doesn't like to give interviews and he distrusts the
press, although he never hesitated to use the press to promote
NASCAR and stock car racing, and at times the sportswriters
couldn't have done a better job for him had they been on his
payroll.

Bernard Kahn, the executive sports editor of the Daytona
Beach *News Journal*, has covered NASCAR since that first
organizing meeting in 1947, and he writes glowingly of France,
the France family, and NASCAR. He has written of France:
"As comes naturally to many successful self-made men, France
has a king-size ego. He is sensitive to criticism in the news
media. He overreacts to it sometimes. 'Not true,' says Bill,
good-naturedly, 'I just want them to print the facts without
distortions.' But the facts, when they are not particularly pleas-
ant, still aggravate him."

One reason that France stepped aside as NASCAR president
was to give him more time to do other things. He wanted to
spend more time on his sixty-seven-foot yacht, but more than
that, he wanted to get into politics. He had courted politicians
from the local level up for many years, primarily to insure that

he got little interference with his racetracks, but also to help insure that no legislation unfavorable to racing should slip past (periodically there have been outcries to ban it altogether). He even named the late Mendel Rivers, the powerful South Carolina congressman, as the commissioner of stock car racing, an honorary position.

In 1972, France headed the campaign that won Florida's Democratic presidential primary for George Wallace. He had become close friends with Wallace, not only because he had built a big racetrack in Alabama, but because he and Wallace were in close agreement on political philosophy. "Christ," says one of France's former employees, "the old man is so conservative he's the John Wayne of the South." After Wallace was shot, France switched over to lead the Democrats for Nixon organization in Florida. Now he is working for Wallace again, is expected to be a key man in Wallace's 1976 presidential campaign, and, who knows, Bill France could be the next Secretary of State.

The Old-Timer

IN CASTING AROUND for an old-time driver to write about, I knew what I was looking for. I wanted somebody who had started as a bootleg runner, gone on to rank among the very best of the early-day drivers, been loved by the fans, had the grace to quit before he'd become a pitied has-been, one who had been in the thick of things and lived the high old life that was expected of a stock car racing hero. Most important, I wanted somebody who liked to talk about it all, to tell the stories. That was going to be the hard part. So many stock car drivers are reserved, seldom offering little in conversation except to their closest friends.

As soon as I met Tim Flock, however, I knew I had my man. There was just one problem. He wasn't old.

Not yet fifty, his hair had just begun to gray, but he kept it carefully styled in a youthful manner. He wore double-knit suits and broad, colorful ties. Although he had lost the thinness of his youth, he was still far from being heavy. His eyes wrinkled smilingly at the edges and they had that mischievous twinkle that seems to convey special messages to a great many women. In his time, Tim Flock had used that to good advantage.

One spring afternoon, I sat in a cluttered corner that served as the office of Tim Flock's little furniture store in Charlotte,

North Carolina, with Flock and a few of his friends who had stopped by to visit, and he began recalling old times.

There had been a time when Flock was probably the best-known name in stock car racing. The Flock boys were feared wherever they went. There were three of them, brothers: Tim, Fonty, and Bob. Tim was the youngest; Bob, six years older, was the eldest. Now Tim was the only one left.

He was born on a farm near Fort Payne, Alabama. His father, who died when Tim was four, farmed and drove a taxi, but he had adventure in his soul. He taught himself to be a tight-rope walker.

"He started off in the backyard with a big ol' rope stretched across the backyard," Flock said. "He'd walk that thing. Then he started racin' bicycles. He run bicycles."

There were eight Flock children, and most of them seemed to inherit their father's adventurous spirit. "The whole family done somethin' crazy," Tim Flock said. Carl, the eldest son, became a champion speedboat racer. Bob, Fonty, and Tim raced stock cars. So did sister Ethel. Another sister, Reo, became an early parachute jumper and wing walker. One of her stunts was to hang by her ankles from an airplane wing without a parachute.

Carl was the one who got his brothers into stock car racing. He left home after his father died. "Carl went to Atlanta," Tim Flock was recalling. There was a gentleman there, Peachtree Williams was the man's name, was my uncle. Peachtree Williams was the greatest bootlegger that Georgia has ever known. This was way back yonder. Way before the Depression. So he got Carl over there and Carl got in the likker business. So Carl started haulin' likker and started makin' so dern much money he didn't know what to do with it so . . .

"Finally Carl got out on his own. He knew that Mama was having all kind of trouble with all these other kids, so he got me, Bob, and Fonty and got us moved to Atlanta and put us in school. We was done out of school, didn't have no clothes, starvin' to death. So we was growin' up in Atlanta with Carl.

So his likker business got so big when we was growin' up, we started haulin' for Carl."

Bob began driving first, then Fonty. They would make runs to the Georgia mountains, to Dawsonville and Gainesville and Dahlonega, where the manufacturers were, and bring the stuff back to Atlanta. "We'd put eighty, ninety gallons in a '34 Ford back then, '39 Ford later on. When I started ridin' with Bob and Fonty, I was about eleven or twelve years old. I wasn't, you know, old enough to drive. I couldn't even see over the steering wheel when I started. . . . My job was to try to keep the stuff from gittin' broke, them ol' fruit jars. Let's see, Fonty was haulin' at sixteen.

"Comin' out of Dahlonegee—the sheriff knew when you'd go in. The ol' car was jacked up, when you'd go in there and put a load on it, it'd kinda level it comin' back. But this sheriff, he'd just set on the side of the road with a double-ought shotgun with double-ought buck in his hand and just shoot your radiator out. You'd go by about eighty, ninety mile an hour, you know. He'd just put his gun up and git his car around, 'cause he knew about three or four miles down the road, your radiator, all your water was gone, and you'd git out and run, leave the whole eighty or ninety gallons on there, see.

"So this kept happenin'; and they kept catchin' cars and the po-leece come out—anybody caught one of these bootleggin' cars, it'd be sold in front of the courthouse in Atlanta, and the po-leece that shot the radiator out or caught it, got half the money that it brought. So, boy, they got tough.

"They started shootin' these radiators out. So we took and put a big ol' steel plate right up there where the radiator was and started runnin' the engine in the rear. We drove this for maybe nine or ten months before they caught on. They'd shoot the radiator out, and they git in the car, you know, and come down and there wouldn't be no car. We'd go on in with the load and set it off. We got by with that for eight or ten months.

"Then they come along with this deal where they had a thing like an ol'-timey ice tongs. They'd run up behind you. On a hill they could catch you with all this likker on. The cars wasn't

souped up. We didn't even know what cams were back then.
But on a big hill they'd run up behind you and they'd hit you
and this thing would tap your bumper, and they'd just put on
the brake and this thing'd slow you down. You'd git out and
run.

"So we started puttin' on our bumpers with coat hanger wire.
So they'd run up behind it and grab it and we'd give it the gas,
or catch second gear and jerk it loose, and the bumper would
fall down in front of their wheels, and by the time they got all
that out from under there, we'd be gone.

"See, we used everything in our head that we could to git
that likker in, to keep from gittin' caught, and it worked. If you
didn't git the likker in, you didn't git paid. That was the main
thing.

"We wasn't the only ones in the bootleggin' business. Remember, they was about twenty or thirty different people bootleggin' in Atlanta. So these cars—seemed like they was always
arguing about who had the fastest car, so they had a little place
about twelve miles outside Atlanta. On Sundays they wouldn't
haul any likker. They'd git out there in this cow pasture, is what
it was, wasn't no racetrack or nothin'. But they'd git out there
and go around, cut furrows out and make a racetrack with one
of the cars, and they started racin' out there on Sundays. These
bootleggers was the only ones out there, wasn't no fans or
nothin' except the drivers, and they would be fifteen or twenty
thousand dollars change hands back then, bettin' on the cars.

"So people started linin' up along the fences, wasn't no
boards up or nothin'. They could stand there and watch these
cars run on Sunday. So the drivers, we were still haulin', you
know, maybe gittin' twenty-five or fifty dollars a load, if we got
back without tearin' the car up out of Dahlonegee, we'd go up
there with our caps or anything and go down the line, and people'd put quarters and half dollars in it, git up our purse, you
know. So finally, it got so big they was eight hundred or nine
hundred people comin' down there on Sundays."

After the Second World War, when stock car racing tracks
started popping up all around the South, the Flock boys
started making the rounds, driving cars backed by the big boot-

leggers and bug men (lottery operators) in Atlanta. Tim Flock drove his first race in 1946 at North Wilkesboro, North Carolina, in a car owned by the father of Speedy Thompson, who later became a top stock car racer.

"I started winnin' races the first year I drove," Tim Flock recalled. "'Cause Bob and Fonty had took me out and showed me everythin' in the world in cars. They'd spin me out in their cars, not in a race. I more or less knew how to drive a race car the first time I set down in one. I started outrunnin' Fonty and Bob the same year that I started.

"Yes sir, it was dog eat dog. I'd ruther outrun them than anybody on the racetrack, because they told me at one time when I was tryin' to git them to start helpin' me, they said, 'You'll never become a race driver, we goina send you through school.' I said, 'One of these days I'm goina outrun you,' and I did. But I'd ruther outrun them than anybody else because I knew I was outrunnin' the best back then."

Bob was Tim's favorite driver. "His eyes would completely change in a race," Tim recalled. "You could see it. He'd run under you, around you, or over the top of you to git by you. Rough. Real rough driver. They used to start a hundred and sixty cars on the beach at Daytona, it was a real slaughterhouse. I've seen Bob Flock start in a hundred and fifty-third place. It was one mile and six tenths to the first turn. He went into that turn first." Bob Flock was just as rough outside his car. "No one ever touched Bob," his brother was saying. "He'd hit you. All you had to do was touch him. He couldn't stand nobody to touch him. A man, I mean. Now, a woman was all right. He broke his arm twenty-two times hittin' people."

Fonty was a good driver, but more flamboyant. He was the first man ever to wear Bermuda shorts to a racetrack in the South, a daring thing at the time. He had a pencil-thin mustache and favored gaudy shirts. He was a real crowd-pleaser, and women liked him particularly. "That Fonty," says sister Ethel, "boy, he was the one. That Fonty had the women, didn't he? And his wife, Marge, she didn't keer. It didn't make a bit of difference to her, and she loved him to death."

Tim was an intense driver. "I'd plan a race," he says. "For

four or five nights before a big race, I wouldn't even be able
to sleep. I'd drive that race before I got in there." He kept
meticulous records on all the tracks, the required tire pressures,
gear ratios, everything. And it paid off. He won races, but he
also had bleeding ulcers. He consumed vast quantities of milk.
He never went to a racetrack without at least a half gallon of
milk.

Their sister Ethel evaluates the Flock brothers this way:
"Now, Tim is strictly a race driver. Tim drives because he loves
racing. Fonty drove for publicity. That smilin' Fonty. Pepso-
dent Kid, they used to call him. Bob drove because, dern it, he
was just a natural-born race driver. He put that foot down and
he'd go. He'd take the brakes off his modified. He'd say, 'Aw,
you don't need no brakes to drive a car.'"

Tim eventually outdrove his brothers. He was twice
NASCAR's Grand National champion, in 1952 and 1955. He
set records that were not broken for years. He quit racing once
in 1954. He had run an Oldsmobile in the race at Daytona and
won. A protest was lodged against his car, however, and he was
summoned before Bill France and other NASCAR officials and
told that he had been disqualified for a minor technical violation. Lee Petty, who finished second in a Chrysler, was declared
the winner. Tim Flock felt that he was being disqualified because France wanted a Chrysler to win. It was the dirtiest deal
he'd ever seen, he said, and he'd never race again. He was so
angry that on leaving the meeting he slammed the door hard
enough to break the glass. He returned to Atlanta, opened a
service station, and raced no more.

The next year a couple of friends talked him into going with
them to Daytona as a spectator. He was standing on the beach
when a white Chrysler roared by, really moving.

"Damn!" he said. "Boy, if I had that car, I'd win this race."

A man standing nearby approached him and said, "Aren't you
Tim Flock?" He said that he was, and the man said he knew the
man who owned that Chrysler, that the owner didn't have a
driver, and if Tim Flock was interested . . .

The owner of the car was Carl Kiekhaefer, who invented and
manufactured Mercury boat motors. He had decided to go

into stock car racing as a means of getting his boat motors known. Whether he realized it or not, he was about to change the sport entirely. There had been no big companies sponsoring race cars before him.

Tim Flock will never forget his first meeting with Kiekhaefer. The car was in a garage Kiekhaefer had rented in Daytona. A whole platoon of guys in clean white uniforms was working on it. The old man was in the back, a chunky guy with a cigar in his mouth and a sneer on his face. He seemed to growl at Tim Flock. "He was *mean*," Flock recalls.

Flock was introduced, but the old man had never heard of him. The guy who had brought Flock over told Kiekhaefer that Flock had won the race the year before, but had been disqualified.

"Yes, sir," Flock offered, "and I'd win it again this year if I had that car right there."

The old man looked him up and down, then took the cigar from his mouth.

"Go over there and sit down in that car," he said.

Tim Flock knew then that it was his to drive. He was back in racing.

"I set there, man, I was just thrilled to death," he remembered.

In qualifying the car, Flock set a new record of 141 miles per hour. But the car had an automatic transmission, and it slowed in the turns. Flock finished second in the race behind Fireball Roberts. The transmission had cost him the win.

Kiekhaefer promised that the automatic transmission would go. It was his first race, he said, and he was learning. He asked Flock to drive for him regularly. Flock didn't have to think long about it. His service station wasn't doing very well, and he was broke. He accepted. Kiekhaefer then told him that he didn't want any of the money that Flock won in the car. He wasn't in racing for the money, he said. This was unprecedented. Drivers usually got only 40 per cent, 50 per cent at most. Flock had won nineteen hundred dollars for placing second, and he was overjoyed.

The next morning Flock was having breakfast in a restaurant

when a friend hurried in with a newspaper. "Did you see this?" his friend asked.

The newspaper story said that Fireball Roberts' car had been disqualified for a technical violation. Tim Flock had won the race and the thirty-two hundred dollars first-place money. From that point on, Tim Flock believed in justice.

Driving for Carl Kiekhaefer that year, Flock won eighteen Grand National races, a record that would stand until Richard Petty broke it twelve years later. He also won the national championship and pocketed fifty-five thousand dollars. The next year, however, he found it increasingly more difficult to get along with Kiekhaefer, who was a demanding man. Flock's ulcers were getting worse, and he quit. The car manufacturers had come into racing by this time, and he had no trouble getting another ride. He signed a contract to drive for Chevrolet.

"Twenty-five hundred a month in the mailbox," he said. "That was nice."

He continued to drive for Chevrolet and later for Ford until 1961, when he was barred with Curtis Turner.

His brothers had quit racing before him. Bob quit in 1954. "Bob just run his life out," his brother said. "He run twenty-two years. Went until he just got too old. He was a hell of a race driver, though. He run like Turner. Wild." Bob Flock retired to Atlanta where his wife ran a restaurant. One fall day in 1965 he came home after eating a hamburger and began to complain of indigestion. He took a dose of soda and sat to watch the horse races on TV. The indigestion didn't go away. He went to the kitchen and took another dose of soda. He didn't make it back to his chair. He fell dead on the floor of a heart attack. The family believed the soda killed him.

Fonty Flock's last race was the Southern 500 at Darlington in 1957. His car wasn't handling well, and he lost control of it. He was all over the track before the car finally wedged against the wall in front of the grandstand. He was facing the traffic, and he couldn't get out of the car. For some reason the yellow flag wasn't dropped immediately. The other cars were coming at him at full speed. Bobby Myers' car hit him head-on. People sitting nearby said the crash sounded like a dynamite explosion. Fonty had seen the crash coming and braced himself, feet and arms against the dashboard. His chest and pelvis were crushed, and he suffered other injuries. Bobby Myers was killed. Fonty later said that the last thing he remembered before the crash was Bobby Myers' eyes and the fear in them. Those eyes, he said, would haunt him the rest of his life. He never drove a race car again. He returned to Atlanta, got into the insurance business, and a few years later came down with cancer. He suffered from it for ten years before it killed him in January of 1973.

Bill France lifted his ban against Tim Flock in 1965, but Flock did not return to racing. He'd been away too long, he said. And he was about to get his stomach straightened out again. For three years he traveled with show cars doing PR work for Ford. Then he went to work for Richard Howard at Charlotte Motor Speedway. Howard, a millionaire furniture dealer, later set him up in the furniture store.

As we sat in the furniture store, Flock and his friends got to laughing and telling racing stories, and the business of all the fighting that used to go on came up.

"I got all my teeth knocked out, eyes gouged, nose broke, scars, see here," Tim Flock was saying. "It was tough. We 'bout tore up a racetrack in New Jersey. Fonty and I had to have the sheriff come git us out of a racetrack at High Point."

He told that story, and that led to others, and somebody mentioned a fight that ol' Curtis was in one time, and that did it. It was Curtis Turner stories from then on. Tim Flock was one of Curtis' best friends, as was Horace Crowe, who was there. The stories naturally got around to the "doll babies," which is what Turner called the girls who chased after race drivers.

"He's been in every motel and every motel room, probably every motel room in North Carolina, from here to Texas. California. Overseas," Tim Flock was saying. "I'm goina bet the man's been with four hundred and sixty women. We used to keep up with it. We had a record goin', who could git the most. I got to three hundred and sixty and I quit countin'.

"Where you raced, even back then, like these drivers now, you had a good name and they knew your number. It wouldn't surprise you a bit if two o'clock in the morning somebody'd be banging on your motel door and you open the door and there's a doll baby. Plenty of girls." He laughed. "This really helped you race, you know, be up all night long havin' to drive a race the next day.

"These women out here, man, you ain't goina turn 'em down. Women like race drivers, or bull fighters. I don't know. It's something about a woman.

"I don't imagine these guys now have any problems findin' girls, but I think they train more than we did. We used to use girls to train with. Now they usin' ropes and chinnin'. We trained with women.

"Now—used to be the mechanic never did git none. He done all the work. These drivers they got now, they in trainin' and they can't party like that. They just turn 'em over to the mechanics. 'Course they slip off. You ain't goina find out about it though."

He asked that my tape recorder be turned off. "I'll tell you something," he said. When the recorder was off, he called the name of a current popular driver. "He called me not long ago. He said, 'Tim, you remember that contest you and Curtis used to have goin'?' I said, 'Yeah.' He said, 'Well, I'm at one eighty-four.'" Everybody laughed.

It was getting late, almost closing time. The story-telling had gone on for hours. Tim Flock had had to interrupt occasionally to wait on a customer or answer the telephone. "Look, I got two deliveries I got to git out this evenin'," he said. The telephone rang again. He answered.

"Yeah!" he said, his voice brightening. "How you doin'?" He talked for several minutes, and when he had hung up, he smiled and winked.

"That was one of those ol' doll babies," he said. "From Atlanta. Hadn't heard from her in years."

No Women Need Apply
(Except with Big Tits)

IN THE FALL of 1972, *Stock Car Racing* magazine ran a special section on women in racing. In it, Linda Vaughn was described as the "most popular female in racing history." That is probably true, and it says a lot about the position of women in racing.

Linda Vaughn is a race queen.

In 1961, fresh out of high school in Dalton, Georgia, Linda Vaughn entered the Miss Atlanta International Raceway contest and won.

"I felt I was going to win in the finals ahead of time," she told an interviewer from the magazine. "Like we qualified, then we ran, and I knew when the last ten laps came up that I felt like a winner. I could just see that checkered flag and I won and I've been supporting racing ever since because it's in my blood."

Clearly, there had to be a place in racing for a girl who thought and talked like that. Especially one with racing in her blood. And it didn't hurt any either that her racing blood coursed through one of the most tremendous sets of tits to ever come around a racetrack. God, what tits! Great flesh pillows. And there wasn't an ol' boy at any of those racetracks where Linda Vaughn appeared who did not dream of resting his head on them.

Even after Linda Vaughn had ended her reign as Miss

Atlanta Raceway and gone on to be Miss Firebird, off to the races every weekend to ride that Firebird float, smiling and waving and thrusting out her chest, grabbing every opportunity to tell everybody how much she loved racing and everybody in it, all the big guys and the little guys with grime under their fingernails, and just everything—there wasn't anything about racing that Linda Vaughn didn't love—after all of this, still it was those tits, those tremendous tits that made all of the old boys at all of those tracks stand in awe, made them punch one another in the ribs and giggle like little boys, and made them want to run out and fill up their tanks with Firebird gas, all of them drooling to take those tremendous tits in hand, or at least, for godsakes, to have one little peek at them. They finally did get that peek when Linda Vaughn put out her own program, a program just like the ones the big racetracks publish for every race, except that this one was all about Linda Vaughn, and while she didn't exactly bare those tits in it, there *were* some pictures of her wearing a wet T-shirt with nothing on beneath and—hot damn!—that was enough. Those tits were all that any of those ol' boys had ever imagined them to be. Tremendous!

Obviously stock car racing was not big enough to monopolize the talents of a girl like Linda Vaughn. She went on to become Miss Hurst Golden Shifter, branching out into all areas of automobile racing, loving every bit of it. What can you say about a girl who says that "the most paramount thing" she has ever done was to ride in the Indianapolis 500 parade?

Linda Vaughn is still supporting racing, as it has supported her for so many years, still a race queen. She is in California now, the lines beginning to show on her beautiful face, training other girls to be race queens, talking of big things for racing, maybe a TV series—one that she would be a part of, of course. When she is asked what advice she would give to girls who'd like to pursue a career like hers, she tells them it's not enough just to be pretty. You have to support racing, she says, love it and live it. She doesn't mention a thing about having big tits.

Almost all companies involved in stock car racing, and there are a lot of them, have one or more beautiful girls to represent them at the racetracks, to smile at the fans and kiss the winning drivers. Some of the companies, like R. J. Reynolds with its Winston Cup girls, and Union 76 with its Race Stoppers, have platoons of girls who must meet stiff requirements before they are hired, the first, of course, being that they must be beautiful. Beyond that, Union 76, for example, requires its girls to have college degrees (two, in fact, are working on doctorates) as well as professional experience in modeling or show business. And they must abide by strict rules. No smoking or drinking on duty, no dating while traveling for the company. Uniforms must be freshly pressed, fingernails clean. Smile, soldier! And thrust out that chest. Keep up that company image. The great bulk of racing queens, however, need suffer no more stringent requirements than having a pretty face, nice legs, and the bigger the tits, the better.

To be a race queen is about the only way a woman can be involved in big-time stock car racing. Oh, wives and girlfriends of drivers are allowed to keep lap scores, but there are no women drivers, no women mechanics or crew members. No women but race queens.

At smaller tracks in some areas of the country, women do race stock cars. Usually they are the wives of the men drivers and race only against each other in "powderpuff derbies," gimmicks to please the fans. Few tracks allow women to race against men. And many do not even allow women in the pits.

Indeed, until 1973, when a female photographer threatened to bring suit, women were not allowed in the pits of most of the big stock car tracks, and the "No Women Allowed" signs remain on the fences at some. The reason for this has never really been made clear. One is apt to hear that women would get in the way, or might get hurt, or might distract the men from their work, or cause hanky-panky and jealous outbursts to develop. Privately, almost all men involved in stock car racing, from mechanics to drivers to promoters to NASCAR officials, say that women have no place and no future in racing—except as race queens. Some of them will even say it publicly. There is probably no more ardent group of male chauvinists than stock car racing men.

It is ironic, in a way, because in the early days of stock car racing, some women did drive against the men. They were accepted, and they didn't do too badly, either.

"They 'fraid that a woman might beat 'em," Ethel Flock Smith was saying. "That is it. I bet you that's it."

She was speculating about why men didn't want women in racing.

"I don't understand it," she said, "'cause the women can drive if they make up their minds."

She would know. In the late forties and early fifties, she raced against men and sometimes beat them.

Ethel Smith is in her fifties now, a jovial, talkative woman. Her hair is red, pulled into a bun to accommodate the big, dangling earrings. She wears a lot of flashy jewelry, diamond rings gleaming on her fingers, and her makeup is heavy, her lipstick bright red. At one time she made a lot of money in the restaurant business. In 1971, she and her second husband, Burrell Smith, who retired from his truck tire business, bought a big brick boardinghouse in an old section of Atlanta to see them through their retirement. Ethel Flock sat at the big dining-room table and laughed.

"Oh, my God, I've gained sixty pounds at this boardin' house."

A black woman, the cook, was in the kitchen, making ready for the evening meal. Ethel Smith took a cigarette from a pack and called to the woman. "Lou, bring me a match, Sugarfoot, and I'll dance at your next weddin'."

She sighed.

"We're all has-beens," she said. "I'm a has-been."

Ethel Smith came to racing naturally as the sister of the famous racing Flock brothers. "I had the feelin' that I wanted to be a race driver," she said. "It was borned in me, 'cause my whole family, see, was, you know, they just felt like, 'we want to git on a track, see, race.'"

Her brother Bob taught her how to drive a race car.

"I'm goina tell you, the first time, down at Daytona, it was a modified, a '39 standard Ford that Bob had made hisself, had built. He put me in that car and . . . my God! He took me down that straightaway—and that's when they were racin' on the beach, they's two miles of asphalt and then two miles up the beach. We went down that beach, honest to God, it felt like we were goin' five hundred miles an hour, and I said, 'Slow up, Bob, slow up! My God, you're fixin' to go in that turn too fast!' You know, I was screamin' at 'im. He said, 'You wanta be a race driver?' and I said, 'Yeah, step on it,' and 'Go on, go on,' and boy, he went in that turn so fast that I don't know whether I was upside down in that seat. When we got back to the pits, you know where I was? Practic'ly standin' on my head in the floorboard!"

She would soon race over that course herself.

"The best race I ever did at Daytona on the beach track, there was Bob, Fonty, and Tim and myself and I had nobody to sponsor me, but I had a Cadillac convertible, and I told Charlie Mobley, my first husband, I said, 'I'm goina go in that race.' He said, 'What you goina drive?' I said, 'I'm goina drive my Cadillac. It must've been, I don't know, it was the latest thing, ever what year it was. I got my tires and the wheels all fixed, got my safety belt put under the seat.

"I qualified, let's see, I qualified eleventh. They was forty-seven drivers in that race. I qualified eleventh and I came in fourth. All my brothers' cars, they blowed up. I beat 'em. Ever' one. And they grabbed me after that *race!* I thought them three boys was goina beat me to death. They liked to tore me up after that race!"

That was her best finish in a big race, although she did win a few small modified races.

The men, she said, learned to respect her. "Bob had done told me, 'If they push, you push back,' and don't think I didn't!"

She sat at the dining-room table for a long time, talking about racing, laughing loudly, smoking one cigarette after another.

"God, it's been a long time, hadn't it?" she said.

She couldn't remember the last race she drove. "Where *was* that last race? My God, I don't know whether . . . I imagine it was Lakewood Park. It must've been. I had a '52 Cadillac and I raced at Lakewood Park."

Her two daughters, who now have children of their own, were still small then. She remembered posing for a newspaper picture, wearing her racing helmet, putting a diaper on her younger daughter on the hood of her race car. It was a hokey picture. Her daughter was too old to be wearing diapers any more, but the photographer had thought it would be clever.

She never made any money racing, she was saying, lost money, in fact, and she just drifted away from it.

"The older I got, the less nerve I got, see. . . . But I never been skeered in my life, thank God, on a racetrack. I never got nervous."

She was, she said, without regrets for her experience. "I'm glad. I wouldn't take anything in the world for it. My daughters, they bragged about it, I've been told. That their mother was a race driver. That makes me feel good. It's something to be thankful for, I think. It's an honor to me, because I'm old now." She laughed suddenly. "I'm not *old!* I won't never git old!"

There were only three cars in the first race that Sara Christian ran. The race was held at a little track that Bob Flock had built at Morrow, Georgia. The other two cars were driven by women, too. Her sister, Mildred Williams, was in one, and the other was driven by Ethel Flock. There would have been four cars in the race, but the other girl took a little too much liquid courage and wrecked her car before the race started.

As far as is known, this was the first "powderpuff derby" in stock car racing.

One fall day, Sara Christian, now a graying grandmother, sat looking at a driving rain in Dahlonega, Georgia, an old gold-mining and bootlegging town in the mountains of northern Georgia, where she now lives, and recalled how she came to drive in that first race.

One afternoon she and her husband, Frank, were sitting with

Bob and Ruby Flock in their restaurant trying to think up something that would draw attention to the racetrack that Bob was trying to develop. Somebody said that maybe people would come to see women race.

"I don't know how the subject came up about women," she said. "I said, 'I'll drive.' You know, just like that."

She didn't know why she volunteered, and it surprised her husband. "I just always liked to drive," she explained. "I never had thought about racing before. I liked Bob and Ruby. I knew they had put everything in that track, and it meant a lot to 'em."

Ethel also agreed to drive, as did Sara's sister, and for two weeks they went every afternoon to learn the tricks and practice. The gimmick worked. A lot of people came to see that race.

Frank Christian bought his wife a '39 Ford to run, and she put the number 7/11 on it, because her daughter was eleven years old and her son was seven months. They were her lucky numbers. She won the race. She looked at a picture of her car streaking across the finish line just ahead of her friend, Ethel.

"Yeah, that's Ethel right behind me. She sure did try. They was a lot of money bet on that race down there that day. Everybody figured Ethel would win because of Bob and Fonty, you know. Nobody didn't think about me winning. I think if I hadn't, it would've just broke Frank's heart. I had to just for him because he had gone out and bought that car, done all that, you know."

After that race, Sara Christian found herself in demand at other tracks, and she soon began to race against men. She always had a good car. Her husband operated a garage and service station, and he'd built race cars for the Flocks and other drivers. He didn't like to race himself. He did drive in one race against his wife, though.

"He started fifth and ended fifth," his wife recalled. "He passed me and waved at me."

Sara Christian discovered that she really liked to race. "Yeah, I got excited. I don't deny that. Now, before a race, before they'd give the green flag, I'd be just like this almost." She held out her hand and made it tremble. "Then the minute they dropped the green flag, I was just as calm and cool as I could be. I don't know, but I never would be nervous running. Then when I flew in to make a pit stop, until I'd get started again, I'd be the same way."

She fared very well against the men. In 1949, her second year driving, she placed high in the NASCAR point standings. Then at the end of the year, she was driving her new Oldsmobile at the Lakewood track in Atlanta. She had a picture of the car, an immaculate car. She was standing beside it in her helmet, smiling, a pretty young woman.

"Not too long after that picture was made I turned over," she said.

She had a picture of the car after the wreck, too. " 'Course, that doesn't look too bad there. But I was upside down. I turned over seven times. I broke my back."

As soon as the car began overturning, her husband started running toward it. He beat the ambulance there. She was knocked unconscious, but remembered coming to as she was being pulled from the wreckage, and she remembered that she didn't want to be put in the ambulance because her mama was there in the stands. After that wreck, her husband said he didn't want her to race again. It took her nine months to recover, but she did race again. Just once. At Reading, Pennsylvania.

"I just wanted to be sure I could," she said. "You know, they say if you ever have a bad wreck, the best thing to do is go back and drive."

She won two heat races and finished second in the feature that last time.

A few years later, she and her husband closed the garage in Atlanta and moved to Dahlonega to care for his aging father, who was alone at the old home place. They raised chickens and ran a motel and restaurant in Dahlonega. Then, in October of 1967, Sara Christian suffered a stroke.

"I came out of it remarkably well," she was saying, lighting a cigarette. "It was two weeks out of my life I'll never know anything about. I couldn't talk, couldn't walk, had double vision. It all came back gradually."

Two months after her stroke, before she had recovered, her husband died suddenly of a heart attack.

"I still like to drive," she was saying. "Driving relaxes me. I can be tired, or nervous, and I get in my car and go, and it just goes away."

If she hadn't had the wreck, would she have continued racing?

"Probably. If I had been younger. And no responsibility. No children. See, it worried my mother more than anything.

"I don't know, though. The speeds they going now—ooo-eee! 'Course, I'm older now, too, you see. When it gets where they goin' so fast you can't see the numbers on 'em, I'm glad I'm as old as I am and got that excuse."

The modest brick house sits at the end of a dead-end street in Greenville, South Carolina, completely surrounded by what is reported to be the biggest junkyard in the South. The junkyard is owned by Noah Smith. He has been in the junk business many years—all of his adult life, in fact. People come from all over the country to buy used-car parts from him. He has parts that are difficult to find anywhere else.

Noah Smith's wife, Louise, is a middle-aged Christian woman, respected in the community. She now tints her once-jet black hair, and wears wigs occasionally. She dresses conservatively and elegantly. She is a successful businesswoman on her own. She has made a lot of money in real estate. She owns a resort development on a nearby lake and a big restaurant. Meeting her for the first time, no one would likely ever suspect that she was once one of the wildest drivers who ever came into stock car racing. Of course, the trophies are there just inside the door of her house, and there on the wall is the oil painting that a fan did and gave to her of Louise Smith peering out from under her racing helmet.

On a blustery winter day, she sat at her dining-room table going through her racing scrapbooks.

"This picture is Lee Petty," she said. "Looks younger than Richard does now."

Louise Smith is a spirited, good-humored woman who laughs a lot and loves to tell racing stories. She was born in Greenville. Her father was a mechanic, her brothers became mechanics. "That's all we've ever known is cars," she said.

She was fascinated by cars at an early age. At seven she was sneaking to drive her daddy's cars. "I stole the car out one time and run it into the chicken house," she said. "I couldn't git the thing stopped. 'Course, we had T Models and A Models before my daddy died. That's what I learnt to drive in."

She learned to drive well, and she always drove fast. She married Noah Smith when she was eighteen, and he couldn't slow her down either. She was always going out on back roads and racing somebody. She got her first chance to race on a track in 1946. She recalled how that happened.

"They come up here one time to race. We hadn't been havin' any racin' around here. I was a purty wild driver anyway around town. I was always outrunnin' the policemen, the state highwaymen, and everybody else. They couldn't catch me. I always had a good car. I had the fastest one and the niggerishest-lookin' one in Greenville 'cause I always had it fixed up with everything on it could be imaginable. They always had a little trouble around town with me, you know, about that.

"When it got around they was comin' up here to race, everybody said, 'Who's goina drive?' They said—it was all over Greenville—'Louise Smith'll drive.' So it started gittin' around town, and they started gittin' up bets all over Greenville. So, the first thing you know, that money'd got into the thousands, and I said, 'Well, might as well go out and try it.' I never had even seen a race."

Hickey Nichels agreed to let her drive his car, and she agreed to give him half the money she won, bets and all. He was late getting to the track, though. He got the car there just in time for the start of the race. Louise Smith didn't even get to practice.

But the crowd was with her all the way.

And the word started getting around. Somebody went down to Florida and told a racetrack promoter that there was the craziest woman you'd ever seen up at Greenville, and it would pay him to get her down there to run. She began getting offers from a lot of distant racetracks, paying offers, and she took them. She was soon making all of the races with Buddy Shuman, Curtis Turner, Lee Petty, Buck Baker, the Flock boys, and all the rest.

Louise Smith held her own with the men, not only at driving, but the other arts that they were accomplished in as well: drinking, cussing, and fighting.

"Oh, it was wild," she said, laughing. "I remember down at Darlington, I guarantee you, 1950, '51, it was wild. All over that town. We got on the fire truck to ride in the parade and Roy Acuff (a popular country singer) was down there and he was drunk, and we was ridin' down through town and Roy Acuff fell off the fire engine and liked to killed hisself. And we liked to tore one of them motels apart. They put every one of us out of the motel. They wouldn't let nobody stay there."

It was just as wild on the track sometimes. "See, now, they used to pull a few tricks on you. They can't afford to do that as fast as they runnin' now. But Buddy Shuman had a technique. He could run up behind a car and he'd just barely touch the bumper and cut you a flip. If you didn't move out of his way, about the second lap around, you'd wish you had. So I went out to the track with him, he showed me how to do that. So I got purty good at doin' that. If they messed with you, if they'd keep aggravatin' you, cut 'em a flip and git 'em out of the way. But then they'd be a fight when you come in, see. Man, you always had to fight.

"See, I had a name for fightin' purty bad anyway. 'Cause I had had a few fights with guys down here at the yard. I mean men. See, if they'd make me mad, I'd jerk 'em down off that truck and pop 'em, or about anything else. They didn't bother me too much on the tracks."

Noah Smith didn't care for such goings-on. He didn't want his wife to race, but she was a strong-willed woman, and there wasn't much he could do about it. Except drink. He did that.

Louise Smith pulled a picture of Bill France from a pile on the table. "He was a *good-lookin'* man," she said. "Ooo-eee." Half the picture had been cut off. She had been on the other half. She cut that off for Noah's sake.

"He's not jealous any more," she confided. "Got too old, I guess. Back then he kindly worried about me, I think."

He worried for more reasons than that, however. His wife was probably the wreckingest driver who ever drove stock cars. She kept running into houses, fences, trees, light poles, cars, anything that happened to be handy. "I won a trophy for turning over in Hatfield, Pennsylvania," she said with a grin. "It was the first one I ever won. It was for joinin' the upside-down club." Turning over was indeed a specialty of hers. "I needed wheels on top," she said. "I'd a drove a lot better. . . ."

She once hit a house at a little track at Asheville, North Carolina. "You know," she explained, "when you first take off, your nerves is kindly drawn anyway." It was an honest mistake. She went into the first turn and forgot to let up. "I went right up that bank—Joe Littlejohn never has forgot that, he was there—I went up that bank and it was purty steep, and that ol' house was settin' there and they was people all over the top of it. I just went right through the front door and out the back. The old house went every way. The people, they flew and fell and some of 'em got hurt. They used to kid me a lot about that. I said the ol' house needed tearin' down anyway."

She turned over into a lake once in Alabama, and got out okay. In a race up North, she got hit by almost every car on the track without getting seriously hurt. But her worst wreck came at Hillsborough, North Carolina, when she got Curtis Turner to teach her his famous power slide, a technique he used in order to get through the turns on dirt tracks.

"He said, 'Lou, I'm goina take you out there and show you how to git around here now.' I said, 'Okay, let's go.' So I squatted down in the car with him and I made about four or five rounds with him and he showed me. He said, 'Now, right here at the end of this wood fence,' he said, 'just give it one

jerk,' and said, 'when you git on the other side, you're headed
down the straightaway and pour the steam on it.' Well, he rode
around with me then two or three times, and he said, 'Well, you
doin' just fine. If you keep that up, you'll do good.'"

Qualifying came, and Louise Smith took to the track. It was
a one-mile track, and she turned the first lap at a little over a
hundred. The slide was working fine. The second lap was good,
too. She went into the third lap. "That thang was runnin' like
a dream that day," she said. "Man, when I hit that second turn,
that tire blew and that thang never did even straighten up. It
sailed off that bank down toward that river like a cannonball.
Hit three trees. The radiator dove and I back-flopped against
a tree. They had to git me out with a torch."

When the ambulance took her off to the hospital, the other
drivers had given her up for dead. But at the hospital she regained consciousness and insisted on going back to the track.
She was bruised and cut and most of her ribs were broken, but
she went back to the track. The other drivers stopped the race
and got out of their cars to hug her. They called her Lucky Lou
after that.

It wasn't the first time she was hurt in a race, though, and it
wouldn't be the last. "I can tell you a week before it's goina
rain anytime," she said. "I've had my collarbone broke, all my
ribs, my legs, my arm. . . ."

She does consider herself lucky. She ran in several races in
which drivers were killed; spectators, too, at times. She was
driving one night at a track in eastern South Carolina and there
was a guy sitting drunk on the guard rail in the middle of one
of the turns waving the cars on like a traffic cop. Her car hooked
up with two others and they all went into the rail and killed
the man.

"They had us up down there on trial," she said. "They low-
rated us down to the dogs. We was crazy race drivers comin'
in there and killin' their citizens. They indicted us for this man
but they never did anything about it. Manslaughter. Then when
it all come out—'course there never was nothin' to it."

Louise Smith raced for many years, up and down the Eastern

Seaboard, and she was always in demand. "I went to New York City, I raced there in dead wintertime and people were still lined up for three blocks tryin' to git in there when the race was over. They said they'd never at that time seen a woman driver." She raced several times a week usually and sometimes got as much as a thousand dollars' appearance money, big money in those days.

"I made money," she said, "but I spent it all. I wrecked so many cars."

She retrieved another picture from the pile on the table and laughed. "Here's Buck's car that he won his first modified championship with. You shoulda seen that car when I got through with it. It looked about like that other'n at Hillsborough. Cut down a telephone post comin' back out of midair. It cut it halfway in two comin' down, then knocked the lower half out of the ground."

Louise Smith's racing career ended early in 1956. It was a Saturday. She was to leave the next day to race at Daytona. A fundamentalist Baptist preacher came to the junkyard that day to get a part for his car, and he started talking to Noah Smith. Noah Smith had been drinking worse than ever, and he got saved that afternoon and quit drinking. The preacher asked about his wife.

"I don't believe you'd be able to do anything with my wife," he told him. "She's fixin' to go to Daytona."

The preacher said he'd come to see her anyway.

Noah Smith came up to the house that afternoon and told his wife that he'd been saved and was going to start going to church.

"Let me tell you one so-and-so thing," she remembered telling him. "It's all right if you want to go to church, it's all right if you want to git saved, but don't you have them blankety-blank preachers after me!" She doesn't use the words nowadays that she once did.

She went down to the junkyard later that day, and the preacher phoned. She chatted politely with him. He said he understood that she was getting ready to go race again, and she said she surely was. "Then he asked, 'Did you ever think about what would happen to you if you was killed in one of them races?' He said, 'You'd go to hell if you've never been saved.' And 'course that makes you stop and think, especially when you stay on your top more than you do anywhere else," she said. They continued to talk for a while, and finally something moved Louise Smith to ask the preacher to pray for her. He said he'd be right over. "No," she said, "I feel like if it's not now, it just won't be." The preacher prayed. "And I got saved on the telephone," she said.

She phoned her friends who were going with her to Daytona to tell them that she wouldn't be going, she'd been saved. None believed her. It was true, though, and Louise Smith quit going to the races altogether. She started going to church and working to raise money for an orphanage. She went to Hollywood twice and appeared on many TV shows, capitalizing on her racing fame to raise money for the orphanage. She was on "You Bet Your Life," "Queen for a Day," "Breakfast in Hollywood," "It Could Be You," and several others, and she brought in a lot of money for the orphanage. One of the dormitories that was built with the money was named for her.

In 1972, Louise Smith decided to go to the races at Daytona. It was the first time she'd been to a race since she had gotten saved. "I could not imagine the changes that had took place," she said. She saw a lot of her old friends and had a good time.

"Yeah, you know," she said, somewhat wistfully, "I miss them, and I miss racin'. It just don't git out of your blood. I can be settin' in here in the den a lot of times in the summer on a Saturday night and they runnin' modifieds out there at the speedway and the sound comes right across. If I got that window up, I have to git up and pull it down. Can't stand it. Boy, git up and start walkin'. . . ."

Stuffings, Part 2

The Small Time

Saturday Night at the Rainbow Speedway

SWIRLING CLOUDS of dust. All those GTOs and LTDs and Monte Carlos and Dodge Chargers and shiny new pickup trucks with chrome on the sides and aluminum covers on the back are turning off Highway 29 onto the unpaved road, kicking up all that red dust to fall on the little rectangular brick veneer houses with attached carports that line the road to the Rainbow Speedway.

Saturday night in Reidsville, North Carolina, home of Lucky Strike cigarettes and the Smothers tobacco warehouses, and here are all these people piling out of their shiny cars and trucks, some of them running fingers distastefully through the fresh film of red dust on the smooth, waxed finishes. Working people, these, country people, even if they do happen to live in town. They work in the cigarette factories and cotton mills, the service stations and garages, in the construction business and on the farms where the tobacco is grown. These cars and trucks are their proudest possessions. They pay for them by the month, big payments, bigger even than their food bills and house rent. So it is no surprise that when it comes to having a big time on Saturday night, they drive these big, shiny, powerful cars out to the Rainbow Speedway to see other cars do battle.

The Rainbow Speedway is a big, red-raw (and bleeding, when it rains) gash in the earth. It is a throwback to the old days, what stock car racing was before it got rich and moved to the other side of town. Now all those hot dogs at the big tracks look down on places like the Rainbow Speedway. Bull rings, they call them. Outlaw tracks, because they are not affiliated with NASCAR or any other organization. But big-time stock car racing began at short dirt tracks with unpainted fences and sagging wooden bleachers. Tracks like the Rainbow Speedway.

Until Bobby Dunlap came along, the Rainbow Speedway had been deserted and idle for fifteen years. He looked at the run-down track and saw opportunity. Bobby Dunlap is a slick operator. He wears open-necked sport shirts and double-knit slacks, and he is a smooth talker. He has a small shopping center on the highway over at Madison, and a trailer park.

Bobby Dunlap had been a race fan for a long time (he hasn't missed a race at Darlington since 1955), and a couple of years earlier, when a couple of boys he knew were trying to reopen the old 311 Speedway, another dirt track, at Madison, he went in with them and helped make it a success.

"Got ol' Curtis Turner down 'ere when he was livin'. Ol' Curtis put on a damn show for us, filled up the grandstands. We pulled 'em out."

He is leaning against a pickup truck near the entrance as all those people from all those shiny cars and trucks throng to the gate to pay the $3.50 admission fee: young dating couples, the boys wearing white socks and loafers, the girls with lacquered hair teased high on their heads; families with rowdy kids, the men sunburned and hardened, the women dumpy, fat thighs squeezed into Bermuda shorts or hidden under plain, straight dresses, carrying foam rubber pads to sit on, some of the men smuggling beer in brown paper sacks past big red-and-white signs that say, "Alcoholic Beverages Prohibited."

"It's a little different drivin' dirt, you know," Dunlap is saying. "That dirt track, it takes a art to that, you know. . . ."

He interrupts to greet some of the people plodding toward the gate. "Hey, how y'all," he says.

"It's comin' back. Dirt track racin's comin' back, I think."

He looks at the line of people at the gate.

"Well, they still like to see it, you know. Like I say, it's a art, you know. The cars hang out, you know. They broadslide, you know."

"I think it's more action," says an ol' boy who has been listening in.

"It is, yeah, it's more action. . . . How y'all." He nods to new arrivals.

Bobby Dunlap did not get the track open until June, missing a couple of good racing months when attendance is usually heaviest after the winter racing drought. It is now close to the end of the season, and he is pleased with how it has gone. Attendance has ranged between eighteen hundred and twenty-three hundred every week, and everybody pays, even the guys who drive and work on the race cars. Each week, Bobby Dunlap pays the drivers a purse of about thirty-five hundred dollars. It does not take an expert mathematician to see that he has had a good summer.

He has not had a particularly good day, however.

"We've had a rough time today," he says. "Had a lot of breakdowns, and the weather's so dadblame hot, you know."

It is almost race time, but the track is not yet ready. Bobby Dunlap walks down the hill through the parking lot toward the infield gate, where a few late-arriving drivers are checking in their beat-up race cars.

"You just stop and think about it," he says, "you take these guys run on these superspeedways, now they're runnin' sorta right on the ragged edge, you know it, and that's what these boys's doin' here, you know. They've really not got a whole lot of control of these cars. They'll bump and bang on each other."

The tractors that kept breaking down all day have finally got the track's hard-packed red dirt broken up, and a big green tanker, which has also suffered a few breakdowns, has just finished wetting down the loose dirt, turning it into thick muck. Dunlap slops through the mud holding his pants legs up. Trucks are now spreading calcium on the track. Soon the cars will be called out to circle the track, packing it into running condition. The races, obviously, will be late getting started.

The infield is jammed with cars and trucks, drivers, and their friends, who serve as crews. The men come from all around, from Reidsville, Danville, Greensboro, Burlington, Graham, Yanceyville, Pfafftown, Altamahaw, mechanics all, if only shade-tree mechanics, men who like to "piddle" with cars. This is their recreation. They race at 311 Speedway on Friday nights, at Rainbow on Saturdays. In the winters, they rebuild their cars, which are usually pretty well battered by summer's end.

The cars are built mostly from junkyard parts in backyard shops and towed to the track attached to pickup trucks, or on trailers. There are three divisions: late-model, limited, and hobby—the differences being primarily in engine size. The cost of the cars may range from two hundred dollars for a hobby car to five thousand dollars for a good late model. The most a driver can win is four hundred dollars for taking first place in a forty-lap late-model feature. Most of the drivers drive only for fun. A few, like Red Justice, or Larry Isley, or Donald Tucker, can make a little money.

The week before, Red Justice and Donald Tucker had gotten tangled coming out of the fourth turn, and Red had lost it. His car hit the little mound of dirt separating the track from the pits and became airborne.

Lynn Johnson, a twenty-four-year-old plumber with a wife and a young baby, was leaning over the front of his hobby car, an old Falcon, making some adjustments to his carburetor. He didn't see Red Justice's car coming.

When Red Justice's car hit, Lynn Johnson was pinned to the front of his car. The doctors at Cone Hospital in Greensboro, where he was taken by ambulance, decided that there was no hope for saving his mangled right leg, and it was amputated. The other leg, broken in several places, was put in traction.

Things like that sometimes happen around racetracks. An accident. That's all. It couldn't be helped.

"Just one of them things, you know," Red Justice is saying.

He is sitting now on the back of his truck, a lanky man with a freckled face, gaunt and lined. He is smoking a long cigar and watching the cars slipping and spinning around the track, throwing up great sheets of mud to coat windshields and make it difficult even to tell the colors of the cars as they try to get the track ready to race.

"It's just bad," he says. "As good as I try to git along with ever'body, it had to happen to me. It tore my nerves up so bad Monday and Tuesday, I just . . . well, I just decided to quit. Right now, you know. I talked to Lynn. Lynn said, 'Red, it's just a accident, you couldn't he'p it.' I could've landed anywhere in here, or, you know, anything could've happened. He said, 'Go on and race.' So I said, 'Okay, if you got that way of feelin' about it, well, I'm goina go on and run.'"

The track is ready, and the drivers have begun to congregate around the back of Red Justice's tow truck. Little Red Justice, short and lean and muscular, his orange hair cropped close, his jaw muscles constantly tensing, stands in the center of the crowd wearing a T-shirt and bright red pants. He is holding a red flag furled on a stick. Little Red is called that to distinguish him from his older brother, the driver. Little Red does not drive. He holds a position of authority. He is the flagman. His job is to line up the cars on the track and see that they stay in proper order if the race has to be stopped for a wreck, or something, which is frequently. He shifts a chew of tobacco into his cheek and says, "Shore a lot of people standin' around. I don't know if I got nerve enough to talk."

When he mounts the back of the truck a few minutes later, however, there can be little doubt that Little Red is in charge. His voice is loud and a bit shrill, the voice of a man who for years has tried to be understood over the roar of powerful, unmuffled engines.

"The track's good and slick and it's goina take a while to arn it out," he begins, "but first we're goina have a drivers' meetin'! Ever'body knows last Sa'rd'y niat that Lynn Johnson got hurt and he got hurt real bad! The widders wanta have a beneficiary race for 'im! It's up to you whe'r you wanta come, nobody's makin' you come! You come, put on a good show, ever'thang is goin' for him! Bobby said he would go a hunnerd per cent to git the track in shape—to run! But—we don't know what niat y'all wanta run it on! That's up to y'all! Y'all pick a niat that you want to run other'n Friday or Sa'rd'y niat!"

"They can run on Saturday if they want to," Bobby Dunlap interjects from the crowd.

"Don't make no difference!" Little Red continues. "Bobby said he can make no difference on Sa'rd'y niat if y'all want it on Sa'rd'y niat!"

"What's wrong with Monday night? Labor Day?" somebody shouts.

"That's right!" another adds.

"Too close," says Bobby Dunlap, shaking his head. He was planning to go to Darlington Monday. He does not miss the race at Darlington if it can be helped.

"Shit!" yells another driver. "I'll help you git the damn track ready! Let's run!"

Bobby Dunlap shakes his head. He is very adamant. No, Monday is out.

"Let's just wait a little while," somebody suggests.

"Y'all just talk it over," Bobby Dunlap suggests. "Y'all git together, whatever you want to do."

"I think it's a good thang!" Little Red is shouting again. "We tuk up for 'im last niat at Madison, got 'im some good money! We goina do the same here toniat. Ever'body'd 'preciate it, and if anybody else got hurt, we do it for ever'body! We don't do it for just one, and I think it's a really good thang! 'Cause the boy lost his laig! He lost it for life! It really hurt 'im! But the boy's got a lotta spirit and I'm proud of 'im! Bobby, git up here! You wanta say anythang?"

"Naw, that's all—yeah! One thing. On this stayin' back behind these posts. We gotta do that. When you go out with your car, just bring it back behind these posts."

"Boys, som'in' else!" Little Red again. This time he sounds angry, his voice rising even more. "Last week the track was a little slick and a little muddy, but a couple of you pulled right over here and said, 'I want a drink of water!' Two of 'em done

it to me last Sa'rd'y niat! Damn it! You do it toniat, you goina be
a lap down when the race stops! Now, if you want your windshield cleaned, here's a pit road, come in it! You just pull up
'ere and park and you come on by that pit road gate, that ain't
biness! But when you go to git your money, if you a lap down,
you cry on somebody else's shoulder! You ain't goina cry on
mine! 'Cause it ain't biness! Y'all know who I'm talkin' 'bout
too!"

"Let's draw, let's draw!" somebody calls impatiently. "What
you say?"

The scorers are standing by with the little numbered slips
that will determine starting positions for the heat races, which
will, in turn, determine positions for the feature races.

"Let's draw!" cries Little Red.

Sweet Mama Sonja! Big mama, too. Plenty of woman flesh
tucked into that red tank top and those pale blue hip huggers,
all of it wiggling and jiggling with every move. Sonie, the boys
call her. Bleached blonde and brassy. Sassy, too, when she wants
to be. Full of wisecracks and loud, shrill laughter. She is passing
out a hug here and a little cheek sugar there, calling everybody
"Honey." Hell, Clyde don't care. Clyde is her husband. He
isn't here tonight, off up in Massachusetts, or somewhere, on
business. They run a speed shop over in Greensboro. But even
if Clyde were here, he wouldn't say a thing, just laugh along
with everybody else, because he knows it's all in fun. That's
just the way Sweet Mama Sonja is!

Oh, but there are some who object—all those "racing widders" up in the stands, the wives of all those ol' boys out there
in the infield, are just burning with envy and jealousy, because
women and children aren't allowed in the infield, yet there is
Sweet Mama Sonja sashaying through the infield as if she owned
the place, and they all know what she's doing down there, hugging up their men, giving 'em cheek sugar, cracking risqué jokes,
and calling 'em "Honey"; they *know*, and they don't like it one
bit. Nosiree.

"Jealousy," Sweet Mama Sonja is saying. "That's all it is.

They's a lot of things that requires me to be in the pits. I come down here to *do my job!*"

Her job. Of course. Sweet Mama Sonja is a track official. She giggles.

"I'm the *head* nigger," she says.

She keeps the records, and pays off the boys after the races, and listens to their gripes. She also handles the publicity. "I guess they figure with my mouth I can do anything," she says, laughing.

And if attendance starts to sag, Sweet Mama Sonja is even willing to hop in a car and drive in a powderpuff derby. A woman's race always pulls 'em in.

"Last year I run three," she says. "I won two of 'em and blowed one. I've run against Wanda. I've run against Goldie. I mean, you know, some of the purty good girls. I've never finished past fourth but one time. I've always finished every race I started in but one time and I blew a *brand-new* motor *all to pieces!*

"One night I was drivin' at Caraway. Matter of fact, I was drivin' for Carl Price, C. L. Price, his little coupe, and this woman hit me in the back and sent me sailin' over the front end of one. I went six feet in the air—and down at Caraway, they have, you know, these earth piles piled up against the light posts. I ran up on it. I came down in the infield. I run up on this dirt pile, I come around on the backstretch, and I come out *leadin'* the race!" She cackles.

"Winnin' really is, it's a joy, but when you do somethin' special, now, like that . . . I broke a rib and mashed a vertebra. I led the whole ten laps!

"Once you git racin' in your blood—Hon-ee, it's there to *stay.* There's no two ways about it—*WELL BUDDY!*"

Some ol' boy off to the side, directly in Sweet Mama Sonja's line of vision, has just dropped his britches down around his thighs in order to tuck in his shirttail, and he is grinning at Sweet Mama Sonja, who is feigning great shock.

"What say, hon?" he says.

"These guys!" she says with mock disgust. "They think I'm

just one of 'em. They don't pay nere bit of attention, just like I'm not even here."

That is the farthest thing from the truth, of course. They all lavish attention on Sweet Mama Sonja, and she revels in it. She doesn't mind at all about being the only woman over in these dark pits with all these rough ol' boys, even when Clyde can't be here.

"Just like last Saturday night," she says. "This Butch Michael that drives this '55, he said—I walked from in the pits back over and got the payoff and I come back down here by myself —he said, 'Sonie,' he says, 'are you not afraid to be up here, you know, to walk across the track and all down through these pits like you do by yourself?' I said, 'Well, no, I'm not, Butch.' I said, 'Let me ask you this.' I said, 'What would you do if you would see a man mistreatin' me or anything?' He said, 'I'd kill 'im.' I says, 'They's not one member in any pit crew that I walk by that wouldn't do that, because they know who I am. They know I'm married to Clyde. They know that I'm married.' But I mean, this is just between you and me, if I was goina run around, I wouldn't do it up here. But I mean, I've got a home and a family. And whenever I was asked to take this job, I asked Clyde first and he said, 'Yes.' Because all the guys know me and they know him and . . . I don't know . . . I was told they couldn't nobody else do it."

She laughs.

"I think this is a high honor. Clyde and I both were honored."

A driver walks by.

"Hey, honey," she says. "How you doin'? Where you been?"

Larry Isley leans against his Dodge with its gold-flake paint job, and he is very cool in his thin red-and-white racing suit. His hair is swept back high on top and sides, held in place by a heavy coat of hair spray. He wears a look that seems to say, "I know that I am above all of this, but . . ."

"Git it, Larry, git it, boy . . ." somebody is saying.

"You met Larry?" Bobby Dunlap asks me.

"Just did."

"He's a true American," says Melvin Brown, who is Larry's friend and is always kidding around. Melvin Brown is a top driver in the hobby division. Larry Isley is a top driver in the late-model division.

"Yessiree, he sure is," Bobby Dunlap agrees. "He's one of the Dodge boys."

"We're predictin' he'll be the next superstar," Melvin Brown says in a mocking tone. "I don't know."

"What happened to the Plymouth?" Dunlap asks Isley.

"Last night?"

"Yeah."

"Burnt a piston."

Somebody says, "How long you been racin', Larry?"

"Oh, about fifteen years."

"Damn," says Melvin Brown, "he oughta be good, hadn't he?"

"What do you do over there in Burlington?" Dunlap asks.

"Service manager over at the Dodge place."

"I *didn't* know you was all that important," Melvin Brown says with a little grin. "I thought you was just a flunky."

"Shit manager," says Isley. "Git all the shit."

A little later, a group of guys is standing around Isley's car talking about dirt track racing, and Isley is saying, "It's a art, all right," and I ask him, "How long does it take to get it right, to learn just how to do it?"

"I don't know," Isley says straight-facedly, "I never have learned yet."

A big howl comes up from all the ol' boys in hearing distance.

"How 'bout that?" one says. "Ol' Larry said he ain't never learnt yet. That's purty good."

"Reminds me of the time I seen 'em interview a ol' man on television," Melvin Brown says. "He run a sawmill up North sommers, and they ask him had he done that all his life, and he said, 'Not yet.'"

"I won't never git away from dirt," Red Justice is saying. "It's a lot more excitement on dirt, you know. You take asphalt's

good but you just set tight. It ain't . . . 'nother words, you
follow the leader more. You don't see as much passin', carryin'
on like that on asphalt, I don't think."

"Do a lot more bangin' around on dirt," somebody adds.

"Oh, yeah, yeah," Red says. He laughs. "You gotta rub
fenders once in a while."

Red Justice is thirty-eight years old now, and he has been
racing on dirt tracks for fifteen or sixteen years, he can't remember exactly. "When I started off, I started with a junkyard
car and a junkyard motor, working in the backyard," he says. He
ran in the hobby division for years, but for the past four years
he has been driving a late-model car, and he is one of the hot
dogs. His car, a '65 Chevelle, is owned by C. L. Price, who runs
a construction company over in Greensboro, and it is one of the
three best at the track. Red—who is salaried by Price, racing in
the summer and working construction in the winter—even has
mechanics to look after the car, just as the big-track racing teams
do. A business.

"I race, I race for money," Red is saying. "Far as for fun,
I'm over with the fun. I'm just kinda like Petty and them is."

The year before, when the Rainbow Speedway was just a
deserted old racetrack, he had run at Madison and at a little
track at Altamahaw, which had closed at the end of the season,
and he had won thirteen thousand dollars. This year Bobby
Dunlap had opened the Rainbow Speedway, so he still had two
tracks to run, and he seldom goes anywhere else to race.

"Hell," he says, "I don't know, it's just two fine tracks, you
know, it's close to home, that's one reason we don't go some-
wheres else. . . . I tell you, 'ough, this is a good bunch of boys.
We have some ups and downs, but if you race, you goina have
ups and downs, you know.

"I mean, anything you go at, you got a crowd, you goina have
some arguments. . . . I try to keep boys down, you know, I try
to talk to 'em and keep the trouble down, 'cause, I tell you,
when I come in it, when I was back racin' hobby and stuff, a
man all he wanted to do was fight. I done got over that, you
see. Right now, I think it's one of the best things a man could

have around here for pleasure. I try to keep all the boys together, satisfied, and happy. They got any problem, they come
to me. I try to help 'em, you know. It's about the only damn
way you can handle it."

"You was bad to fight there one time yourself, wudn't you,
Red," some ol' boy says, grinning.

Red chuckles. "Yeah, yeah, purty bad." He stands up on the
back of his truck.

"Well, let me ride a little bit," he says. "I'm goina see what I
can do. I'm goina do my thing tonight."

At Madison the night before, Red had won. He hoped to
make it two in a row.

"If it was like it was when I started," Melvin Brown is saying,
"I'd be as happy as a cat at a fish fry."

He is wearing a T-shirt that bears his name and car number,
hand-drawn in colored inks. His car is by far the best-looking
of the hobby cars, an immaculate white Mustang with big
orange nines on the sides. He obviously takes a lot of pride in
his equipment. He has a truck to carry the car on, the kind that
the big-time racing teams have. Lettered on the doors of the
truck is "Brown Racing Enterprises, Whynot." Whynot is a
little community just down the road from Seagrove in Randolph
County, maybe seventy miles away from Reidsville. People are
always asking how Whynot got its name, and Melvin Brown
tells them it was because nobody could decide what to call the
place, so somebody said, "Why not call it Whynot?," which is
what they did. That is true. Charles Kuralt did a little bit one
night on the TV news about it, and Melvin Brown and the
other people in Whynot were very proud. Melvin Brown is in
his twenties, and he runs a service station in Seagrove. He has
been racing for several years now. The hobby division races are
twenty laps, and they pay $125 to win. So if nothing hap-
pens to his car, Melvin Brown can sometimes pick up a couple of hundred bucks a week, because he is a front runner. But
he has to work hard to do it, and then he doesn't really have
anything.

"You have to win some money to stay in it now," he is saying. "It gits faster every year. It'll take every penny you can win if you win every race just to keep your car up."

Earlier, when Bobby Dunlap was standing in front of the track watching the people come in, Melvin Brown had approached him and said, "Could we git up and talk to the announcer's booth? What we wanna do—I drive number nine—we wanna make a challenge. We goina give all the money we win tonight to Lynn. We'd like to challenge all the rookie cars to do the same thing. Kinda like a telethon works, you know."

"All right, okay," Bobby Dunlap had said.

"Can we git up there to see 'em?"

"Yeah, yeah, yeah."

And Melvin Brown had gone off to the announcer's booth.

It is an odd lot of cars on the track, maybe fifty or more altogether, lots of old Fords, Chevrolets, Dodges, Plymouths, but heavier cars, too, Buicks, Pontiacs, Oldsmobiles, Chryslers, even an old Studebaker, all of them banged all to hell now that the season is ending, some with hoods missing and bumpers dangling, fenders cut away with blowtorches, leaving jagged, raw wounds in the metal. "Carolina Twister," one of them has written across the front. "Sweet Thang." "Go or Blow." A few carry advertisements for local businesses, "Big Gurney's Pit Cooked Bar-B-Q," "Dogwood Septic Tank Service." But now the cars are all covered with mud.

The track equipment problems earlier in the afternoon have set everything back, and it is now well past time for the heat races to have started. The heat races are only ten laps. Finally, Bobby Dunlap decides to go ahead and start the heat races, even though the track is still too muddy. The cars do a lot of slipping and sliding and spinning as the heats begin, and after the first lap, every driver has his head hanging out the window because his windshield is coated with thick red mud and he can't see a thing, and soon every driver's head is covered with mud, too. Understandably, there is a great deal of bumping and banging around, but nothing serious.

After the first heat, the track announcer comes on the loud-speakers and pleads with the crowd, "Please do not throw cans on the racetrack. This is real, real dangerous. If you are caught throwing cans on the racetrack, you will be arrested."

Sweet Mama Sonja looks at the cars lining up for the next heat and says, "God, they got some fast runners in this race. If y'all don't pull for Fords, just keep ye mouth shut." Then she spots a driver she has not seen earlier and cries out, "Hey, honey, where's your 'mudies?," which is what she calls Bermuda shorts. "Cut them britches off! I want to see them good-lookin' laigs agin tonight!"

All around, drivers and mechanics are making last-minute adjustments to their cars, the engines roaring to life and cough-ing off. Over in the fourth turn, where cars enter the track, the guards swing open the gate, and an old pickup truck scoots across the track with a battered race car bouncing on a trailer behind. The driver finds a spot in the crowded infield, and sev-eral friends go to help him unload his car. "We didn't git an-other motor 'til three-thirty this ev'nin'," he tells another driver, "had to pull the other motor, take the cam out, and put this'un in. Looks like she's doin' purty good."

Soon the heat races are finished, and it is time for a sort of halftime break. There is a drawing for free prizes donated by local merchants in exchange for advertising. Then the announcer tells the crowd about Lynn Johnson losing his leg, and as the announcer makes the pitch, the drivers fan out across the track carrying their helmets and hats to file through the stands and collect the loose change and dollar bills that the fans are willing to cough up to pay Lynn Johnson for the leg he gave for their entertainment. The announcer tells the crowd that at the 311 Speedway the night before the crowd gave more than fifteen hundred dollars. But Sweet Mama Sonja eyes the grandstand ex-pertly and says, "The crowd's off." She doesn't expect that they'll get anywhere near fifteen hundred tonight.

The limiteds are running—older, junkier cars than the late models, but faster and not quite as junky as the hobby cars And it is just as Bobby Dunlap had said. Plenty of action. They

broadslide. They hang out. They slam into one another. Sparks
fly. Mud flies. Bumpers fall off. Somebody is spinning! Wild.
No safety features on these cars. Roll bars, but little else. The
drivers do not wear fire-resistant driving suits. They wear
service-station suits and dungarees and T-shirts. Some do not
even have helmets. Just get in the damn things and go. In the
third turn, several cars come together, and one of them goes
sliding wildly into the bank as a front wheel flies off and goes
bouncing down the track with cars dodging every which way to
keep from running over it. Then up in turn No. 1 there is a car
flying through the air *upside down!* The first turn is cut into a
high bank, and if a car goes into the turn too hard, the bank will
just pick it up and flip it over and send it sailing. So this car
is sailing through the air upside down, and another car shoots
right under it, and then the car falls and two other cars plow
into it, and people are running through the pits to see if anybody is hurt, and Little Red is jumping up and down waving
his red flag for the other cars to stop. Wild. It goes this way, and
Little Red has got his hands full, stopping and restarting, making
sure that the cars are in their proper order, rushing out to
shake his flag at an erring driver, screaming himself hoarse to be
heard over the engines, now and then turning his head to release
an angry spurt of tobacco juice.

Little Red's brother stands beside his car in the pits, saying,
"I'da won that heat race a while ago if I could see."

Out on the track the race is going again, and a car goes into
a slide coming out of the fourth turn, just as Red Justice's car
had done the week before, and it hits the mound of dirt that
separates the track from the pits, just as Red's had done, but
since last week the mound has been made higher, and the car
hangs there, the driver spinning his tires and whipping the
wheel to free it.

"Now if it'd been like that last week," Red Justice says, "nobody wouldn't've got hurt."

Ol' Duke is having a high old time. He is a squat and
muscular young man with sunburned, grimy skin. Ol' Duke is a
character, they say around the track, loud and brash and some-

times funny. He is wearing a grubby T-shirt that is now the color of the red clay, and this funny little rainhat has "Le Mans" written all over it with pictures of fancy race cars, the likes of which Ol' Duke has never seen. The bill of the hat is turned up in front. On each of his forearms, Ol' Duke has a tattooed red heart, and in one of them is the word, "Mother." Ol' Duke was feeling good when he arrived, but with the passing of the night he has grown even happier. This is because he has been making regular trips over to the wrecker that he drives, where he pulls a brown paper bag from beneath the seat. In the bag there is a bottle of Seagrams VO.

These three deputy sheriffs in brown uniforms had arrived to patrol the infield at about the time the boys were gathering around Red Justice's truck for the drivers' meeting. Two of them had climbed onto the back of the truck and approached an ol' boy who didn't seem particularly desirous of their company.

"Which one of your cousins is it that's in the cement business?" one of the deputies, the older one, had asked.

"I don't know 'im," the ol' boy said curtly.

"Yes, you do."

"Well, if I do," the ol' boy had said loudly, "I don't know what the hell he done!"

All of the ol' boys had been watching and listening, and they had laughed at this, and one of them had called out, "Somebody give them boys a drinka likker!" and that had gotten another laugh.

Now, several hours later, Ol' Duke is feeling good enough to take up the challenge. All three deputies are sitting on the back of Red Justice's truck, where they have been all night, watching the races. Ol' Duke appears beside the truck and takes a defiant stance.

"Hey!" He is addressing the oldest deputy, who is sitting nearest him. The deputy pays no attention.

"Hey!"

The deputy looks at him.

"You wanna drink?"

"Drinka what? Ice water?"

"Naw. Likker."

The deputy laughs. He doesn't want any trouble.

"Take a drinka likker!"

The deputy shakes his head and laughs again.

"You skeered, say so!"

The deputy can see now that he is not going to be able to laugh Ol' Duke away, and all of the ol' boys within hearing range are perking up, punching one another and saying, "Look at Ol' Duke."

"I don't see no likker," the deputy tries.

"I done drunk one fifth."

"You ain't drunk no *fifth*."

"Shit I ain't! Bet you a dollah. You wanna bet?"

The deputy laughs again.

"I show ya."

Ol' Duke goes off to his truck and comes back waving an empty liquor bottle.

"See. I got a'nud'un, too. It ain't empty—yet."

He climbs onto the truck and sits down close to the deputy, who winces at his breath, makes a little waving motion, and laughs.

"Don't you wanna drinka likker? Come on, have one drink."

"I might git drunk," the deputy says.

"Shit, I git drunk ever' nite durin' the week. I might even git drunk tonight."

"You ain't got far to go, have you?" the deputy says, laughing.

Ol' Duke gets up indignantly and walks back toward his wrecker.

"Well, don't say I ain't never offered you nothin'," he says.

The late models take to the track for the feature race of the night, and as soon as the green flag drops, it is obvious that these drivers know what they are doing. They are much smoother, coming off the turns in wide, slow-motion slides, then shooting quickly into the straights. It is also obvious from the beginning that only two drivers are really in competition: Red Justice and

Larry Isley. They pull away from the other cars and are soon passing them, gaining a lap each time they do.

It is easy to see why Red Justice commands respect from the other drivers. He goes deeper into the turns than any of them, and comes out quicker, and when he comes up on a slower car that does not get out of his way immediately, he reminds the guy that he is back there by slamming repeatedly into his rear end, and if that is not enough to convince him to move over, then Red does not hesitate to knock him out of the way. To make any money, you have to be rough and run hard, and Red, as he said, drives for money.

The track has dried now, and instead of mud, the cars are beginning to kick up dust. There are few spinouts, and no wrecks bad enough to stop the race, and the forty laps go quickly. With only Justice and Isley in contention, it appears that it will be a close finish, but as the end looms, Red Justice suddenly backs off, and Larry Isley shoots past the checkered flag.

After having taken his victory lap carrying the checkered flag, Larry Isley pulls his car into the pits, and several young men who help him with the car run out jubilantly to greet him, piling onto the hood and trunk of his car. "Atta boy, Larry," they are saying.

Red Justice climbs out of his car, red-faced, dripping with sweat, and looking upset.

"I had to back off," he says to one of his mechanics. "It was gettin' hot, I had to back off." He seems apologetic.

"'At's all right," the mechanic says. "Man, I'll take a week like 'is anytime, one and two! Purty damn good."

Red Justice plops onto the back of his truck and sits spraddle-legged, looking at his car. Steam is now pouring from beneath the hood. He wipes the sweat from his face with a rag and sticks the stub of his cigar back into his mouth.

"Any other race we'd-a had two or three restarts." Then he points to his radiator and says, "Looky yonder at them bugs. No wonder I'm runnin' hot."

On the back side of the track, Larry Isley has gotten out of

his car, still looking very cool, and has taken off his helmet and
run a hand over his hair to put it back in place. A big group is
standing around congratulating him, and suddenly something
goes *pop!*, and with one big swoosh of air, his right rear tire goes
flat.

"Goddamn tire blowed out," one of the boys says. "How
'bout that."

"Let me tell you," Larry Isley says with a grin. "It went down
at the right time."

Over the loudspeakers, the track announcer is saying, "Melvin Brown, donating all he takes in tonight with car number nine
to the Lynn Johnson family. He said he would like to have
all the other boys donate what they win here tonight. He would
challenge you to do this. Melvin Brown, the car number nine
hobby, goina donate all he wins to the Lynn Johnson family. We
certainly 'preciate this."

Melvin Brown is out there now, driving like hell for Lynn
Johnson's leg, and for a while it looks as if he is going to win,
for he leads most of the way, but near the end he goes into the
fourth turn a little too high, and another car shoots below him
and wins. Melvin Brown takes second and one hundred dollars
for Lynn Johnson. Only one other driver has accepted his challenge, and that is Bobby Sprinkles, who is driving Lynn Johnson's car. He finishes fourth for sixty-five dollars.

It is almost midnight when the final race ends, and the
stands begin to empty. The wives and girlfriends and children
are now free to come into the infield, and they all do, huddling
around their men while cars and equipment are loaded.

Over the loudspeakers, the announcer is saying, "Car number
five is for sale for twelve hundred dollars. Contact Lynn Johnson's wife in Greensboro. Car number five *is* for sale."

Sweet Mama Sonja comes sashaying across the infield from
the scoring booth carrying the final results and the checkbook
for the payoffs, and she was right, she says, about the collection
for Lynn Johnson. The total was $724.57. She spots Larry Isley

and goes over and says, "Come here, honey, and I'll give ye some victory sugar, if you won't tell Clyde." He bends down to kiss her cheek, and she says, "Hell, that ain't the kinda sugar I want," and gives him a popper on the lips.

At the little building in the infield where she makes the pay-offs, she is encountered by several drivers, one of whom is upset because he has just learned that he was set back a lap by Little Red for some infraction.

"The red flag was out," he is protesting.

A friend of the driver steps in and speaks up for him. "I mean the red flag was out and he just slid into 'em. He wudn't involved in the wreck, not whatsoever."

The argument goes on for a while, and finally Sweet Mama Sonja says, "That's the way it goes. You win a few and lose a few and a whole lot of 'em's rained out. Cheer up, babe."

And somebody is asking, "Where'd I finish?"

"I'll have to check. Let's see . . . thirteenth."

"Goddamn, I thought I finished higher'n 'at."

"They goina pull that sixteen?" somebody says.

"I don't know, are they?"

"Somebody said they was."

"I hope the hell they do," another driver adds.

"I hope they pull somebody tonight," says another.

"I do too," says Sweet Mama Sonja. "I don't want to go home tonight."

"I don't want to go home neither."

"I don't neither."

"Hell, I wanta stay all night!"

Across the way, No. 16 is indeed being "pulled." Some driver has lodged an official complaint, meaning that he has put up money, and the engine must be broken down and inspected to see if it is too big. Two angry young men are bending over the engine now, taking off small parts, and a small crowd has gathered to watch. One of them pulls out a spark plug that is burned all to hell and tosses it to the other. "Ain't burnin' too good there, Cleo."

"They better have somebody to do it," one of the young men says. "We ain't lettin' no fuckin' jackleg . . ."

"Clyde," says the other, turning to a friend, "find out who put up the green."

Nearby, Ol' Duke lurches to a halt in his wrecker, hangs his head out the window, and yells, "Hey, you boys wanna drink?"

And out in the parking lot, all of those shiny new cars and trucks are filing onto the dusty road, leaving behind the excitement of the Rainbow Speedway for at least another week.

California Dreamer

BILLY SCOTT was cruising again. Down the broad boulevards of San Bernardino. Just for old times' sake.

"Low riders," he said. "That's the thing now. You've never seen one of the low riders? I'll show you one."

He drove down by the corner where Big M's Drive-In had been. "That was the original McDonald's right there," he said. The building had been torn down. There was a new, busy McDonald's across the street.

Big M's was where he had hung out in high school. That was where he picked up girls and made arrangements for late-night races out on Green Spot Road. He'd won a lot of money and gotten in a few brawls racing out on Green Spot Road. They called him Billy the Kid in those days. He was winning three hundred dollars a week then, driving two-hundred-mile-an-hour double-A fuel dragsters, but that didn't mean all that much to the other kids in San Bernardino. To them he was known for having the "baddest car in town."

It was a '55 Chevy with a big GMC motor. Billy Scott had spent a lot of loving care and money on that car. He could, as he put it, "smoke" anybody with it. "Most guys wouldn't want to race me," he said matter-of-factly, "'cause they knew they'd get beat. Kids went in for speed then, but now things were changing. Low riding was the thing.

"There's one right there," Billy Scott said.

The low rider was sitting on a side street waiting to turn into the traffic. The car was an old Chevrolet painted metal-flake purple, decorated with elaborate, weird, pin-striping designs, a skull discernible on the driver's door. The body had been lowered so that it barely cleared the pavement. It would have played hell negotiating a respectable pothole. The driver's head was barely visible above the door, a ghostly pale, thin-faced young man's head covered with long, stringy hair; a thin goatee looked as if it had been pasted on the front. Billy Scott pulled alongside the car and stopped, rolling down his window.

"Hey, man, what's happenin'?"

"Hey, man." The young man shrugged. "Nothin'," he said.

They chatted briefly, neither looking at the other, both examining the other's car, each displaying signs of disdain. Billy Scott was driving a sleek new black Porsche. He drove it for one main reason: It got him a lot of pussy.

"Well, I'll be seein' you around, man," Billy Scott said, easing away.

"That was a low rider," he said. "Far out, huh? He's about the weirdest one in town. All his cars are weird. He had a pickup truck with a coffin in the back."

Low riding obviously had no appeal to Billy Scott. It might have had a few years earlier when he was in high school, but— no—that would never really have appealed to him. Speed was his thing. It had been *the* thing when he was in high school: fast cars with racing wheels and the rear ends jacked up. He was sorry to see that changing, sorry for more reasons than one. He and his father ran a speed shop in San Bernardino, selling all those parts that a guy needed to make a car really fast. Already they had begun to feel the drop in business.

"Most of the people in California are just going to fix-up items instead of fast-guy items," Billy Scott said. "You know, they're putting wheels and tires on their cars, maybe a set of headers to make it sound good, but they're not putting on the camshaft, the trick heads and the roller rockers and the tunnel rams and the blowers and stuff like that. They're just staying with the stock equipment. It's all this ecology stuff, too. It's hurting the high-performance industry out here. But mainly they're going for looks more than speed."

Speed had been bred in Billy Scott. That was why he raced stock cars, why he got so many speeding tickets in his Porsche. His father had raced. He had run roadsters in the old days of dry-lake racing in California, had been in on the early days of drag racing. Then he ran a wrecking yard in San Bernardino and built his own cars. He had put his son in a race car at the age of five, and Billy had been racing ever since.

As a kid, Billy Scott raced quarter midget cars. He has a scrapbook that his mother made, and it is filled with pictures of himself looking cute in his helmet, tearing around the corners in his little car (always in the lead), posing with his trophies, grinning shyly as cute little girls, toddler racetrack queens, kissed him on the cheek. His father gave him one basic instruction: Drive hard. Those little cars would run sixty-five or seventy, and Billy Scott pushed them as fast as they would go. "Every place we'd go we were feared, man," Billy Scott says. "We were the baddest in the land." He won so many trophies that he gave them away to friends and cousins.

When he aged out of quarter midget racing, his father put him into a dragster immediately. He ran over two hundred miles an hour for the first time when he was fifteen. In the year that he graduated from high school, he won the American Hot Rod Association's double-A fuel dragster national championship. But in November of that year the brakes on his dragster failed at the end of a run. The parachute that should have popped out to slow the car did not pop out. The car left the track at two hundred miles per hour, hit a big mound of dirt, and took flight. Billy Scott remembers nothing of the wreck after that. The car was destroyed. He almost was. His back was broken in six places. He spent four months in a hospital. Five months after the wreck, he was back racing a dragster.

He went on tour nationally that year, pulling his dragster in a trailer behind his new GTO. He went to the South first, then up the East Coast to New England, across the Northeast to the Midwest, racing several times each week. It was a wild, hectic tour. The drivers usually traveled in a pack, veering off to chase girls or lounge in pool rooms. Crazy. The whole bunch was crazy. They bought slingshots and shot marbles at cows as they breezed through the countryside, chased each other flinging cherry bombs from their car windows. And raced. Barreling down the turnpikes at 120, pulling their race cars behind.

"It was really the most fun I've ever had, I believe," Billy Scott says.

But it was hard. "Really rough," he says. The constant moving from day to day. The pressures of driving. And the work. He had to do it all himself, repairing the car, the booking, everything. Something was always breaking on the car. Sometimes he had to sleep in his trailer at the racetracks. Sometimes he didn't get to sleep at all. It was all wearing, nerve-jangling. And little, irritating things happened. In Pittsburgh, for example, he lost his wallet with $750 in it. It all began to show on him as the season wore short. One Saturday night in Wisconsin his engine failed in the last race, just before midnight. He had to be in Gary, Indiana, for another race the next morning. He worked all night on the car, then drove like hell to Indiana, barely making it in time for the race. The whole business finally came to a head at a race in Illinois. He red-lighted. Jumped the gun. A stupid mistake. He climbed out of his car, pissed off at himself, and dropped his helmet. His goggles broke. That did it. He started screaming, jumping, flailing, yelling, throwing things. His tantrum and the tour ended, he headed back to California. He had made forty-two thousand dollars for his summer's effort, and he had made up his mind about one thing. He wasn't going on any such tour again. "Just too much work for the money," he said.

For the next year, Billy Scott drove mostly at tracks in Southern California. He was losing interest in drag racing. He started driving sprint cars. Then, at the beginning of 1969, a San Bernardino businessman, who also built race cars, asked Billy Scott to drive one of his cars in a NASCAR race. It was the Permatex 200, a race for sportsman cars—older-model stock cars

—that is held at Riverside Raceway on the day before the five-hundred-mile Grand National race that draws all the big-name southern drivers each January. Billy Scott had never been in a stock car before, but he agreed to drive. He was running second, gaining on the leader with seven laps to go when the radiator blew. Still he had made an impressive start in stock car racing. He continued driving in sportsman and modified cars at tracks near his home after that, driving for somebody else until he decided to build a car of his own for the bigger races. As always, he ran hard, and he didn't let anybody push him around. He quickly became a hot dog, seldom finishing out of the top five.

"You gotta go out there to win," he was saying. "If you go there to finish fifth or sixth, why go at all? You know what I mean?"

He was sitting now in a San Bernardino restaurant, eating a cheeseburger with bacon, drinking a tall glass of milk. A few days earlier, he had driven his Chevelle, a '66 model, in the big sportsman race of the year at Riverside. He'd had problems with his car on the first day of qualifying, had to qualify later with the third-class runners, and ended up starting in thirtieth position, almost at the back of the pack, although when he finally did get his car running right, his qualifying speed was third highest. When the race began, however, he was clearly running faster than everybody on the track. He was forty-five seconds behind the leader on the second lap. On the twentieth lap, he was eighteen seconds behind, gaining more than a second a lap. Then his engine started misfiring. He pulled into the pits, and a spark-plug wire was discovered to have come off. When he went back onto the track, it happened again, and he had to make a second pit stop under the green flag. This time the problem was found. The spark plug had exploded. It was changed, and he was soon back into the race, but too far behind to catch up. He finished ninth, which paid $225. He had spent $175 just to start the race, the money going to buy his NASCAR license for the year, his pit passes for this race, and to pay the entry fee. He'd lost money this time, but that was racing.

Before the race, the Riverside newspaper had carried a story about Billy Scott in a special racing supplement. The story was headlined: *"Bill Scott New Star on the Horizon."* In the article, Billy Scott was quoted as saying, "The big money in stock car racing is in the South . . . but the experience is on the West Coast. . . . Once I get the experience, I'm heading where the money is."

That was why I had sought him out. I wanted to talk with an ambitious young driver, a good one, who was intent on making the big time.

"Next year," Billy Scott was telling me now between bites of cheeseburger. "I was going next year. That was kinda on my agenda."

He wasn't sure yet just how he was going to do it. There was the problem of money, of course.

Stock car racing was becoming more popular on the West Coast, but not popular enough for the drivers to make big money. NASCAR has a division called Grand National West, with the big-newer-model cars running on small tracks in California, Oregon, Washington, and occasionally in other states, but only a few drivers win as much as ten thousand dollars a year. Mediocre drivers in the South would win as much as the top West Coast drivers, and few West Coast drivers could be really competitive in the South. Most stock car racing in Southern California was sportsman and modified cars, or junkers running figure-eight races for the crash fiends. Few drivers could make a living racing. Most of them were amateurs, guys who did it just for fun.

Billy Scott said that he couldn't afford to run Grand National West races. The expense was too much. He could make money running modifieds and sportsman cars at little tracks close to home. "We run hard," he said. "If we finish in the top five every race, we can make a little money. I could live off of it, but I wouldn't be driving a Porsche, or taking out expensive girls." He has to work with his father to be able to do that.

He began to talk about how he might sell his sportsman car,

build himself a Grand National car, and head to the South to
give the big-league boys a run for their money.

"I figure I could leave here with two guys, a race car, and five
thousand dollars, and I'll come back at the end of the year and
have some money when I come back," he said.

I told him that drivers in the South would laugh at him for
believing that, that he'd be lucky to get through a couple of big
races without going broke.

"I would bet any amount of money that I could go back
there, and . . ." His voice trailed away. His eyes were following an attractive girl who was making her way toward the cash
register. ". . . Oh, yeah, very nice . . . uh, what was I saying?
Oh, yeah, being a West Coast guy, I could go back there . . ."

He had been doing that all through the lunch. Every time a
pretty girl walked by, he had become totally distracted. "Oh,
my goodness, look at that. That's nice," he would say. Or, "Oh,
boy, she's good-looking, huh? What do you think?"

Now he was saying that he realized that if he did go to the
South he couldn't be competitive the first year because he
wouldn't know the tracks, but that there wasn't all that much
to being competitive, and after the first year all those ol' southern boys had better watch out, because Billy Scott from California would be smoking 'em. He would be the hottest hot dog
the South had ever seen. All of those big-car owners would be
begging him to drive for them. He would take the big money
and he would go on to drive and win at Indianapolis. That was
his dream. And he was just that confident, just that cocky.
There was no better race driver in the world than Billy Scott.

"Anything you want to win at, you know, you have to go at it
right," he said. "Just like Janis Joplin's song says, 'Try a little
harder.' You know. That's all you gotta do.

"Everybody says, 'Well, you need money.' Really, money is
the big thing, but if one guy's got the same amount of money
as the other guy, the guy that's trying hardest is the guy that's
goina win.

"The guy that stays out chasing girls . . . see, that's my big thing. I chase too many girls, you know. I don't—I don't chase *too many of 'em* but, you know, I like to do that."

If anything would keep Billy Scott from becoming a stock car racing star in the South, it might well be girls. Girls are like speed to him, an obsession.

Billy Scott used to have a garage for his race car that was very nice. It was big enough so that he had fixed up a little apartment in the back. He had moved in rugs, sofas, lamps, a stereo, the whole works. Very cool. It was a very elegant garage. Think of it. He could take girls there and make it with them in the same room with, and almost in reach of, his race car! Wild. There was something about that that seemed to turn girls on.

Billy Scott no longer had that garage. It cost too much. He had moved his car into a smaller garage at half the price. There was not room for all the expensive furnishings, but he *had* managed to squeeze in the couch.

It was afternoon, and Billy Scott had stopped by his garage. A black dude, a very cool cat, dropped by. Billy Scott had known him for several years. The guy was roly-poly and had a little goatee. He looked like Charlie Chan. He had brought a few items for Billy Scott to inspect. One was an expensive slide projector. Another was an eight-millimeter movie projector. Both had been used previously.

"Bill and a half," the dude said. "These are nice things, man."

Billy Scott had bought from him before. This guy could get a person almost anything he wanted. He always offered a good deal. Billy Scott never asked where he got the stuff.

"You don't have to pay me now. Keep the stuff, check it out."

The dude had a good line of jive. He walked over to Billy Scott's race car and caressed the fender.

"I was out there Saturday," he said. "This baby run like a motherfucker. Oh, she was *sweet*."

They talked about the race.

"What you take for that tach?" the black dude said, looking inside the car.

"Twenty on the top."

The dude took a big roll of bills from his pocket, peeled a twenty off the top, and laid it on top the car. Billy Scott got a screwdriver and removed the tachometer.

"How about that?" Billy Scott said, smiling, pocketing the money. "Sell the damn tach right off the car."

The dude held the instrument up to the light, examining it as if it were a precious stone.

"Shit, man," he said, "I 'onna tell everybody that mother-fucker run at Riverside!"

The race car needed some work done on it, and Billy Scott was planning to do it that night. A friend was coming over to help. But that night Billy Scott was sitting at a table in his garage unreeling a roll of eight-millimeter film onto the floor. The film was looped together in a cartridge. It was one of those peep-show machine films. Somebody had picked up two of the films in a peep show room of a local dirty-book store. They were just lying there on top of one of the machines. It seemed obvious that nobody wanted them.

Billy Scott had been trying to show the films on the projector that the black dude had brought. He wanted to test the machine, but he wasn't having much luck. He didn't know how to run it, and it didn't come with instructions.

Several guys were in the garage on the pretense of coming to help Billy Scott with his car. Most of them were high school kids who liked to hang around the garage. They never were much help. Billy Scott had bought a couple of six-packs of beer for the evening. He finally decided that what he needed to show the films was another reel, and he sent a couple of the kids to a nearby discount store to try to find one. They came back with several of different sizes.

After much unreeling and rewinding of film and a lot of tinkering with the projector, Billy Scott finally got it to work, and the films began to flicker on one of the garage walls.

Billy Scott drank more beer and showed the films several

times. He was expecting a couple of chicks to drop by after while, he said. When the girls had not arrived by eleven o'clock, Billy Scott said the hell with them. Their loss, he figured. He wanted to go out to a couple of joints he knew. The others left, and he locked up the garage without having touched his car all evening.

The joints were on the edge of town, seedy places, side by side. They sold beer and featured nude dancers. Big signs advertised "BOTTOMLESS."

Billy Scott was wearing faded blue jeans that drooped in the seat with a blue plaid wool shirt and a little knit cap on his dark, curly hair. He was not a particularly good-looking guy, not at all the Robert Redford type, but there was something about him that attracted girls. He was always making off with the best-looking women, and other guys did not understand how he did it. He got a beer and sat at a table at the back of one of the joints, away from the stage.

A dark-haired girl was dancing to a hard-rock tune. She looked to be in her late twenties. The scars where the silicone had been implanted were visible under her firm, heavy breasts. A raunchy dance. She poured white lotion onto her breasts and stomach, smearing it with her fingers. She pulled one finger through the lips of her twat with elaborate motions and licked it. She lifted her breasts to her mouth and licked them.

"What a fucking pig," Billy Scott said.

A fat Mexican girl, a waitress, sat down beside several guys at one side of the stage. One of them whispered something to her and she laughed wildly, pulled back the edge of her costume, and exposed pubic hair.

Several black guys occupied the other side of the stage. They were having a big time, yelling and laughing. The girl on stage seemed to be dancing for them.

"Look at that," Billy Scott said. "She's a fucking nigger lover. I hate a goddamn nigger lover!"

Billy Scott got another beer from a tall, leggy waitress. She was wearing a thin, white body-suit with nothing on beneath. Billy Scott thought that she had a fantastic body. He slipped an arm around her waist and put a tip on her tray.

"You goina dance?" he said. "We wanta see *you* dance."

She smiled and slipped away.

Billy Scott decided to go next door.

This joint was decorated in red. Dim red lights glowed. A slim blond girl, blank-eyed, lank-haired, and nude danced languidly on a stage above the bar. She looked very young, and her pubic hair was very fine. Several guys sat slumped around the bar sipping beer and watching the girl.

A tall girl in a red, abbreviated outfit brought the beer. Her outfit included red mesh stockings. She was a very big girl, not fat, but big-boned. She towered over Billy Scott. Her face was pretty, and her blond hair was teased high on her head. She smiled. When she took the money back to the cash register, Billy Scott confided to me that she had given him the eye.

The music stopped, and the naked girl strolled limply off the stage. She looked spaced-out. On drugs probably. Billy Scott took his beer to the back of the room. A guy that he recognized was shooting pool alone on a coin-operated table. The guy was younger than Billy Scott, and he had an artificial leg that caused him to limp slightly. Billy Scott shot a game of pool with him.

"Hey, man, I finally run Patti," the guy said.

"You smoke her?"

"Yeah. That girl can drive, though."

Billy Scott returned to the bar to finish his beer. "That guy's a street racer," he said, explaining that was how the guy had lost his leg.

"Any good?" I asked.

"He's pretty good. He wouldn't've been shit back when I was street racing. None of these guys would have."

The limp girl was displaying her body again. Billy Scott began to talk about his two great passions. "If a man can fuck and drive race cars, man . . . I mean, what else is there?" He told about this girl he had met at the race a few days earlier. She was a Miss Something or Other, a professional model from L.A., a real knockout. He'd taken her out. She had invited him to go on a weekend skiing trip. He had turned her down. He was explaining why. The girl was a great skier. Billy Scott knew nothing about it. He'd probably bust his ass.

"I ain't letting no chick outdo me at anything," he said.

"Another beer?" The big blonde.

When she brought the beers, she stayed around a few minutes to talk. Billy Scott leaned across the bar talking quietly to her. He seemed to have captured her with his eyes. He did not take his eyes from hers. His eyes were the most striking feature of his face. They were wide-set. She seemed to have trouble breaking their grip, and when she did, she went back to the cash register.

"Watch this," Billy Scott said, grinning. "I'll bet anything she's over there writing down her telephone number for me. This is goina be good how she gets it to me without all these other guys knowing."

He made it easy for her when she came back. He took off his knit cap.

"How you like my hat?" he said, passing it to her.

"That's nice," she replied, twirling the cap on her fingers. "Where'd you get it?"

She handed the hat back and went off to serve another customer who was calling for beer. Billy Scott took a quick peek inside the hat and smiled. He slid it across the bar to me. I looked inside. The girl's name, address, and telephone number were there, scribbled on a scrap of paper.

"What'd I tell you?" he said, gloatingly. He was laughing, flushed with success. "Goddamn! It's great! Great! It's just like winning a heat race!"

The Site of Excitement...
Vermont?

SUNDAY AFTERNOON. The road up the mountain is jammed, and I am caught in the middle of it. The car ahead of mine is a flashy purple Plymouth Satellite with a white vinyl top. Plastic letters affixed to the back spell out "The Fugitive." On the left rear side window are decals advertising "Champion Spark Plugs," "Edelbrook Manifolds," "High Performance Holley Equipped," "Hijackers." The car edges along impatiently on wide racing tires, and it is jacked so high in the back that it looks as if the passengers have to harness themselves fast to the seats to keep from falling into the windshield. The passengers are one girl and three guys. They all look to be in their twenties. The girl is with the driver. She is sitting very close. He is wearing a clinging yellow shirt that is cut low in the neck and has no sleeves. His left arm, resting in the window, is still pale, for the warm weather has just arrived. They are headed, as am I, as are all the vehicles in this long line snaking up Quarry Hill, to a racetrack that has been cut into the top of the mountain. The track is named Thunder Road. It bills itself as "The Nation's Site of Excitement!"

Near the mountaintop, the line of vehicles is directed into a big green field, and I park beside the purple Satellite. The girl gets out of the car carrying a blanket. Two of the guys cling to the remainders of six-packs of Colt 45. One is wearing a T-shirt with a pack of cigarettes rolled into the left sleeve. As they get out of the car, I notice that a pair of large foam-rubber dice dangle from the rear-view mirror. Across the dashboard there are little footprints made of yellow fake fur. All around us are other people scurrying along carrying blankets, ice chests, and folding aluminum lawn chairs, all well prepared for another Sunday afternoon of excitement. Soon the mountainside will reverberate with the inharmonious roar of stock car racers. Thunder Road! Visions of Robert Mitchum and mountain boys on midnight moonshine runs. As I near the gate, I can hear country music oozing from the public-address loudspeakers. Ol' Hank Snow is singing about drinkin' wine. Spo-dee-oh-dee.

This is too much. I have to keep reminding myself that this is not a mountaintop in Carolina, or Tennessee, or Georgia, or Alabama. This mountain hovers over Barre, Vermont, home of the world's largest granite quarries. This is a *Yankee* mountain, for godsakes, but if I didn't know better, I'd swear I was in the heart of Dixie. What is going on here, anyway?

The day before, I had sat in a silo house in the ski village of Stowe asking just that question of Ken Squier, who built Thunder Road. Ken Squier is a man who knows a great deal about stock car racing all over the country, and I had asked him if there was any difference in these people and those one might find at a southern racetrack.

"None at all," he'd said. "I think Mississippi and Vermont and Alabama and Vermont are very much alike. They're agrarian, not the richest places in the world, and folks work hard. The main difference is that we never had a real black and white problem."

It shouldn't have come as a surprise then, I suppose, that Vermont would be the center of the most extensive stock car racing circuit north of the Mason-Dixon line. It was a rural state, after all, and stock car racing was a rural sport, basic and simple. It had developed in Vermont much as it had in the South, with country boys coming home from World War II, money in their pockets, looking for excitement. They pushed off dirt tracks in farm fields and raced almost anything that would run. Even pickup trucks. "Those were really wild times," says Ken Squier. "How anybody lived through it, I'll never know." As in the South, stock car racing became very popular in Vermont. At one time there were four dirt tracks in the city of Burlington alone.

Ken Squier grew up with stock car racing in Vermont. His father, who owns a radio station in Waterbury, used to announce harness races at fairgrounds tracks, and it was at these tracks that Ken Squier, as a child, saw his first car races. Those were sprint cars and they greatly excited him. "They were just unbelievable," he recalls, "I just couldn't get over them." He saw his first stock car race shortly afterward and was quickly hooked. He remembers hitchhiking at the age of fourteen to Morrisville, where a dirt track had been pushed off behind a garage, to announce his first race from the bed of a logging truck. By the time he was in college in Boston, he had his own stock car racer and was driving regularly at stump jumper tracks around New England. When he wasn't driving, he was announcing races.

"I would love to have been a really good driver," he says now, with a touch of disappointment, "but I discovered I could do the announcing far better."

After returning home from college to work with his father, he gave up race driving, but not racing altogether. He and others joined to build Thunder Road in the late fifties, and a few years later he was a partner in the construction of Catamount Raceway in Milton, a little town bordering Burlington. These two tracks now make up the core of the NASCAR Northern Circuit for the Late-Model Sportsman Division—cars not quite as new, nor with engines quite as big as the Grand National Division—although four other tracks are included in the circuit. The season opens when the winter snows have cleared, and closes in September, just before they begin again. Races are held on Friday nights at the Plattsburgh International Speedway (leased by Ken Squier) in New York, just across Lake Champlain from Burlington (the race cars are hauled over by ferry), at Catamount on Saturday nights, Thunder Road on Sunday afternoons, then at Devil's Bowl Speedway in West Haven, Vermont, on Sunday nights. It makes for a hard weekend for drivers and mechanics, almost all of whom work at regular jobs during the week. Occasionally, races are also held at the Seekonk Speedway in Seekonk, Massachusetts, and at the Sanair Speedway in St. Pie, Quebec. But Vermont is the bedrock. Stock car races are held in every other state in New England, but in no other is the sport as popular as in Vermont.

"Our sport is auto racing," said Ken Squier. "That's it. It's the only sport the state has. It's a really big thing here."

I didn't really comprehend how big until that Saturday night, when I went to Catamount Raceway with Ken Squier. Here was this big field packed with cars, and the grandstands filling with more than four thousand people. There were many families. It was like a community gathering. I had never seen such a crowd at a small racetrack, and there was an air about the place that was different from that at other small tracks. This was more like Grand National Racing, the big tracks.

Ken Squier had told me that the local drivers were heroes, that more kids in Vermont wanted to grow up to be race drivers than football players, baseball players, basketball players, or any other sort of hero. Kids and grown-ups alike were lined up at souvenir stands to buy programs, photographs of favorite drivers, T-shirts emblazoned with sketches of Jean-Paul Cabana, Bobby Dragon, and other local drivers. They lined the pit fence clutching cameras and autograph pads, calling out to drivers they recognized, but most of the drivers were too busy making last-minute adjustments to their cars to respond.

Ken Squier does not get to spend a lot of time at his racetracks. When his tracks became affiliated with NASCAR several years ago, he met Bill France, who offered him a job as track announcer at Daytona. He took it. That job led to another as announcer on the Motor Racing Network, broadcasting seventeen of the year's biggest races on radio stations nationwide. This had led to a job with CBS sports, doing TV reports on auto racing and other sports. Ken Squier had become a big man in motor racing, and all of this kept him busy and away from home a lot.

On this night, however, he was home, and he was upset about a few things. So when the drivers' meeting was called in the pits, he climbed onto the back of a truck to make a little speech. The Indianapolis 500 had been run the week before with its usual carnage, and once again the cry to ban this brutal sport, auto racing, had gone up around the land. There had even been a letter to the editor of the local paper; Ken Squier hadn't liked that letter at all.

"As long as Indy continues to fuck up," he told his drivers, "we're the ones who're going to suffer for it, because all the bleeding hearts think we're the same, and goddamnit, we're not! . . . All we gotta do is get one guy hurt like that poor guy of Granatelli's and we're all in trouble. . . ."

Some of the boys had been engaging in some potentially dangerous practices, and he made it clear that he wanted it stopped. He went on for a while, talking about several things, until some guy in the back of the crowd called out, "Why don't you come more often, you won't have to talk so much." Everybody laughed, and Ken Squier stepped down and let Archie Blackadar, his partner, the chief steward, the man who keeps things running, get the amateur cars (the Hurricane Division, it is called in Vermont) lined up to start the heat races.

While the heat races were being run, I wandered through the pits and chatted with some of the drivers and mechanics. I was impressed by the equipment, especially the late-model cars, all far better and more carefully tended than at most small tracks. There was an air of professionalism here akin to big-time racing, one of the reasons, I suppose, that the NASCAR Northern Circuit annually produces some of the top Sportsman Division drivers in the nation. The circuit is so well respected that the year before, when some of the top people in stock car racing formed a group to help Ritchie Panch, the promising seventeen-year-old son of Marvin Panch, one of stock car racing's best drivers of an earlier day, get his start in racing, they had sent him to Vermont for a season to gain experience. One reason that the competition was good was that enough people came to races to make the purses worthwhile. A driver could pick up five hundred dollars for winning a thirty-lap feature race. In the previous season, five drivers had won more than twenty thousand dollars, one more than thirty thousand dollars, all in Vermont. Not bad for a summer.

Bobby Dragon was the driver who had won more than thirty thousand dollars the year before. He had won twenty-two feature races to do it. Muscular and raw-boned, he was a soft-spoken, modest man, married, his wife expecting a child. Now twenty-seven, he had been racing for ten years. He had followed his brother Beaver, five years older, into racing. "He'd made a big name for himself," said Bobby Dragon. "It looked like a lot of fun. I really liked cars. I really enjoyed the sport. I thought maybe I could drive too."

As it turned out, he could. Very well. He and his brother dominate the circuit. They had won the first four races of the season. Bobby Dragon was at the top of the point standings, followed closely by his brother.

"I've been lucky to have real good mechanics," says Bobby Dragon, with the modesty of a true champion.

Bobby Dragon drove a '66 Chevelle. He and four others owned it. They all worked on the car. "All of us have got an eight-hour-a-day job," said Bobby Dragon, who works as a facilities repairman at the Burlington IBM plant, "and evenings, it seems like every evening, and every weekend, we spend on the car."

For all of that effort, Bobby Dragon and his four partners cleared a profit of about ten thousand dollars the year before, but they had put most of it back into equipment. They had bought a wrecked school bus and rebuilt it so that they could carry the race car and themselves in it. This year, because of their success the year before, they had picked up a sponsor. "The Howard Bank" was painted in big letters on the bus and the race car.

Like almost every small-track driver, Bobby Dragon dreamed of bigger things. He wanted to win a national Sportsman Division championship (he was ninth the year before) and to drive at Daytona ("Right now," Ken Squier had told me, "every kid here dreams of going to Daytona. Boy, going to Daytona, that's like dying and going to heaven.").

I asked him if he wanted to get into big-time racing, and he said, "Well, it would take a lot of money, but I'd be willing to give it a try. You'd have to have a real good sponsor."

After that, Bobby Dragon had to go out and run a heat race. He'd blown an engine the week before, and he was a little concerned about the new one, but it ran well enough to win the heat race.

Before the feature race started, I climbed into the scoring tower at the back of the grandstand to watch it. The official scorer, Dr. Gordon Neilsen, an entomologist at a nearby college, worked over his sheets. The track announcer, Ken Miller —a thin, thirty-eight-year-old ex-minister from Pennsylvania, bearded, long-haired, with a bald spot in back, hippie-attired, he had come to Vermont seeking truth and had found stock car racing—hunched over his microphone, a Marlboro smoking in his left hand. The night had turned very cold, and the windows in the scoring stand kept fogging, making it difficult for everybody.

"Don't forget," Ken Miller announced as the cars lined up for the feature race, "next Saturday night here at Milton's Catamount Stadium, it's the Milton 100, the first national championship race of 1973, one hundred laps of fantastic, torrid, late-model sportsman competition, next Saturday night here at the home of the brave, the Milton 100!"

All was ready now. The cars had been making their way slowly around the third-mile track behind the safety trucks. "Safety trucks come in," said Ken Miller. "And there's the green flag!"

Mac Miller, who had started on the pole, led into the first turn with the whole pack trying to burst past him. By the time the first lap had been completed, cars were spread out all around the track. "Tight, tight running," Ken Miller was saying dramatically over the roar of the engines, "as number ninety-nine,

Mac Miller, takes to the underside of . . . OH! HE T-BONES
HIM IN THE FACE OF THE FIELD! A ROUGH MO-
MENT ON THE BACKSTRETCH!

Cars were slamming into one another all over the place. The
yellow flag went out. The race was stopped.

The wreckage was cleared away, the race restarted, but it had
no sooner picked up momentum than Ken Miller was shouting
into his microphone, "OH, WOW! BAD NEWS! BAD NEWS!
YELLOW ON THE SPEEDWAY!"

Ken Squier was upset that the hot drivers were taking off
on the starts before the green flag was dropped. He kept barking
orders into telephones and radios. "Assistant flagman, tell Tom
Newton to watch on this restart. Johnny Rosati really jumped
that last one. All the big shoes did, but Johnny was right up in
front, very obvious in front of the crowd here.

"Archie, you go out and warn Cabana, warn Rosati about
jumping that flag. He really took a jump."

It went on that way, one wreck, one restart after another,
each giving Ken Miller a chance to throw in another commercial for a local business establishment—"In the event you
have the munchies following the racing action tonight, a great
way to take care of that problem is with a Domino's pizza"
—until it began to look as if this race would never be finished.
Then to cap it off, communications between the scoring booth
and flagman's stand broke down, just as the end was looming.
The flagman, Tom Newton, had no way of knowing a winner,
and he stood looking helplessly at the scoring booth as the race
went past its allotted thirty laps, until, after much frantic
waving and shouting from the scoring booth, he finally understood and dropped the checkered flag.

"We must've run thirty-three or thirty-four, but that's between us," said the scorer with a shrug.

Ken Squier was angry. "I wanta talk to the flagman," he
snapped. "I wanta talk to the electrician." It had not been a
good night.

The checkered flag had been given to Jean-Paul Cabana, a
handsome, curly-haired, blue-eyed Canadian, a favorite of the

women fans with his heavy French accent, a professional driver who had been racing for nearly twenty years. Bobby Dragon had gone out of the race with another blown engine.

Now it is Sunday afternoon, and the drivers have brought their cars to Thunder Road, and all of these people are plunking down three bucks a head to watch them go around and around the quarter-mile track.

This track is incongruous with its surroundings. The setting is simply too beautiful for a racetrack. It is hard to imagine why anybody would want to put race cars here to spoil the scenery. But these are race fans, and they are a breed apart. All around me there are people wearing racing jackets, Daytona Raceway T-shirts (there are large numbers of people in Vermont who take their vacations every year at Daytona Beach during Speed Weeks), and other items of apparel that bespeak their loyalty to their sport. Many of them have filed into the grandstands near the track, but many more sprawl in the grass beneath birch trees and sugar maples on the hillside, sipping beer and munching hot dogs and waiting for the action to start.

They are not disappointed. Thunder Road is known as a track that is "good" for wrecks. In the second heat, car No. 51 performs a sudden somersault on the frontstretch and comes to a stop on its top in front of the grandstand, smoking, water and oil pouring onto the track. Everybody is on his feet, straining to see. People from the infield run toward the car carrying fire extinguishers. After a long pause, the driver crawls out meekly. "He's out on his feet!" Ken Miller cries over the loudspeakers, and the crowd breaks into applause.

As the afternoon proceeds, there are several spinouts, a few collisions, another flipper. Nothing serious. All in the course of an afternoon.

The feature race is an exciting one, a head-to-head battle all the way between Bobby Dragon and Jean-Paul Cabana. The night before, Bobby Dragon and his crew had hauled his crippled car back to their shop, got the parts manager of the local Chevrolet dealership to open up at midnight to provide them with parts, and they had worked all night to get the car running again, finishing just in time to get it to the track. Dragon had won at Thunder Road the week before. Cabana wanted this one badly, however. His win at Catamount the night before had given him two in a row. A local beer company had posted a bonus award of eight hundred dollars to any driver who could win three in a row. He could pick up thirteen hundred dollars by winning this race.

As the race nears the end, with the crowd on its feet, cheering and waving, Cabana is leading, with Dragon right on his bumper. As they start down the frontstretch, Dragon makes a move to pass on the inside, and Cabana moves over just enough so that Dragon's front fender clips the wall, spewing sparks. As Dragon's car limps into the pits, Cabana takes the checkered flag. Some fans are ecstatic, others angry, throwing their beer cans toward the track.

"That's racing," Ken Miller is saying over the loudspeakers. "Tough break for Dragon. The Canadian ace was not to be denied—Jean-Paul Cabana puts together the hat trick! Three in a row!"

In the pits there is now a feverish loading of equipment. It is almost five o'clock. At six o'clock the races start at Devil's Bowl. That is more than sixty miles down the road.

"Do you think Bobby could catch you?" somebody is asking Cabana.

"I don't know," he says. "You never know."

I catch up with Bobby Dragon and ask him what happened.

"Just trying to get around him," he says, "tire hit the wall. I'm not blaming him. It would've been hard to get around him. He was loose. Every time I tried to get around him, his ass end was all over the place."

"Damage it badly?" I ask.

He shakes his head.

A kid wearing a Bobby Dragon T-shirt runs up, calling, "Hey, Bobby! Hey, Bobby! You should've won, Bobby."

Dragon smiles faintly and hurries off to his bus. There is another race yet to run.

Stuffings, Part 3

The World's
Number One,
All-Time Great,
Stock Car Racing...

Driver

THE COMMUNITY of Level Cross lies on the edge of the North Carolina Piedmont, a crossroads on U. S. Highway 220, twelve miles south of Greensboro, five miles north of a little river-town called Randleman. There isn't much in Level Cross—neat, comfortable, middle-class houses, a trailer park, a couple of churches, a nice brick community center with a lighted baseball field out back, the new volunteer fire department building across the road —but it may be the best-known crossroads community in the South. The reason is Level Cross' only industry, No. 1 tourist attraction, and leading family. All bear the name Petty.

Stock car racing people do a lot of arguing about who is, or was, the greatest stock car racing driver of all time. Some say Fireball Roberts, some Curtis Turner, some David Pearson, and so on. But if the criteria for judging are to be the number of races and amount of money won, then the question is settled: Richard Petty is the greatest. He is so far out front that no other driver is ever likely to equal his record. He is *the* superstar of stock car racing.

Richard Petty lives less than a mile down the road from the volunteer fire station in a modest, red brick "ranch style" house. His younger brother, Maurice, one of racing's best mechanics, lives in another brick house across the road. Next door is a stately white house with a big front porch and a stone foundation, a house that Richard Petty's grandfather built. Here, with his wife Elizabeth, lives Lee Petty, now the family patriarch, a man who decided to go racing in the late forties and took his two young sons with him. Lee Petty became one of the great drivers of his day and held the record for winning races and national championships until his son came along and blitzed it. Next to the big white house, built around an old farmshed where Lee Petty put together his first race cars, is the center of Petty Enterprises, a cyclone-fence-enclosed compound of big blue-and-white steel buildings—a factory, no less, and the only product is race cars.

"Looks like a dealership," the governor said, glancing around the big parts warehouse.

"That's what it is," Richard Petty replied. "It's a little dealership and a little factory."

This was a warm, sparkling fall day in 1973, and a big crowd had gathered at the Petty Enterprises compound. A few years earlier, when the Pettys had finished a new building in the complex, somebody got the idea to hold an open house to inaugurate it. More than twelve thousand people showed up, tying up the community for a full day and ruining Lee Petty's spacious lawn with their cars. The highway patrol had to send out several cars and a contingent of troopers to help clear up the jam. Richard Petty sat for more than eight hours signing autographs without interruption that day.

This crowd was more manageable, only about three hundred people, delegates to the second annual Richard Petty Fan Club convention. They had come from seventeen different states, representing the five thousand fan club members throughout the country (chapters in forty-five states). Some of them had driven all night from such distant points as Long Island and Cincinnati. In the morning, they had toured the compound; then they had gathered under the big oaks outside the community center and stood in groups talking racing, almost all of them wearing something with Richard Petty's name on it (one man was smoking a pipe painted "Petty blue" with Petty's car number, 43, embossed on the sides of the bowl), while the ladies of the community prepared a sumptuous spread of "country cook-ing" inside. It all had the air of a country church homecoming. The governor, a short, elfin man named James Holshouser, the special guest and featured speaker, had arrived late by helicop-ter, his landing sending kids scurrying in excitement. The gov-ernor's aides apparently had not fully understood the nature of the occasion, for the governor obviously thought it was just a community gathering to pay tribute to Richard Petty. But there were few local people present. Nonetheless, after speaking about the contribution the Pettys had made to the state, he had gone on to talk about a new river bridge that he had just authorized to replace a rickety old one in Randleman.

Now Richard Petty was giving the governor a brief tour of the compound before the highlight of the day, the pit crew races in which he, the governor, and some of the fans would partici-pate. They saw the top-secret room where the engines are assem-bled, paused to look at the antique cars in the old farmshed where it all began, and took a quick tour through the new body shop.

"We started building here about 1953, and we're still build-ing," Petty said, laughing. "Keeps our North Carolina taxes from goin' up."

"Don't do that!" said the governor. "We need all we can get."

"We have to do something with it or Uncle Sam gets it all."

One of Petty's race cars was parked in a sort of courtyard outside the shops awaiting the pit crew races.

"Have you ever looked at one of the race cars up close?" Petty asked.

"Yes, I got to look at them down at Charlotte last fall," said the governor, following Petty over to the car.

"This one we're runnin' at Rockingham this comin' Sunday."

"That's a nice track down there."

"Yeah, it's one of the nicer tracks that we run."

The governor stuck his head into the window of the car.

"You've got a halfway decent set of protection, don't you?"

"Oh, yeah."

"I guess you have to."

"Yeah, there's no way that you could run and run and run without *somethin'* happenin'. With me ridin' in 'em, I'm goina make it just as safe as I can. If I'm goina ride in it, you can bet I'm goina make it safe."

Everybody had begun to line up for the start of the pit crew races, and Petty, wearing his usual open-necked sport shirt and jeans, turned to the governor, who was wearing his usual conservative blue suit. "You goina do it with your necktie on?" Petty said, grinning. "Git with the crowd."

The governor took off his coat and tie, rolled his shirt sleeves, and the amateur pit crews set to their competition to much cheering, picture-snapping, and shouted encouragement. Everybody laughed when a sportswriter turned jackman went sprawling over his equipment and one of the women in the crews put the lugs on backward, and they applauded the governor's efforts as a tireman.

But the governor had arrived this day with a problem of which he was unaware, as it was not a particularly windy day. The seat of his conservative trousers had a long rip in the seam, and his executive white boxer shorts were shining through. Some people had noticed this, although his aides and bodyguards apparently had not, but those who had noticed it had not been able to muster the courage to approach the governor to tell him about it. As he bent to his work changing the race car tire, however, the governor's sartorial gap became embarrassingly evident to all, and his aides had rushed to effect a cover-up, as political aides are so apt to do. The governor abruptly disappeared into a garage, where, surrounded by several burly state highway patrolmen, he removed his trousers. They were rushed to Richard Petty's mama, who did a quick repair job with a needle, and the governor was soon back for another round of competition, grinning somewhat sheepishly and saying that he wouldn't have missed this for the world.

Elizabeth Petty thought no more of darning the governor's trousers than she had thought of sewing up rips in her sons' overalls when they were boys. ("She's a mama," one of the highway patrolmen had said, "she knows how to handle these things.") Governors, presidents, emperors—it didn't matter. They were no different from anybody else. Nobody awed her, and she believed in treating everybody the same. That was just the way she was. It was the way all the Pettys were.

One of the delegates to the convention, Don Irwin of Lancaster, Pennsylvania, had summed up the way most people felt about the Pettys after they had met them: "I like to come down here," he had told me. "Everybody's always so friendly. These Pettys are just great people. They always have time for you."

The Pettys were country people, simple, decent, God-fearing, and friendly, as most country people are, and they had remained country people. Perhaps as much as any other family, the Pettys represented what America was supposed to be about. They had believed and worked hard, and all the good things that were supposed to happen as a result had come to them. Yet it hadn't changed them. They were still the same down-to-earth people they had always been.

If any of the Pettys were going to change, it should have been Richard, for all the pressures and opportunities had surely been his. He had become rich and famous, a hero. He had paid his respects at the White House and toured Vietnam to visit the troops. Hollywood had made a movie about his life, and he had played the leading role (doing a creditable job, too; he was at least as good an actor as, say, Elvis, or Rory Calhoun, both of whom had starred in dreadful stock car racing flicks). But his friends, neighbors, and the people around the racetracks would be the first to say that Richard Petty had never gotten "the big head."

"Same ol' Richard," says Ronnie Hucks, who has been a friend since high school days.

Richard sums up the Petty attitude succinctly: "A man don't want to git above his raisin's, you know."

Those "raisings" were humble indeed. One of Richard Petty's earliest and most vivid memories came at the age of six, in 1943, when his mother splashed some kerosene into the wood cooking stove one morning and it exploded, burning down the small frame Petty home before she had time to get anything out

except herself and her two sons. The family moved into Richard's grandfather's house, where they stayed until the war
ended, when Lee Petty built a tiny three-room house out of a
construction trailer. He was doing a little farming then, growing
tobacco and trying to make a go out of a little trucking business
(some say that Lee Petty and his brother, Julie, also did a little
likker hauling, although the Pettys do not acknowledge this).
But a great deal of his time was spent breaking down cars and
putting them back together with his brother Julie. The front-
yard was always strewn with old cars and car parts. Lee Petty
had been obsessed with cars since he was sixteen and gotten his
first Model T. Nights he and Julie raced their cars on the red
dirt roads around Level Cross. Guys with hot cars would come
from as far away as Atlanta to race against the Petty brothers,
and oftentimes there would be big money bet on those races.
Some people around Level Cross would see Lee Petty speeding
by, throwing up big clouds of red dust, and they would shake
their heads and say that he was sure to come to no good—if he
didn't get himself killed first.

By 1947, organized stock car races of a sort were being held at
the Greensboro Fairgrounds and at a little track near Martinsville, Virginia, and the Petty brothers went to almost all of them.
They were confident that they could put together a better car
and drive it faster than anybody they saw at those races, and
they began making plans to do just that. They bought a '39
Plymouth coupe and put a straight-eight Chrysler engine in it.
By the time they'd finished rebuilding and refining it, they'd
sunk nearly four thousand dollars into the project. It would take
a lot of races to get that much money back, and the car would
likely be torn up before they did it. Lee Petty made his formal
racing debut in that car in 1948, however, and he was astounded
when he finished only second. He had expected to completely
dazzle the competition.

The following spring, the recently organized NASCAR announced plans for its first "new car" race at Charlotte, and Lee
Petty was itching to get into it. He talked a friend into letting him
borrow his '48 Buick Roadmaster for the race. He had raced the

car on the back roads before and knew that it would really run. He spent days preparing the car, and when the day of the race came, he loaded his family into it and drove off to Charlotte. The car gave him all the power he needed. He was about to take the lead in the race when a sway bar broke and the Buick rolled four times. It took two wreckers to haul it off. The family had to hitch a ride back home, and Lee Petty had a lot of explaining to do to his friend, but that wreck had convinced him of one thing: He was going to have to get a lighter car.

By the time the first race was held at Darlington in 1950, Lee Petty had his light car. A Plymouth. Thus began an association between Plymouth and Petty that was to last for years, with only brief interruptions. At Darlington that day, the heavier cars began falling out under the pressure of the mounting mileage, but Lee Petty and Johnny Mantz, who was also driving a Plymouth, kept plugging away, always staying at the front, with Mantz finally beating out Petty to win.

But Lee Petty took second place in the point standings that year in his Plymouth, third the next, and in 1954 he finally won his first championship. Two more would follow.

Richard was twelve and Maurice ten when their father started racing full time in 1950, and they both fancied themselves as racing mechanics. They went to all the races, and although there was a rule prohibiting anybody under eighteen from the pits, they usually managed to sneak around it. Their summers were hectic and exciting times, traveling to tracks around the South and into the North and Midwest, racing several times a week. They found themselves heroes to their classmates when they had to return to school in the fall, not so much because of the racing as for the traveling they had done.

High school had held no real interest for Richard except for athletics. He was 6 feet 2 and weighed over 180 pounds and he played football, basketball, and baseball for Randleman High, while managing to maintain a grade average close to B. Nights, he hurried home to help his father work on his car. He and Maurice had begun to learn the mechanics of a car when they first started traveling with their father. He let them do simple things at first, advanced them as they were ready. By the time he was eighteen, Richard was already building engines.

Lee Petty lived by maxims: Anything worth doing was worth doing well, he taught his sons. He also taught them that the person who works the longest, tries the hardest, always puts forward the extra effort, is the one who wins. Richard and Maurice listened to this advice and saw the results.

When he was twenty-one, Richard decided he would like to try his hand at driving in a race. He'd expressed some interest earlier, but his father asked him to wait until he was twenty-one. It wasn't something that Richard had a burning passion to do. It was something he thought he ought to try, just to see if he liked it. He liked being a racing mechanic, and was sure that he would be happy making that his life's work, although he had once given some thought to going to college and becoming a high school coach, which was what his wife had hoped he would do.

"I never set out to be no superstar or nothing like that," he told me one night. "It was just something that happened over a long period of time. It was a gradual thing. One thing just builds on another, and I never had much time to think about it."

He and his cousin Dale Inman got ready an old Oldsmobile convertible that had been sitting near the house, and they took it off to Columbia, South Carolina, for Richard's first race. Lee Petty didn't go. He had another race that night. Lee Petty knew that there was no way to tell his son how to drive a race car. It was something that he would have to learn for himself. His only advice was: "Never drive a car faster than it feels good to you." Richard remembers that he was not at all nervous before that race. Driving a race car with other cars banging against it seemed to him a perfectly natural thing to be doing. He finished sixth that night, but he wouldn't have that good a finish again for a long time. He entered nine races his first year, tore up a lot of equipment, and won only $760, not a particularly impressive start.

Lee Petty had known that it would probably be like this, and he was not critical.

"After every race," Richard recalls, "he would set us down and say, 'Now, what did you learn from this race?'"

He was learning, and the next year, 1959, proved to be a good one for the Pettys. The new speedway at Daytona was opened that year, and Lee Petty won the first race there, although it was so close—three cars streaking across the line side by side—that it took the officials three days of studying photographs to decide who had won it. He went on to win an unprecedented third national championship for the year. Richard ran twenty-one races that year, racing against his father in most of them, but he says that there was never a father-son rivalry. He managed to finish six races in the top five that year, enough to bring home almost eight thousand dollars, although still not enough to turn a profit. He was showing promise, however, and NASCAR named him its first Rookie of the Year.

In July of that year, Richard had slipped off to Chesterfield, South Carolina, with a cute cheerleader from Randleman High School named Lynda Owens, and they were married by a justice of the peace. They had been going together for three years, having met while Maurice was dating a friend of Lynda's, and they hoped to keep the marriage a secret, because Lynda still had a year of high school to finish. The secret was soon out, and they moved in with Richard's parents until they got themselves a trailer and parked it next door. Their first child, Kyle, was born the following year.

Richard won his first race in 1960, the year his son was born. That was at Charlotte. He thought he'd won one the year before at Atlanta. He had taken the checkered flag, but another driver had kept on charging around the track and later demanded a recheck, claiming that there had been a scoring error.

"You didn't win," he told Richard. "*I* did."

The protesting driver, Lee Petty, was found to be correct and was declared the winner.

"I want the boy to win," Lee Petty told a reporter, "but I want him to *really* win. He didn't, so he doesn't deserve it."

There were three Pettys on the track during some races in 1960. Maurice had begun to drive, but his eyes were bad, and after he destroyed a car at Columbia, he quit and went back to building engines, at which he had turned out to be a whiz. Richard came into his own as a driver that year, winning three races and more than thirty-five thousand dollars, finishing second in the national championship.

He had little time to enjoy his success. Racing has its own way of humbling men, and it went to work on the Pettys early in 1961. They arrived at Daytona that year with two new Plymouths. Richard found himself starting in the first of the twin hundred-mile qualifying races. His father was to run in the second. On the last lap of the first race, Junior Johnson ran over something on the track and lost control. He hit Richard's car, sending it high up on the track—and over the wall, crashing into the parking lot far below.

For a moment, Richard sat stunned in the broken car. Then he crawled out through the empty space where the windshield had been and fell to the ground, spraining his ankle as he fell. He sat on the ground looking at the remains of his car until he realized that the engine was still running. He had crawled over to shut off the engine when the ambulance arrived.

At the track dispensary, the doctors found nothing seriously wrong. He was bruised and his ankle was painful, but he hobbled back to the pits, where his father was getting ready to start the second race. Just before the race began, Richard was suddenly struck by severe pain in his eyes. He was taken back to the dispensary, where the doctors discovered that his eyes were filled with tiny slivers of glass from the shattered windshield.

It took the doctors quite a while to get all of the glass out, and when Richard finally left the hospital, the race was almost finished. In the last lap, Banjo Matthews suddenly got sideways going into the first turn. Lee Petty, close behind, also started sliding. Johnny Beauchamp hit Lee Petty squarely in the side— T-boned him, in racing parlance—and froze with his foot full on the accelerator. Both cars went over the fence at the top of the bank and took flight. Richard started running toward the wreck, falling and stumbling because of his ankle. When he got to the wreckage, breathless and in pain, his father was being loaded into an ambulance. Richard had never seen race cars so badly damaged. His father was unconscious on the stretcher, limp and bleeding profusely. Richard climbed into a second ambulance and followed his father to the dispensary. There was a trail of blood leading inside when he got there, and the doctors were working hurriedly to stop the bleeding.

Lee Petty lingered near death for several days. He had been severely cut and bruised, a lung was punctured, and one leg was so badly smashed that the doctors feared that if he did live, he'd never be able to walk again without braces. When Lee Petty finally did regain consciousness for the first time, he looked up and saw Richard and told him to go on home, get another car ready to race, and he'd be on in a few days.

But Lee Petty remained hospitalized for four months. And Richard, at twenty-three, and Maurice, at twenty-one, were left to run the family racing business by themselves. Neither of them knew anything about the business end of it, their father had always handled that, although Richard luckily had attended business college for several months after high school. They began to learn quickly, however. They got another car ready, and Richard ran all forty-two races on the circuit that year, bringing in twenty-two thousand dollars, not a profitable season by a long shot, but it kept the Petty racing business alive.

By the 1962 season, Lee Petty was fully recovered. He walked with a slight limp, but he didn't need braces. He drove in a couple of races that season, but the spirit was no longer in him. It wasn't fun any more, he said, and he quit, leaving the responsibility of the family fortunes to Richard—who responded by winning eight races that year and eleven the next for more than a hundred thousand dollars in purses. In 1964, he won ninety-nine thousand dollars and his first national championship.

Except for brief flings with Oldsmobiles, Chryslers, and Dodges, the Pettys had driven Plymouths exclusively. Lee Petty had made No. 42 famous. There was no special significance to the number. A sign painter had simply taken it from a license plate. Richard had followed by using No. 43, and he also painted all of his cars a certain brilliant blue that came to be known as "Petty blue." The color had no special significance either. It was the result of mixing a can of blue paint with a can of white because there wasn't enough of either to paint his car. But the color became one of the most popular on Plymouths sold in the South. When the car manufacturers were in racing, the Pettys were the Chrysler Corporation's No. 1 team. The manufacturers had come back into racing in 1963, and in 1965, when Chrysler pulled its drivers out to protest NASCAR's ban of its hemi engine, Richard and Maurice built a Barracuda, named it "Outlawed," numbered it "43, Jr.," and went drag racing.

At a dragstrip in Dallas, Georgia, something broke, Richard lost control, and the car careened up an embankment and hurtled into the crowd. Petty crawled from the car and sat, dazed, on the ground. A man came over angrily screaming, "You've killed a boy!" The boy was eight years old. Several other people were hurt. Petty, whose own son was five at the time, quit drag racing after that. That accident, he now says, is his only regret in all of his years of racing.

Chrysler and Petty returned to stock car racing in 1966. Petty won 8 races that year, finished 20 out of 39 in the top 5, and won $79,000. The next year was to be a record-setter. Everything seemed to fall into place, and Petty won 27 of the 48 races that year, 10 of them in a row, an unbelievable feat. That brought him $130,000 in purses and his second national championship. It took him three years to win that much money again, and it was not only unlikely, but almost impossible that anybody would ever win that many races in a season again.

But in 1971 he came close, winning 21 of 46 races and nearly $310,000 in purses, more money than any driver has ever won in a single year. That was the year that Chrysler finally pulled out of racing again, the last of the car manufacturers to do so. Petty quickly worked a deal with Andy Granatelli to have his STP Corporation sponsor the Petty Plymouth (later Dodge). *Time* reported that STP was funneling as much as

$500,000 annually to Petty. "It might be that over a couple of years," says Petty, who, like most drivers, doesn't particularly care to discuss his financial affairs.

Richard Petty's third national championship came in 1971; his fourth, breaking his father's record, came the following year, when his winnings came to $227,000. By midseason of 1974, Petty had won 158 races (including 5 Daytona 500s) and more than $1,700,000 in purses in his career. His nearest competitor, David Pearson, had won 77 races.

Unlike some of the other good stock car drivers who have gone on to attempt other forms of racing, particularly in championship cars at Indianapolis, Petty, except for his brief stint in drag racing, has never ventured outside stock car racing. For that reason, racing experts have been reluctant to classify him as an all-around great race driver. That doesn't bother him. He replies that other kinds of racing simply don't appeal to him, and he prefers staying with what he knows best.

Just how long he will stay with racing is a constant subject of speculation. Sportswriters ask him when he is going to retire at almost every race. He has set all the records, made himself wealthy, they point out, so why go on? What else is there to prove? Every driver knows that the more he races the greater the chance that the day of the final wreck will come, so why continue to face the risk?

Petty laughs and shrugs off the question, pointing out that at his age (he was born in 1937) his father was just beginning to race. Besides, there is all that money, the race purses, the appearance fees (he gets three thousand dollars just for showing up at the big tracks, fifteen hundred dollars from the small ones, plus varying amounts for other away-from-the-track appearances), the money from commercial endorsements, and all those people who depend on him (some thirty-five working for the Petty racing organization alone). Nobody walks away from all of that—not until he has to.

Risk? Well, maybe a little. But he doesn't pay it any attention. No driver does. A driver who worried about risk wouldn't be able to drive.

Richard Petty is a careful race driver. He is known as a driver who "drives with his head," as opposed to a flat-out, stay-in-front-at-all-costs driver. "I don't worry about him," says his wife, Lynda. "I know that *he'll* be careful. It's the other drivers I worry about."

Richard Petty really does not know fear or anxiety, not in the sense that most people do, anyway. Driving a race, making a movie, appearing on TV, meeting the President, eating supper, playing with his kids—it's all the same to him. He goes about everything in the same way: Take it as it comes, inspect it, decide the best way of going about it, and do the best you can. If anything bothers him, it never shows. He doesn't get scared, excited, or nervous, and he doesn't worry.

"I guess I'm not a very emotional person," he says. "I never have been."

He is, in fact, almost eerily even-dispositioned. It would be hard to imagine what it would take to shake his unemotional, easy-going, level-headed, common-sense approach to life.

Wrecks on racetracks certainly don't do it, and he has had many of those. In the spring of 1970, he survived one of the most spectacular racing wrecks ever seen at Darlington. Coming out of the fourth turn, his car swiped the outside wall, took an abrupt turn to the left, sailed across the track, and smashed almost head-on into the inside wall. It then began a series of end-over-end flips, added a few rolls for good measure, and came to rest on its top, destroyed. Some people who saw the wreck remember it as seeming to happen almost in slow motion. The most vivid part of the memory was seeing Petty's left arm flopping limply outside the window as the car flipped and rolled, and to some it seemed that the car would never come to a stop. Drivers and crew members in the pits ran to the car fully expecting to find Petty dead. He looked dead hanging there in the remains of the car with his limp arm still outside the window. He was taken to the track hospital unconscious, but although badly battered, his worst injury was a dislocated shoulder.

"Hurt my dang shoulder," he told the worried-faced doctors when he had regained consciousness.

Later, when he talked with the sportswriters, they asked him what caused the wreck. He grinned.

"I got a little behind in my steerin'," he said.

His even disposition is one of the things that has made Petty an effective spokesman for racing (as well as for a number of products). He does not believe in "bad-mouthin'" anybody or anything, but especially racing. He has had his disagreements with NASCAR and with others in racing, and he has let some of his criticisms be known, but he has never spoken out against the sport, and he doesn't like those who do. People who make their livings from racing have a special obligation to support and promote it, he thinks, and he has worked hard to build the image of stock car racing as a "clean" family sport. He probably has done more toward accomplishing that than anybody.

Racing has, of course, been good to him and the other Pettys. It has made them millionaires. Petty Enterprises, of which Lee is president, Richard and Maurice vice presidents, not only builds Richard's race cars, but also handles all of Chrysler's racing business, cars and parts, from its Level Cross headquarters. It has also expanded into other fields. The Pettys own a motel, a series of airport warehouses, an interest in a "minority" bank (with blacks and Jews) in Charlotte, widely scattered rental properties, a plastics business, an electronics business, a share in a chain of miniature recreational racetracks, and so on. In addition, Richard Petty is a familiar face on southern television, endorsing everything from hamburgers to "mobile homes" to lawnmowers and soft drinks. And not far from his present home, he is constructing a huge new house on several hundred acres of Randolph County land, where he plans to raise cattle.

Petty takes his hero image seriously. He practices clean living, doesn't drink, is careful of his language, sometimes speaks to church and youth groups, and regularly attends the Methodist church in Randleman when he is not on the road. He is perhaps the biggest supporter of Brother Bill Frazier, who calls himself the chaplain of stock car racing and ministers to racing people. Petty is also quick to give his name, money, and time to any number of good causes. When he is not racing, he prefers to spend his time at home with his family. And when the races are close to home, as many are, they become outings for the entire Petty family.

At nine o'clock in the morning on one of these racing Sundays, Richard Petty was still in the bathroom combing his wavy hair. The hair was only moderately long now. Earlier in the year, he had worn it much longer and accentuated it with a Fu Manchu mustache, but his wife had won out and he had shaved the mustache and shortened his hair.

He came into the kitchen a few minutes later wearing a sport shirt and flared brown slacks with a big western belt. He had the lanky, raw-boned good looks of a TV western star, and when he smiled he displayed a set of shiny white teeth that would put a piano keyboard to shame.

"Everybody ready?" he said.

"Just about," said his wife.

The van was pulled up to the back door. Ice chests and boxes of food—fried chicken, sandwiches, ham biscuits, homemade pies, cookies, persimmon pudding, a great feast—had already been loaded into the back. The van was really a small bus, with four rows of seats. Dodge had built it specially for Richard Petty and painted it in the same design and brilliant red-and-blue colors as his race car. The van always attracted attention because everybody who knew anything about stock car racing knew that it was Richard's. Lynda Petty usually drove it around home, going for groceries, or hauling kids around the countryside, but it was the perfect vehicle for race day trips. For these they needed lots of room.

The race was at Martinsville, Virginia, sixty-five miles to the north. Some of the Petty clan were already at the track. Others were now rolling northward. Richard was getting eager now to get under way so that he could avoid the heaviest traffic.

There would be the full load as usual: Richard and Lynda and their four children (the baby was four months old now, and this would be her first race); Dale Inman's wife, Mary, and her two children; Martha Jane Bonkemeyer and her two. Martha Jane was Lynda's best friend. Her husband, Willis, had been one of Richard's closest friends since high school, and they almost always went to the races with Richard and Lynda, although this day Willis was off at a sales meeting for the building supply company he worked for. Kyle's buddy would come too.

Kyle was thirteen now, Richard's and Lynda's only son, a big boy with long, flowing hair. He was outside, wearing an old gray fedora with the brim turned down, tossing a football with his friend. His father came out the back door and began knocking down the passes playfully, kidding his son.

"Whatsamatter? Can't you throw it?"

Everyone was out of the house now and finding seats in the van, the kids all crowding into the back, Lynda, already looking a little harried, shepherding them. Richard put on his wraparound sunglasses and lighted a long, thin cigar (outside his house he is seldom seen without either) and climbed into the driver's seat.

"Well, have we got everybody?" he said, starting the engine.

"I think so," said Lynda, a little tiredly.

"Don't want to forget nobody."

He looked down at the baby, who was in a bassinet beside his seat, and clucked at her as he headed the van down the long driveway.

"Turn down his collar," Lynda said in that tone that wives use when they want to say, "How in the world would these men ever get along without us?," and Martha Jane, who was sitting behind Richard, reached up and straightened his shirt collar.

At a stop light in Greensboro, the van came to a halt behind an old pickup truck with a gun rack in the rear window. Three men were in the truck, and one of them turned around and saw that Richard Petty was sitting right there behind him, big as life! It was obvious from his expression that he was excited about it. He told his friends, and they all turned around, grinning and waving. Richard smiled and threw up his hand.

"Them boys is going to the race, I bet."

It had been warm, with the sky overcast by high light clouds when the van left Level Cross, but as it neared Martinsville, the air took on a chill and the clouds became darker and heavier, scudding low over the hills. A fine mist began to fall.

"Well, the weatherman said sixty per cent chance," Richard said.

"I'll bet they don't run today," said one of the women.

"I hope they call it off in time to git home and watch the football game on TV," Richard said.

Martinsville lies in the foothills of the Blue Ridge Mountains, and the Martinsville Speedway is set in the side of one of those hills a few miles south of town. It is an immaculate track, probably the finest and most beautiful half-mile track in the country. The grounds are grassed and landscaped, lots of trees, shrubs, and flowers, a pond with geese and ducks. Fences, walls, concession stands, and rest rooms are all whitewashed and kept clean. The concrete grandstands are covered. This was Richard Petty's favorite track, maybe because he had won more races here (twelve) than anybody.

"Hey, there's Richard Petty!"

The race was to start at one, and that was still more than two hours away, but people were already thronging into the track, and they all recognized Richard as he drove slowly past in the line of traffic. They called and waved to him, and he waved back. Each car and truck was being stopped at the infield gate, and as he waited his turn, Richard rolled down his window and chatted with a cop about the weather.

The Martinsville infield is tiny and cramped and figure-eight-shaped because of the pit areas that have been cut into it on both sides. It won't hold many cars. Fans who want to get their cars inside must arrive early. By the time the Petty van rolled through the gate, the infield was almost filled. Richard drove slowly toward the top of the eight at the first and second turns, where the Pettys always gather. Cars were already parked four-deep from the fence.

"Don't park on that side," Kyle warned, as his father began to turn toward the backstretch, "you won't win."

"I'm not, I'm just goina back in."

Every time that Richard Petty had won at Martinsville, he

had parked in the same area, near the frontstretch, and a super-stition had grown around it.

Before Richard could get the van parked, a swarm of people was around it, peering closely into the windows, calling his name, aiming their movie cameras, Polaroids, and Instamatics at the van.

"I've done messed up now," he said, looking at all the peo-ple. Some were now running from distant areas of the infield. "I should've got out up at the pit gate."

"You'll be lucky to get in there in time for the race," his wife said.

"Where's a pen?" he said, searching around the dashboard. "You gotta pen?"

Lynda handed him a ballpoint pen, and he opened the door smiling to face the people who were already thrusting racing programs, photographs, postcards, autograph books, and scraps of paper at him.

"Sign my shirt, Richard!"

On the first piece of paper, the pen only made an indenta-tion. He bore down, but still it produced no ink.

"Gimme another pen," he said, opening the van door, "that'n there don't write."

"Oh, look at their little baby!" somebody squealed. "It's Richard's little baby!"

"Oh, I want to see his little baby!" said a woman, breaking for the other side of the van.

While Richard signed autographs with his usual artistic flour-ish, Lynda opened the side doors of the van and held up the baby for a sizable adoring crowd who oohed and aahed and snapped pictures for their scrapbooks.

"Ain't she the purtiest little thang!" somebody was saying.

"Richard, do one on my hat," a boy said.

Petty signed the back of the hat while it was still on the wearer's head.

"If you git hit on the back of the head, you'll know why," he told the boy, and turned to sign a girl's proffered arm.

"Pam, you'll just wash that off when you git home," the girl's mother protested.

"I won't neither!"

It took Petty about fifteen minutes to make his way to the pit gate, a crowd trailing all the way, and all the way he smiled and bantered amiably.

When he finally made it through the gate, a snaggle-toothed old man called out, "Richard, you better win today, you hear?"

Petty's car occupied the first spot on pit row. His crew was working over the car, putting on the wheels, making last-minute adjustments, waxing again the gleaming finish. Richard huddled for a few minutes with his brother and cousin Dale Inman.

"It's working," Inman said, putting the air breather back in place. "It's working today."

Fifty feet away, people clung to the pit fence calling, "Richard! Hey, Richard Petty!"

A small-town radio announcer thrust a tape recorder microphone into Petty's face and began asking how things looked for the race, and what about the rain?

Petty gave the usual answers that race drivers give to microphones. Things looked pretty good, but then you never know.

"The weather's somethin' we have no control over," Petty was saying to wrap it up.

After the announcer had left, a fidgety, mustachioed freelance writer wearing a tag that said, "Bill Neely, *Playboy* mag.," bounced over and grabbed Petty's hand and told him how good it was to see him again. Neely had written Petty's as-told-to autobiography a couple of years earlier. The book had sold out two editions, and now the two of them discussed the possibility of another updated edition before the paperback was issued. Petty's sponsor, STP, was interested in the new edition, interested in having a picture of Richard's new car with its new STP insignia on the cover, interested in a new chapter about the two seasons that Petty had now run for STP.

"Well, we're not makin' any money on it the way it is," Petty said. "We could be sellin' books."

Money. Richard Petty had become an astute businessman,

and he didn't like to let a dollar slip by if he could help it. With his continuously diversifying business interests, he was constantly surrounded by sharp young business types, wheeler-dealers who either handled his businesses or worked for him in one way or another. A small troop of them, all wearing the red-and-blue uniforms of Petty's crewmen, accompanied him to almost all of the races. In fact, he conducted a lot of business at the tracks.

He was sitting now on the back of his equipment truck· ("King Richard holding court," the sportswriters call this), while one of his business sharpies demonstrated a video tape machine that one of his companies was considering marketing. They were looking at some footage of an earlier race that had been shot on the machine. His business manager came up after that to discuss plans for a forthcoming event, and he was followed by one of the Winston Cup girls, a dark-haired, sultry beauty from Atlanta, who dropped by to chat and to try to get Richard to give her a pair of his sunglasses.

"I done give you one pair," he protested.

"I know, but Ralph chewed 'em up."

"You goina have to do sum'in' about Ralph."

The young man who had been demonstrating the video tape machine also worked on some of Petty's contract negotiations, and somebody said to him now, "Ol' Richard sure is getting in a lot of businesses, ain't he?"

"Well, he has to. You know, it's an economic thing. He's not going to run from now on, you know."

Brother Bill was standing on the pit road wall at the starting line ringing his heavy bell to announce chapel services, and Petty jumped from the back of his truck and ambled in that direction. To ward off the chill wind he had put on a thin silver-colored jacket bearing a patch identifying him as a NASCAR champion, and an expensive brown leather Stetson cowboy hat. He pulled the brim of the hat down all around. A group of worshipers had gathered on the track, seated in a semicircle around Brother Bill. A young gospel group called the Joyful Noise was playing when Petty arrived and sat on the fringe of the group, tucking his feet under his thighs. Two women in rescue squad jackets closed in on him immediately, a plump blond one with teased hair edging close and saying sweetly, "Can we set beside you?"

Brother Bill, spotting Richard, brought one of his children over for him to watch. Petty took off his hat when the service started.

The drivers' meeting was held in front of the concession stand a short time after the chapel service. Petty stood cracking jokes and laughing with other drivers as the familiar rules were being explained. The meeting over, he went back to his equipment truck and climbed into the back. As crew members shielded him from the prying eyes of people in the stands across the track, many of whom were using binoculars, he stripped to his blue boxer shorts and donned his driving uniform. Then he put back on the thin jacket, funny-looking hat, and sunglasses, and sat with his feet dangling from the back of the truck to wait.

The rain began shortly before the race was to start. It wasn't a hard rain, just a heavy mist driven by the cold wind. Most of Petty's crew members had now sought shelter in the back of the truck, and it was quite crowded.

"They ain't goina be no race today," somebody said. "No way."

In the uncovered sections of the grandstands, spectators huddled under umbrellas, blankets, and big sheets of clear plastic. The track was wet and slick and growing wetter, but the promoters were proceeding as if confident that the rain would stop. Brother Bill was called on to offer up another prayer, a rain-halting prayer, over the public-address system.

"What they doin' now?" somebody in the deep reaches of the Petty truck asked.

"They got the preacher prayin' agin," said Maurice.

After the prayer, the driver introductions began. Richard Petty was still sitting on the back of his truck talking as the introductions proceeded.

"They introducin' drivers, ain't they?" he said. "I might better git up 'ere."

Petty was starting in sixth position, unusual for him to be so far back, especially at this track. When his name was called, the grandstands erupted in a great roar, a lot of it booing and cat-calling. Petty flashed his keyboard smile and sauntered onto the track giving a little wave. Unlike most of the drivers who had been kissing the Winston Cup girl waiting to greet them, Petty shook her hand and fell in with the other drivers min-gling in the rain.

"Hey, Richard!" some guy in the stands called. "Where'd you git that hat?"

The track officials had decided to start the race despite the rain, hoping that Brother Bill's beseechings to heaven would take hold. The first laps would be run under the caution flag as the cars attempted to dry the track. Not long after the cars took to the track, running slowly in a big pack behind the pace car, the rain stopped, the sky began to lighten, and Brother Bill smiled knowingly. The track was drying slowly under the heat of the passing cars, and after fifteen laps, the president of one of Petty's fan club chapters, a man standing in the back of the Petty truck wearing flashy trousers with "Richard Petty" spelled out up and down the sides, a transistor-radio-connected set of earphones clamped over his head, held up two fingers indicating the race would start after two more laps, some forty-five minutes late.

When the green flag dropped, the pack roared into the first turn at a little over eighty miles per hour with Cale Yarborough, who had started in the pole position, in the lead. Before Yar-borough had made it out of the second turn, however, Petty had already jumped two positions to fourth. Yarborough stretched out his lead gradually until he was a half lap ahead, and he seemed to have the fastest car on the track. But at a track like Martinsville, it is skill and not speed that really counts.

It took Petty half the race to jockey into third position. Five laps later, he eased around Bobby Allison into second, and be-gan to close on Yarborough. Petty was losing time in the stretches, but gaining in the turns, and within two laps he was on Yarborough's bumper trying to "root him out of the groove." On the 259th lap, he did it. Yarborough went into the fourth

turn too hard, and Petty cut to the inside and sped around
him.

Lap 340. Caution flag. Buddy Baker and Bobby Allison had
bumped in the third and fourth turns, and Baker had skidded
out. Petty, still in the lead, made for the pits, Yarborough right
behind him. Both took on fresh right-side tires and gasoline, then
roared back to make another lap while their crews got ready to
replace left-side tires.

Excitement on the track! Buddy Arrington had pulled away
from the pits too soon. A gasoline can was still attached to his
car, and one of his wheels was not fully bolted. The wheel
came off and the gasoline can caught fire. Meanwhile, Petty
had come back in, with Yarborough still fast on his tail. Their
pits were side by side and the crews were now in a frantic race,
each hoping to get its car out first. Yarborough's wheels
touched the pavement a split second before Petty's, and they
both spun away, new tires squealing and smoking, but Yarborough had the advantage and won the lead.

For the next hundred laps, Petty fought to regain the lead,
never allowing Yarborough to escape the nagging vision in his
rear-view mirror of the red-and-blue car hugging his bumper.
Occasionally, just as a reminder that he was still back there,
Petty would give Yarborough's bumper a tap.

On the 452nd lap, Petty got the break he needed. Something
cut Yarborough's right rear tire, causing him to slow just enough
for Petty to pull around him. And the rain began to fall again.
A few big drops splatted on the windshield seconds after Petty
passed.

"Let 'er pour!" Petty's jubilant crew members were shouting.

Two laps later, Yarborough, running on the inner liner of
his cut tire, came in to replace it, and Petty gained a full lap.
The rain had begun to fall harder, and on the 456th lap, the
caution flag came out, sealing Petty's position.

"Well, if she just don't fall apart now, we got it," a crew member said.

The cars bunched behind the slow-moving pace car as the
rain continued to fall, and on the 480th lap, the red flag finally

came out, halting the cars in position. Crew members hurried to cover the cars with tarpaulins. Petty climbed out of his car and headed toward the control tower at a half run. A couple of his crew members returned to his truck laughing.

"Ol' Richard come out of that car, he said, 'Man I gotta go pee,'" one of them said.

Petty put his jacket, sunglasses, and funny hat back on and stood with his crew members in the back of the truck, waiting to see if the rain would stop so that the last twenty laps could be run. Benny Parsons, the driver who was leading him in the point race for the national championship, crowded into the truck out of the rain.

"Where you been?" Petty asked him.

"You seen me back 'ere, didn't you? Slippin' and a-slidin'."

Petty sat down in the back of the truck, and after a while the announcement came over the loudspeakers. The race had been called.

"Looks like ever'body's done give up," he said, jumping to the ground.

"Did they call it?" somebody asked from farther back in the truck.

"Didn't they call it?" Petty was saying, a little uncertain now. "Yeah, they called it."

So he had won the 155th race of his career sitting in the back of his truck.

Yarborough was upset about the whole thing. He had been motioning to the flagman to throw the caution two laps before Petty passed him. "Why did they wait so long to throw the caution flag?" he was saying in the back of Junior Johnson's truck, which was parked beside the Petty truck. "It was raining thirty minutes before the caution came out, but they waited until he passed me before they brought it out." Despite his complaint, he had won eleven thousand dollars: one thousand for getting the pole position, five thousand for taking second place, and another five thousand for leading the most laps. Petty would get only ten thousand for winning.

Petty, meanwhile, was back at the starting line getting his

kiss on the cheek from the Winston Cup girl, when his brother came over and whispered to him. Petty interrupted the ceremony and hurried across the pits to the fence where Lynda was waiting with their nine-year-old daughter Lisa and two rescue squad volunteers. There had been an accident. A car door had been slammed on one of Lisa's fingers, cutting the tip of it, and it was bleeding badly. The rescue squad men said she should be taken to the hospital. Lynda got into an ambulance with her daughter, and the rescue squad men told Richard that they would bring them back from the hospital. Petty returned to the starting line to hold aloft his trophy, shake hands with the track president, and pose for the photographers.

"Let's have a hand for RICHARD PETTY, ladies and gentlemen!" intoned the burly track announcer.

A driver was waiting nearby to take Petty to the press box for the winner's interview.

Petty sank into the back seat of the car.

"Whew," he said.

He spotted a couple of sportswriters as the car started to back away, threw open the door, and called to them.

"Y'all wanta ride, come on!"

"That's a nice way to win a race," said one of the sportswriters, settling into the seat beside Petty, "spend the last twenty laps just cruising, enjoying things."

Petty laughed.

"I tell you, the way he was runnin' there, I didn't have much damn choice."

The other reporter wanted to get right into the interview. He had an early deadline.

"Richard, was it raining hard enough out there to throw the caution before you took the lead?"

Petty grinned. "For me it wudn't."

"That's not answering the question."

"Answered mine," he said, laughing, then added, "Well, you know, not really, because the track never got wet. 'Nother words, all it done was just—blap! blap!—on the windshield, and even when they stopped the race the track still was not wet. I mean it was not shiny wet. It was damp, but it was not runny wet—I believe I could've walked up there this quick. I don't reckon nobody's in no hurry anyway."

The car was bogged in the traffic trying to get out of the infield, and the reporter who had an early deadline was getting fidgety.

"Let's make this thing short," he said.

The car had turned into a surging throng of fans trying to leave the track near the press tower.

"This is about as good as we can do, I expect," said the driver.

Some of the fans had already recognized Petty in the car, and as soon as he opened the door, they crowded around, thrusting things at him to sign. He moved along briskly, signing as he went. When he got to the stairs leading to the press box, he paused, signed a few more autographs, and said, "Be right back," as he turned and bounded up the steps.

The press box was crowded with sportswriters, most of whom had just been served coffee and strawberry shortcake. Petty made his way to the front and sat on a work desk by the big windows. The reporter who had ridden over with him in such a hurry took out his wallet and handed some bills to another reporter.

"You see that?" he said to Petty. "You just cost me thirty-five dollars."

"Sorry 'bout that. You bet on the wrong one. Good enough for you. Gimme somethin' to drink up there, bein' I done cost you some money."

"Richard, do you think you'd caught him if he hadn't had problems?"

"Well, y'all set here and watched the race and I really shouldn't have to tell you who was the fastest car and who was the quicker car."

That had always been Petty's racing philosophy: It's not the faster car that wins, it's the quicker. Meaning it's the driver who uses his head.

"Just wanted you to say it," said the reporter who had asked the question.

"I was quicker around the racetrack and he was a damn right smart faster down the straightaway. You know, I mean somethin' like three or four car lengths. . . .

"I run good all day, that's as good as I've run up here in a long, long time."

Somebody handed him a Pepsi in a can.

"Thank you, sir."

One writer asked about the new curb on the inside of the turns. Petty didn't like it. Another wanted to know how he got around Yarborough.

Somebody asked about the purse, and Petty shook his head.

"I just don't understand. I'm goina have to talk to Clay, him givin' away all this money for leadin' the race and then not payin' me for winnin'. Second-place man wins more money than the first-place man."

Other questions came:

"What about the point race? Richard? What about the point race?"

"Do you believe there's such a thing as Martinsville luck, Richard?"

"Where'd you get that hat?"

Petty fielded all the questions with an easy air of good humor. He knew most of the reporters well. One of those who had known him a long time said, "Once you start banging around out there, do you have a tendency to get a little reckless, regardless of who it might be?"

"I done all the beatin'. Cale . . . I mean, you know, I hit him three or four times, you know what I mean. 'Nother words, I'd go in and he wouldn't git on when I'd think he should—when I'd think he was goin' to and I'd tap him, you know what I mean. Then I'd back off and let him git straight and go on, but not enough to git him sideways. The only time I really hit him—well, I hit him down here when I went by him, then one time I run into him here, but I backed off, let both of us git straight. Then when I passed him that last time I didn't touch him."

"You couldn't touch him on the straightaways, could you?"

Petty laughed. "Not a whole lot."

"When y'all get to banging around like that, like you were banging him, where is the point of no return? I mean, where does the guy decide that you're doing it some intentionally and some not?"

"You purty well know."

"If he hits you and he doesn't back off? If he keeps on hittin' you?"

"Well, yeah, if he keeps on. 'Nother words, if he hits you and gits you sideways and just stays on the thing, but if he hits you and backs off and lets you straighten up and stuff, you know what I mean, then it's just one of those things that you run into in racin', you know."

Some good-natured banter, a few more questions, and it was over. Somebody said, "Thank you, Richard," just as somebody always says, "Thank you, Mr. President," at the close of a presidential news conference. Petty stayed in the press box another fifteen minutes or so, doing a couple of radio interviews and chatting with the sportswriters. "We just got all the breaks," he was telling one group. "He got the bad breaks and we got the good breaks."

Outside, a small group of fans was still waiting in the rain for Petty to emerge. When he finally did open the door and step out onto the little balcony, a little cry went up.

"There he is! There's Richard Petty! I tol' you he was still in there!"

He came down the steps quickly, and as the crowd pressed in, thrusting forth timid children, model cars, race programs, and eight-by-ten pictures of himself, Petty sat on the third step from the bottom and began signing his name.

"Bonnie Lou, git one for Jack."

"You can't stay with 'im, darlin'," a mama was telling a reluctant child, "you gotta go home."

"Richard, where'd you git a hat like 'at, boy?"

A man wearing a Richard Petty T-shirt, Richard Petty racing jacket, and Richard Petty hat appeared with his two young sons, one of whom was wearing a Richard Petty T-shirt, the other a Bobby Allison.

"I got two boys," the man told Petty, "one of 'em pulls for Bobby, the other'n pulls for you. What do you do with a feller like 'at?" He pointed at the son in the Allison shirt, who seemed to be holding back.

"I don't guess you got no peace and quiet at home at all, have you?" Petty said.

"He's a turncoat," said the son in the Petty T-shirt of his brother.

Petty smiled at the boy in the Allison shirt. "Well, that-a-way ever'body has his day, don't they?"

The boy grinned and nodded.

Petty was up and moving again, people still crowding around him. A shabbily dressed, almost toothless man pushed into the crowd leading his homely, well-worn, and bashful wife. He handed Petty a postcard to sign, and moved in very close, as if he had something to confide.

"Richard, she said if you don't kiss 'er, she ain't never goina pull for ye agin," he said of his wife.

"Yeah?"

"You silly!" his wife protested.

"Uh-huh, kiss 'er, go ahead."

"Lord, she would die right here on the spot," said a woman friend of the pair.

"Go ahead, kiss 'er."

Petty handed the postcard back, leaned over, and gave the woman a peck on the cheek.

"Oh!" she said, and her face flushed.

"I tol' ye I was goina tell 'im," her husband was saying gleefully as he led her away by the arm.

Petty broke away from that group, saying, "We'll see y'all later, okay?" only to have another group form around him a few feet away as he tried to make his way down through the grandstands to cross the track. He posed for pictures, usually staring straight at the camera, his arm around some woman's shoulder, as her husband operated the camera. A pretty teen-aged girl snuggled close, putting both arms around his waist, her head on his chest, for her picture. "I want it like this," she said.

Petty hadn't eaten since breakfast, so when he finally made his way back to the van, Martha Jane Bonkemeyer poured him a cup of milk, and he rummaged through the picnic basket and found an egg salad sandwich. He stood in the rain eating his sandwich and talking about the race with his brother.

"Cale was runnin' so mother fast down the straightaway," Richard was saying.

"That's what I say. You wudn't goina compete with him. No way."

"No, but I'm tellin' you, we run real, real good. That's as good as we've ever run."

"See, what he would do, if there was anybody anywhere in the corners and he seen 'em, he quit. He outdrove hisself on that one. He outdrove hisself. He didn't drive hard all day."

"He drove as hard as he could hold it," Richard said, "'cause it wudn't handlin' too good." He laughed.

"Boy, him and Allison had it today," said Maurice.

"He just knocked the piss outta Allison. He'd watch Allison, Allison'd go on the outside, he'd do this way, and Allison'd go on the inside and he'd pull over. I just sorta set there and watched 'em. He knocked the fire outta Allison. Then I got by Allison and just drove up there and then he cut me off and I just drove on the side of 'im . . ."

"Then you got by 'im."

"Yeah, and went on."

Another man had been standing there sort of halfway taking part in this conversation. He had been doing some of the planning for Richard's expensive new ranch house, and now he had some business that he wanted to discuss, and he said somewhat awkwardly to Richard, "Uh, so you wanta—on what we was talkin', you wanta figger less . . ." And Maurice walked away chuckling.

"Yeah," Richard said. "We goina have to set down and figger this deal out." And the two of them went over to the man's truck to go over the drawings of the house plans.

The track was almost deserted now, darkness closing fast, and Lynda Petty and Lisa still hadn't gotten back from the hospital.

"Where is the hospital?" Richard asked, as he wheeled the van across the infield. The baby, lying in the bassinet beside him, had kicked her socks off again and was growing fretful. Martha Jane picked her up, soothing, and searched around until she found a bottle of juice.

"I don't know if she gives her juice," Richard said.

"Well, that's what's in the bottle."

Petty parked the van at the end of the pit road to wait and turned on the heater to ward off the damp chill. He was still talking about the race.

"See, when I got on his tail," he was saying of Yarborough, "he got to watchin' me and then he started makin' mistakes. We aggravated 'im out of it is what we done."

After a few minutes, Petty pulled outside the track to wait on the street near the gate. The last fans leaving the parking lots tooted car horns and waved as they passed. It was dark when the ambulance finally pulled up behind the van and Lynda and Lisa got out and crowded into the back, Lisa wearing a big bangage on one of her fingers.

"I got three stitches!" she said proudly. "It was just hanging off!"

"Cut it, broke it," Lynda said.

"Did it break it?" Richard asked.

"Fractured it right at the end of the bone."

"Did it cut any of it off?"

"They sewed it back on."

"He numbed it," Lisa said excitedly, "and he just tickled me real much!"

"I'm sorry," Lynda said, wearily.

"I'm sorry anybody got hurt," said Richard. "I'm just glad nobody didn't git hurt no worse. Least it wasn't a joint."

"Well, was she okay?" Lynda inquired of Martha Jane about the baby.

"I gave her some juice. She didn't take much."

Lynda began telling now all about how the accident happened. Lisa held her finger up for all to see.

"Oh, she'll be proud of that," her daddy said, then added, teasing, "I want to see her play the pianer now."

The weather was dismal on the drive home, raining hard all the way. In the back the women talked quietly. The day's activities had tired the children to silence. Richard hunkered over the wheel, and throughout the long ride he talked about his favorite subject: racing.

It was after eight when he turned into the driveway at home and pulled the van up to the back door.

"Well," he announced. "We made it. We made it again."

Promoter

THE THING that Richard Howard dreaded most for this day had happened. He pulled himself out of the motel room bed after only a few hours of sleep, and the first thing he did was to pad to the window, peek around the edge of the curtain, and emit a low groan. It was raining. Today of all days. This rain could cost Richard Howard untold problems, a certain headache, and many thousands of dollars. All racetrack promoters feared rain.

He dressed quickly and drove directly to the track, going straight to his office in the back of an old two-story frame house. Not so many years before, the house had been a farm home, but then the Charlotte Motor Speedway had arisen in the backyard, and the house became the speedway's office building. It would be a hectic day for Richard Howard, especially with the rain. All the big work was behind him now, and his main job today would be to keep people happy. That, he knew from experience, would not be so easy with the rain.

The Charlotte Motor Speedway, of which Richard Howard was president and general manager, had had an erratic history. It was conceived by Curtis Turner and Bruton Smith, a Charlotte area race promoter. They planned to build a mile-and-a-half track that they hoped would bring in crowds to rival those Bill France was getting at his new track at Daytona—and make

them both rich. Their plans were big. They were going to hold
a six-hundred-mile race, something that had never been tried
before (there were those who said that a race car couldn't hold
together for six hundred miles, just as there had been those who
had said they couldn't go five hundred miles), and they were
going to give it the grand title of "The World 600." They got
together the money to start construction of the Speedway in
1959, and ran into trouble almost immediately. The site they
had chosen turned out to be almost solid rock. Construction
costs soared. The builders fell deeply in debt.

The first World 600 was held in June of 1960, only a month
later than originally planned, although the track facilities were
still far from being complete. But neither that race nor the sub-
sequent races brought in as much money as Turner and Smith
had hoped, and within two years, their creditors were demanding that the track be sold to meet the debts. The track was
about to fold. There were some, however, who believed that it
could be saved and made into a profitable venture, and Richard
Howard was one of them.

Richard Howard was born in Sherrill's Ford, a small community in southwestern North Carolina. His father was a public
school teacher who reared his children on a farm. When Richard finished high school at the age of seventeen, he joined the
Marines and went off to fight in World War II, winning a Purple Heart during the Battle of Okinawa. After the war, he returned home, married his sweetheart, got a job in a cotton mill,
and settled in the nearby town of Denver. He was restless in his
job, however, knew that it would lead nowhere, and he recognized his own ambitions. Those ambitions began to take direction after he started helping a friend sell furniture. He was soon
making more money selling furniture than working at the mill,
and he decided to build a furniture store beside his house. The
new store did well, and he began opening stores in other small
communities.

Richard Howard made his first million selling furniture and
expanded into other businesses. He opened a chain of bowling
lanes, got into car washes, restaurants, insurance, real estate,

construction. He continued to prosper and thus could afford to indulge some other interests. Such as softball. He bought himself a slow-pitch softball team.

"I've got my own softball field in my backyard," he proudly proclaims. "Where a lot of people's got swimming pools, I got a lit ball field."

He doesn't play himself. His team uses the field. "We've been regional slow-pitch champions four years in a row. We go to the nationals every year. This year we're goina win the world championship (a prophecy that proved true). See, what you do is you set your goal and then go after it."

When the Charlotte Motor Speedway was being organized in 1959, Richard Howard bought a couple of thousand dollars' worth of the stock, as much because he was a racing fan as anything else. He believed that the Charlotte track had great potential, and when it went broke, he was one of the stockholders who appealed to a federal judge for a chance to save it. "It irked me to lose two thousand dollars without trying to do something about it," he said.

In an unprecedented move, the judge gave the stockholders their chance. He ordered the track reorganized under Chapter Ten of the Federal Bankruptcy Act. No business but railroads had ever been placed in such an arrangement. His decision was based on a promise from the stockholders' group that they would raise enough money to get the track out of trouble.

Richard Howard put a lot of his own money into the track, buying additional shares of stock. He also headed the stockholders' committee that borrowed money to stage the year's two races. He was named vice president and assumed management of the track at a salary far below that of other track managers. The track then began a slow recovery that made it free of debt in five years.

And Richard Howard found himself being hailed as some sort of genius at racetrack management. Other tracks were seeking his advice, and the stockholders (there are more than three thousand holding stock valued at six million), at last receiving regular dividends, made Richard Howard the track president.

"I've got a free hand," he says. "The directors don't bother me. I mean, really, what could they say except, 'Keep gittin' it'?"

Of the ten major speedways where stock car races are run in the United States, only half are successful, and three of those (Darlington, Rockingham, and Charlotte) are within a hundred miles of each other. The others are Bill France's Daytona and Talladega tracks. Richard Howard believes that those tracks that get in trouble do so because of poor management. What makes a track succeed? What makes a good track manager or promoter?

One spring morning Richard Howard had sat in his cluttered office (it's decorated with racing posters and photographs, of course) trying to answer questions like these as he puffed on a cigar.

It's difficult for a track to get a good manager or promoter, he was saying.

"There's no way for a guy to train because there's not that many tracks, and the good management normally stays where it is. Lot of the other tracks come here and we talk, you know, lot of times it may be a man's personality that, you know—like people! I mean, I like to talk to people regardless if it be about racin' or just about softball, or about what. And then how he handles the press to the drivers to the mechanics to NASCAR is how good a manager he becomes. That's part of it. Just like any other business.

"Lovin' racin', that's one of the key things that makes a man work a little harder, you know, somethin' to make it grow. We like for ours to be the best track in the South, and now, through the press and through the drivers, relations with all the people we got, we got one of the best names of havin' the best put-together show, because we generally spend some extra dollars to have the best cars available, the best drivers, give people their dollar's worth when they come. And so a lot of the other tracks is tryin' to take a pattern of us, because we have been successful. I mean, everybody wants to follow our success. . . .

"They's two things that makes up a promotion. First, you

git the very best cars and drivers, git the best possible field, and then you tell the public about it.

"The press, they either make a show go, or people don't know nothin' about it. Usually the press will tell it. Take, for instance, I'm in the furniture business. The press, if they need furniture, I don't give a thing, but they can buy furniture from me at about half price. Well, that gits you good relations with 'em. If they need something, really—'cause really they're workin' people, and they need some extra. The drivers, the mechanics. We keep the best relations all around, and this doesn't hurt us."

Richard Howard is careful to keep the sportswriters happy. If they need tickets for friends, he sees that they get them. He sees, too, that the press box is supplied with plenty of good food and beer on race day. He is always available to talk, but more than that, he always comes up with something to make good copy, some little gimmick to draw attention to every race.

He would bring in top drivers from other types of racing to run against the stock car boys. He would bring back top drivers who had retired. Once he put Wendell Scott, the black driver, in a competitive car, a car capable of running with the front runners. This year he was running a contest to let the fans vote for a driver to be given a competitive car. But his best gimmick, by far the most profitable, was to bring Chevrolets back to racing in 1971. Chevrolets had not raced competitively since the midsixties, when General Motors pulled out of stock car racing. Richard Howard knew that if he could get a competitive Chevrolet on the track it would bring in thousands of Chevrolet fans who had lost interest in racing. He went for help to Junior Johnson, who had once built his own Chevrolet without factory help and outrun all those factory-backed Fords. They formed a partnership, and Junior came up with a Chevrolet that could compete. They got Coca-Cola to help sponsor the car and Bobby Allison to drive it, and in 1972 he outran almost everybody. That Chevrolet had rejuvenated racing, and it had made a lot of money for Richard Howard and Junior Johnson.

In the early days of racing, promoters used every trick they could think of to bring the folks in. They ran women against men, blacks against whites. Promoters would make up wild stories, start fights, even cause wrecks to happen, do anything they thought might bring in the crowds. There are some who say that Richard Howard is not above that sort of thing. He was accused of being behind the flare-up between his driver, Bobby Allison, and Richard Petty in the fall of 1972. There had long been some tension between Petty and Allison, as there sometimes is between top drivers. The tension had broken into open dispute on a few occasions. But at the fall race at North Wilkesboro, Allison, who is known for his aggressive driving style, had clearly tried to put Petty into the wall. A tremendous fender-banging battle ensued, with Petty charging after the race that Allison could have killed him. The sports pages were filled with stories about the "Petty-Allison feud." Some people thought that it was not mere coincidence that all of this occurred just one week before the race at Charlotte, and everybody was just dying to see what would happen when Petty and Allison got back on the track again.

Richard Howard denies any involvement in that incident, although he admits that it probably helped attendance at his race.

"You'd draw a crowd if you never did have one bump another'n," he says. "You got a certain old hard core that'd come if you didn't have nothing but T-model trucks runnin' around out there and called it a race. But if you got competition, just the natural drama of a race, having the finest equipment and the finest drivers available is all you need.

"They's a certain amount that likes to see spinouts and wrecks and all. I'd say they'd preferably rather not see 'em git hurt, but they do like a certain amount. Why do people like football so well? Because of the body contact. And anytime you got a car spinning, or hit a wall, it seems like it does 'em a little good. I mean, you know, people go to a bullfight to see something git hurt. . . .

"But we don't have to use the type of promotion the old promoters did. They used to make somethin' happen. In other words, they would start somethin'. My thinkin' of promotion is havin' confidence of the press of what I tell them is the truth. Where, if somebody calls me from the press and I tell 'em somethin', he don't have to check it out to see if it's right. He knows that I'm goina be settin' here the next day to back it up. . . . Times is changed. Whether it takes a fight to do it, to git people in, I mean, rasslin' ain't all that great. People's smarter now. You can't hardly fool 'em."

But then you can't help but wonder why the sportswriters sometimes call Richard Howard the P. T. Barnum of stock car racing.

By midmorning, the rain had stopped, although the clouds still hung heavy and black. The weather had not seemed to deter the crowds. Traffic was backed up for miles along the highways leading to the track, and the huge fields used as parking lots, the infield, and the grandstands were already beginning to fill. Richard Howard sat behind his desk receiving a steady stream of visitors. He clearly was worrying about the rain.

"Nobody really knows how much problems it is when it rains," he said. "Ain't no way to tell nobody."

If rain stopped the race today, it would be rescheduled the following day, Monday, Memorial Day. "That would cost twenty thousand dollars more just for the labor alone," he said. Nearly 3,700 people were working at the track this day, including the drivers and their crew members.

An employee stuck his head in the door.

"They say they can't git another damn car in the infield," he said. "That rain has got 'em jammed up down there. You wanta cut the cars off or not?"

"Do what?"

"Cut the cars off, just walk 'em in."

"I'd cut 'em off if it's that way. And if they'll stress to 'em that we got four-dollar seats, they'll go in there and buy that, tell 'em."

Richard Howard is always scheming to bring in an extra dollar. That is another secret of his success. The four-dollar seats in the infield are new this year. They are bleachers set up near the beginning of the front straightaway. They were installed for drag races that are occasionally held at the track, but Richard Howard decided that it would be a good idea to try to sell the seats to the infield crowd. The four-dollar charge is in addition to the regular six-dollar infield admission. He is always doing something like that. A few years earlier he moved the fence back at the top of his grandstands and created an extra row of seats that brought in another thirty thousand dollars a race. When the scoreboard in the infield became outdated and had to be replaced, he didn't take it down. He cut the top off, installed seats, and sold them for eight dollars each in the infield. For this race, his new luxury seats were finally ready. They were in a new steel tower built atop the frontstretch grandstand. The tower was divided into eight lounges, each with carpet, cushioned chairs, a bar, and air conditioning. Richard Howard had built the lounges to rent to companies that wanted to bring in important guests for the race. A couple were held open for general admission, the seats selling for fifty dollars each. Each of the lounges would hold sixty people and give a good view of the entire track. Every seat was sold for this race.

Richard Howard's office remained full of visitors all morning. Few of them seemed to suspect that he was worried. He laughed and joked and talked easily. He is a totally unpretentious man. A very big man, he usually weighs about three hundred pounds and stands under six feet tall. His clothes look as if they might have come off the rack at a discount house. He almost always dress in open-neck sport shirts, slacks, and loafers with worn heels. On this day, the maroon sport shirt he wore was frayed at the collar. Richard Howard likes for people to think of him as just another good ol' country boy, and that is how he comes off. He is easy-going and willing to talk with anybody. People come away from Richard Howard saying, "You'd never think he was a millionaire, would you?" That pleases him.

"Hey, how ya doin'," he kept saying to his visitors. "Glad y'all could come."

Beauty queens had been in, giving him kisses on the cheek. Susan Raye, a fresh-faced, apple-cheeked country singer, who had been hired to perform for the prerace ceremonies, stopped by. Del Reeves, another country singer, came in wearing flashing red pants, a red jacket, gleaming white shoes, and silver-rimmed sunglasses, his long, graying hair swept back and held in place with a heavy coat of hair spray. His business manager was with him, and they talked with Richard Howard about the possibility of putting on a Saturday night show at the track before next year's race.

"You fellows want to gamble a little," Richard Howard said, "you put the show together and we'll split the gate. If we win, we win; if we lose, well . . ."

"*Fan*-tastic!" said Del Reeves. "Outtasight! I knew somebody wuz on the same wavelength we wuz."

"That was Del Reeves," somebody said when he had left.

"There," Richard Howard said to one of his employees, "you've met another movie star. Not a movie star but a sanger."

Barney Wallace, the president of Darlington Raceway, stopped by to say hello. Special friends came to pick up tickets that Richard Howard was holding for them. The telephone rang continually. Employees popped in to ask questions or give information. A friend came in to talk about bird hunting. "We had a good season. First week we killed three gobblers." A sportswriter came to return two complimentary tickets that Howard had given him.

"I had a cancellation," the sportswriter said. "I figgered since you been takin' keer of me . . ."

"You a good man, Granger."

"Well, you takin' keer of me."

A guy came in to tell Howard that he'd worked out all of the arrangements for him to go to the race at Indianapolis the next day—tickets, room, car, VIP treatment.

"Go to the Holiday Inn right across the street from the speedway," the guy was saying.

A track official came in to tell Richard that an important person was waiting outside thinking that somebody was holding two tickets for him. Obviously there had been some kind of mixup. There were no tickets. Did Richard have them?

"No, but I got two complimentaries that Granger turned back in. Go give 'em to him, tell 'im to be our guest. That'll take keer of 'im."

The official went out the door, saying to the waiting man, "Yeah, Richard Howard had 'em!"

"I didn't have 'em but we made 'em." Howard shrugged and smiled.

"See that's the big part of promotion. You move as many people in and out as fast as you can and hope they leave happy. And when the sun's shinin' they're happy, and when the sun ain't shinin' it's terrible. Sun looks like it's comin' out a little now."

He walked to the window to check the sky, which was lightening.

"Our most hectic time has been gittin' ever'thing prepared up to now. . . . As long as the sun shines, there's not a lot of decisions. . . . See, now I'll go over in a little bit and help them make sure that all these things go right. I wonder who that is parking their car right there?"

An employee got up to check.

"Don't holler at 'em, just see who it is."

Later, after giving final instructions to some of his office help, Howard went out and got into one of the track cars to drive inside the track. Another car was waiting to follow him, driven by a woman who was taking her terminally ill husband to watch the race from the pits as Richard Howard's guest. Howard's twenty-three-year-old son, Rick, approached his car.

"I got a radio if you need me," his father told him. "Ever'-thang's fine. Sun's shinin' and all. You see that sun up there. I'm talkin' to the Man Upstairs. If He'll just let me git by another six hours, He can let the showers come."

As he drove toward the tunnel under the track's fourth turn, Richard Howard was talking about the crowd, which was now in the final crush of getting into the track.

"Another two hours, it'll be chock full, won't it? The infield and that back grandstand's what you have to worry about fillin' up."

A long line of cars was waiting to get into the tunnel. The gate guards had started letting more cars in. When Richard Howard had made his way to the gate, he stopped to chat with one of the ticket sellers for a moment. "Let this girl behind in," he told him.

Inside the track, a young man was directing the incoming cars off to the left. Richard Howard drove straight ahead. The young man yelled and stopped him, obviously unaware that he was stopping the boss.

"Ain't no room up 'ere to park it," the young man called.

Richard Howard had opened the car door. "Look, I'm in the damn parade thing," he said with a little irritated laugh. "I'm all right. Let this girl behind come on, too. I mean, you doin' the right job, but when you see this car, wrote up like this," indicating the speedway signs on the side, "let it go."

The young man still wasn't sure who this was, but he didn't want to take a chance on contesting him further and stepped aside. Richard Howard closed the car door.

"Shit!" he said. And then he laughed, "Heh, heh, heh."

The car had come to a stop in a long line of cars waiting to pass through the pit gate. Nothing was moving. Richard Howard began to grow fidgety, increasingly impatient.

"I wonder what the situation is up yonder. . . . I'll be damn if I've ever seen anything—exactly what's goin' on up yonder?" He craned his head out the window. "I don't understand exactly what we're doin' up 'ere, I mean what the holdup is or what . . ."

He opened the car door abruptly and got out.

"Bring 'is if it starts movin'," he told me and strode off past the line of cars, moving surprisingly fast for his great bulk. I could see him directing cars up by the gate, and the tie-up quickly dissolved.

The prerace activities had been going on since about nine-thirty when the Country Travelers, a U. S. Army country music group, had started playing on the start-finish line. The Great Lindini had already performed his blindfolded driving act. The parade was finished. Daredevil driver Joe Chitwood had made his "world record" attempt to drive two laps around the track with two of his car's wheels in the air, and Brother Bill Frazier had already preached. The go-carts were now racing, and they would be followed by more country music from Susan Raye and Del Reeves. The parachute jump by the 82nd Airborne Division team had been scrubbed because of the weather. But the weather had not grounded the helicopters that kept flitting in and out of the infield taking fare-paying fans up for a brief aerial view of the track.

Richard Howard was smiling when he got back to the car. He was a man who made things happen, and that he had been able to clear up the traffic jam so quickly while others just stood around was further proof of it. "Gits kinda hectic around here when all these people—you know that infield's gittin' solid, boy! But I just got out there, you know, they blocked the place," he said exuberantly. "I tol' 'em to be sure to keep them roads open for 'mergencies and things like that."

He'd no sooner got in the car than a man came rushing up.

"Which way'd you send that truck with the hay bales on it?"

"I sent 'em out this way, 'cause, really, they ain't no place this way."

The man explained that he had the tickets for the girls who had been riding on the float and that they wouldn't be able to get to their seats without them. Richard Howard told him to get in. They would find the truck. He drove down the pit road toward the fourth turn, past the four-dollar bleachers. Only a few people were taking advantage of this bargain so far.

"Here's something that we should be advertising to the people over there," Richard Howard said. "See now, this here we're sellin' the four-dollar ticket, see. So many of them infield people don't even know it, see. If them guards out yonder would tell it . . ."

He drove to several spots around the track looking for the truck and the girls without success.

"See if you see 'em," he told the man in the back seat, as he drove out onto the track.

"Man, I hate to take all your time like this."

"Oh, no. Shit. I'm just in here. When I see some problems or somebody tells me somethin' on this radio, I can answer 'em as good in here as I can out there."

Keeping the car on the bottom edge of the high-banked track, Richard Howard drove toward the backstretch. Looking for the girls would give him a chance to make a quick check on the crowd. The back grandstands were not filling as fast as the front.

"'Nother hour and that'll fill plumb up," he said. "Ever'-thing'll be jam-packed. This up here's the best seats in the house. Eight bucks. See, general admission. Then you'll find these banks gits right full." He laughed happily. "See, I got a special place there for the highway patrol. That makes 'em happy. Yeah, wood chairs, all that. I just make it for 'em. I cook 'em big steaks, git 'em good seats there where they can take their wives and all. If you don't think they'll work their balls off . . .

"See, I don't worry about the front grandstand. It's just jam-packed. We sold out over there. See, you know, we don't have to worry about it. You ever rode up on the bank? We'll have a little fun."

He gunned the car up on the bank in the third turn, running about ninety.

"Richard," said the man in the back, laughing nervously, "I only brought one pair of pants, Richard."

Several stops later, still unable to find the missing girls, Richard Howard decided to call the tower and have an announcement made over the public-address system.

"Tell the girls that's on the Kar Kare car to come to the flagman's stand to pick up their tickets from . . ." he said into the microphone, then turned to the man in the back seat.

"What's your name agin?"

"Bill Woods."

". . . from Bill Woods."

"Okay," he said, wheeling the car toward the flagman's stand. "I'll take you over here now and you just stand there and you'll git it done."

The man got out, thanking him profusely. For a moment, Richard Howard just sat looking up at the crowd.

"Isn't it beautiful to see people settin' down here on the bottom rows? See, that's where it's hard to sell. 'Nother words, when you see 'em settin' down 'ere, you know you got somethin'."

He picked up his microphone.

"Richard to John Bruner agin."

"Go ahead, Richard."

"They don't have a radio up in PA booth, do they?"

"They got one right next door to it up there."

"I just thought, my radio ain't actin' up the best, and . . . uh . . . I was just goina git Hal to announce agin on this paddock down here, them seats at the scorers' stand, tell people in the infield there's plenty of seats there, four dollars a head. I'd like to fill that thing up. . . ."

"All right, I'll pass it on to 'im."

"Tell 'im to repeatedly announce it the next hour, you know, now and then. I believe we can fill that up if they know."

He flipped off the mike.

"Really, you git a good seat," he said. "But until they know it . . . it's a shame all them people pilin' on top of each other and that's why I wanted him to repeatedly announce that. I mean, that's what I like to do is to see what ain't fillin' up. That infield is so jam-packed—and they got rest-room facilities and all down 'ere. Food. It is, see."

A call came over the radio.

"Go ahead. This is Richard."

"You're wanted to call extension thirty-seven."

"Ten four. This is Richard to three seven."

Three seven came on. "The people up in the governor's box don't have any food or likker and they're comin' and askin' me about it. What am I to do about it?"

"If there's anybody up there that can go over and tell Jim Kirkman, he's not goina put any food over there 'til twelve o'clock, and I don't know whether they'll put any booze in there or not, because we just goina put food about twelve o'clock.

But if somebody's up there, tell 'em to tell Jim Kirkman. He's furnishin' the press box, too. Okay? Did you git that, three seven?"

"Right."

"I think that ought to do it," Richard Howard said, laying the mike back on the seat. "If they don't understand that, they don't understand shit, do they?"

He drove onto the grassy area at the start-finish line where a speaker's stand with microphones had been set up.

"Isn't it something, all this work and ever'thing for just four and a half hours," he was saying. "It's amazin' that that many people wants to see somethin' and it comes down to the last four and a half hours of race time. But it's really excitin', I mean, you know.

"Now, as soon as this'un's over, we'll go right to work on the next'un. 'Nother words, you go immediately to start preparin' new brochures, workin' toward your program, toward updatin' your mailin' list that somebody his reservations didn't go right or somethin', and tryin' to revalue things that really didn't go right up to the point that you can tell it don't happen agin. That's why things is goin' as smooth as they are right now. We've had years of experience of knowin' that this has to be done beforehand, see. I got some good people workin' for me, and I can trust. You got to have people to work for you that you *know* can git the job done when you're not there. You know, there's a lot of people goina set on their cans. But they're as interested in makin' this thing go as I am."

When Richard Howard got out of his car, people began to come over to shake his hand and chat.

"Richard, you got 'em today, ain't you, boy?"

"Ever'thing's goin' good. If we can git ever'body out without gittin' hit in the head." The sun eased behind a cloud, and Richard Howard looked up. "Come on, sun, stay out." The cloud slipped past. "Ah! We got it made."

Air Force colonel Quincy Collins, a Vietnam War POW from the close-by town of Concord, was serving as grand marshal for the race, and he was brought over to meet Howard. The colonel, resplendent in formal dress uniform heavy with decorations, was smiling broadly.

"Hear you've got a race here today," he said, extending his hand.

When the colonel left, Del Reeves came over, a bloody mary in one hand, a cigarette in the other. He draped an arm around Richard Howard's shoulder and talked again about the show they would put on together next year. "Listen, baby," he said. "I know where the goddamn fortune is! I promise you. I promise you."

"I hope y'all brought the good weather with you," Richard Howard said to a group of special guests.

"We tried."

"Y'all just enjoy yourself."

"Thank you, old buddy."

Richard Howard wandered through the crowd that had gathered on the grass for the prerace ceremonies, stopping to talk with drivers, crew members, beauty queens, sportswriters, and PR men. He walked over to the pit road where the cars were lined up and huddled for a few minutes with Cale Yarborough, the driver of his No. 11 car. Then, spotting Susan Raye standing nearby, Howard whistled and called to her.

"I got to git me some sugar," he said, starting to kiss her.

"Not on the mouth," she said, turning her cheek.

Richard Howard grinned. "That's my dividend," he said.

"What's your wife say about that, Richard?" somebody teased.

He laughed. "She says, 'Daddy, as long as you've lived with me,' see, I been with her twenty-five years, she says, 'I don't worry about you.'"

At a little before noon, the speeches began. The colonel made a few remarks. Richard Howard stood at the back of the speakers' stand.

"I'm just goina make a few little welcomin' remarks," he said as he waited to be called to the microphone. "About three minutes. Make that three seconds. The fans don't want to hear that stuff. Bein' a race fan myself, I know what they want: twelve-thirty to come and let's git on with it."

"Ladies and gentlemen," the announcer was saying, "the Charlotte Motor Speedway president: RICHARD HOWARD!"

He tried to keep his promise. The remarks were short. He closed by asking who was pulling for Chevrolet, for Ford, for the Dodges. The crowd cheered each one. The drivers were introduced then, each receiving two pairs of panty hose in plastic eggshells from a leggy girl in a scanty costume, gifts from a hosiery manufacturer that was putting up some of the prize money for the race. Then came the presentation of checks to drivers winning the top money in the final leg of the point race, followed by a prayer by Brother Bill, the National Anthem, and the call for the drivers to report to their cars.

"They can come git this stand now," Richard Howard said, taking charge. He climbed onto the stand and picked up a microphone. "Here, take this off and let 'em come git this stand."

Workmen began scurrying around. Satisfied that everything was getting done properly, Richard Howard headed for the pace car. He was going to drive it to start the race.

"Go tell the people in the Cadillac that Colonel Collins is goina ride with them," Richard Howard told a worker. "He's goina start the engines."

Two convertibles would precede the pace car for one parade lap, carrying the colonel and the beauty queens. Susan Raye was to ride in the pace car with Richard Howard.

"Oh, I love it!" she kept saying. "Isn't it exciting?"

Richard Howard tested the radio.

"This is Richard here, are you readin' me?"

"We read you clear. Those two cars in front of you are going just one lap and get off, right?"

"That's right."

"We're in pretty good shape. We'll be ready to go on time."

The radio crackled steadily, checking different points around the track. "Are we all ready down through there fourteen?"

"Ten four, ready to go."

"Okay, Richard, we firin' 'em up now. We'll let 'em set there around about half a minute or so and I'll let you know when to ease off there."

Orders continued to sputter over the radio.

"Okay, move out, Richard. Hey, put those lights on!" Talking about the flashing yellow lights atop the car. "The switch is there under the dash."

The pace car moved out onto the track and up on the banked turns, picking up speed. The beauty queens in the convertibles ahead began to ease down into the seats, clinging to their hairdos. The race cars followed, two by two, tense and jittery with power, eager to leap to speed. Everybody in the track was standing for the start, cheering, waving the cars on.

The apple-cheeked country singer in the pace car was bubbling with excitement. She turned in her seat to watch the pack of race cars behind.

"Oh, I'm so excited," she said. "Aren't they beautiful!"

"It's something, ain't it," Richard Howard agreed. He seemed excited himself. "Have you ever *seen* so many people?" His voice was glee-filled. "Look at all those beautiful people!"

"I meant the cars," she said.

"Oh, I was lookin' at all these people. It's full up. That infield is jam-packed."

"You were counting money," she said, laughing.

Richard Howard grinned. "That's what it's all about."

The first caution flag of the race was out. Peter Gregg, the sports car champion, had found these big cars too much to handle, and had crashed. Richard Petty was leading the race. Richard Howard paused in his office to hear the details over a speaker, then went into the bathroom and combed his hair. On his way out of the office, he stopped to fill his shirt pocket with fresh cigars. He wanted to make one more round outside the track to make certain that everything was in order. He spotted his son, Rick, and stopped to talk.

"I'm goina go upstairs," he said. "That's where I'm fixin' to go in a little. I just want to go around one time. Roads is open good, Rick, and ever'thing. I think ever'thing's good."

Not quite everything. A few minutes later, he saw some people perched atop a rental truck in one of the parking areas watching the race for free, and he summoned security guards to have them removed. Finding all else satisfactory, he returned to the office, parked his car, and commandeered a passing track golf cart to take him up the steep hill to the top of the grandstands. The cart slowed on the hill, straining mightily under the weight. All riders but Richard Howard were forced to abandon it, and it looked as if he might have to climb the hill under his own power, but the cart struggled valiantly on and made it.

He visited all eight of his luxury boxes, shaking hands, talking, slapping backs, keeping people happy. In his own box, an associate handed him a drink, and a white-jacketed black waiter fixed him a plate of prime rib, asparagus, and potatoes. He gobbled the food and hurried to the press box, where he greeted and talked with most of the sportswriters.

"How 'bout this crowd?" one of them said. "Feels good, don't it?"

"You know it does. If the rain'll just hold up now."

The rain didn't hold up. It came at three-thirty. The race had gone 241 laps. Under NASCAR rules, any race that has passed the halfway mark, as this one had at 200 laps, can be canceled because of weather and declared completed. The drivers, therefore, had all been using their rain strategy all day: driving all-out, hoping to be in front if the rain should start. Richard Petty's strategy had worked best. He was leading when the yellow flag came out for the rain. It would have been all right with him if a regular downpour had set in. He had never won a race at Charlotte.

Richard Howard was in his private box when the rain began. He had rushed, almost run, to the press box and climbed, panting with the effort, to the control room above where the NASCAR officials presided. The year before, when Richard Howard had had rain, the NASCAR officials had ordered the checkered flag thrown ending the race well short of the scheduled laps. Richard Howard had not been happy about that. Fans feel cheated if a race ends before it should. They do not go away

happy. Richard Howard wanted to make certain that every fan
felt he got his full dollar's worth at the Charlotte Motor Speedway. He wanted to make sure that what had happened the year
before did not happen again if it could possibly be avoided.

As the rain fell harder, the red flag went out, and the cars
came to a halt on the frontstretch, the crews running out to
cover them with tarpaulins. Richard Howard went on the
public-address system to assure the fans that the race would
resume as soon as the rain stopped. A mighty cheer went up.

The rain stopped after forty-five minutes, and the cars started
drying out the track under the yellow flag. No more rain came,
and the race continued. Richard Howard went down to the
press box to talk with the sportswriters.

"See," he was telling them, "I know what the fans want. I
been a fan, see, and I know what they want. . . . You can go
around and talk to any one of 'em and they'll tell you. They
know we goina try to do right."

"Did you hear that roar when you announced they're goina
run that race?" one of the writers asked. And Richard Howard
smiled.

The race was over. Buddy Baker had won. He'd said all week
that he had a feeling he was going to win. The grandstands
were empty now except for the garbage. Most of the racers had
loaded up their equipment and gone. The infield was almost
empty. In the press box, the sportswriters were finishing their
stories, drinking Richard Howard's beer. The official attendance had been set at 85,250, not quite as big a crowd as Daytona
gets, but bigger than any other stock car track draws, and the
biggest in the history of the Charlotte Motor Speedway. Richard Howard was very happy about that. He was pleased with
the way the day had gone. As Richard Howard walked along
the top of the grandstands, the concessionaires were counting
their money and loading up their unsold goods. He stopped at
the back of a caterer's truck, reached inside, took a big slice of
cheese and another of ham off a tray, rolled them together, and
ate them as he walked down the steep embankment toward his
office.

"You know what I'm goina do now?" he said. "I'm goina go around and thank all my help, all my top men. That's more than their pay. You wouldn't believe it."

In a few hours, he would be on a plane headed for Indianapolis and the big race there the next day. He doesn't like that kind of racing. It has no appeal to him at all. Why was he going? I asked.

"Oh, I'm not goin' to see the race," he said. "I wanta see how they handle that crowd."

Of course. Indianapolis draws the biggest crowd of any race. Someday, with luck, Richard Howard hoped to have a crowd like that himself.

Fan

In the gaudier and more raucous days, before stock car racing got so slick, so conscious of image, he had it painted in big red letters on the side of his car, so that everybody who saw it would know. But that, he came to realize, was not really becoming for a man of his position. He is more subtle now, more . . . well . . . professional. Now he uses business cards.

"Red Robinson," the cards say. In red, of course. "World's Number One Stock Car Racing Fan." But just for good measure, and because it is in his nature to advertise, he still buys license plates that read: "Red R."

Red Robinson has been the world's No. 1 stock car racing fan almost as long as organized stock car racing has been around. Nobody ever really gave him the title. The position was just there, like virgin land, and Red Robinson laid claim to it. His claim has never been disputed.

"I've seen ever' race at Charlotte, Rockingham, Darlington, Daytoner, A'lanter, and Tallerdeger," he will tell you. "Racin', it's about the only thing I've ever liked. I like football, but I don't like the golf, and I don't hunt much. I mean, I don't hunt any. It's a good buncha people, racin' people. 'Course, you have your nuts in it, and your crazy folks, and a few drunks, or whatever, but I've always liked the racin'. I go now when the racin' season starts, I'll be at a race on Thursday niat, I'll be at one on

Friday niat, I'll be at one on Sa'rd'y niat, and I'll be at the big'un on Sunday. That'll be about four races a week, and a lot of times I'll see one on Sa'rd'y ev'nin' up Shelby, see anudn down at Cherokee Speedway Sa'rd'y niat."

Red Robinson is a fixture of the big-time stock car racing circuit, as much so as the drivers and crew members. He is always there with the special passes that the track promoters give him, prowling through the pits before every race, slipping an arm around the beauty queens, stealing a little "sugar," posing for pictures, his pockets bulging with chewing gum.

The chewing gum. That is how it all started. Red came out of the Air Force after the war and got himself a job in a textile finishing plant back at home in Gaffney, South Carolina. He started hanging around at these little dirt racetracks that started popping up all over. He even tried his hand at driving a few races. "Wudn't what you'd call really drivin' in a race," he says. "We usta have them little ol' thangs ever' Sa'rd'y over in Spartanburg. All we had was '39 and '40 Fords. Wudn't much racin' to it. They'as just little ol' thangs with local boys. That was in '46 or '47. All the drivin' we done was just more or less playin'. All we knowed to do was put ether in the gas tank and put bigger tires on the back and maybe a quick-change rear end, and maybe shave the heads and put a dual carburetor on it. Over here in Spartanburg, little ol' track. Now they've got a drive-in theater on it."

That was back in the days when David Pearson, the superstar, was just a kid hanging around the Spartanburg racetrack. It would get awfully hot and dusty around those tracks. Red usually carried a pack of chewing gum to keep a little moisture in his mouth. He well recalls how the chewing gum business got started.

"David and some of them other boys, just out at these dirt tracks, I'd carry it myself, and first thang I knowed, 'Gimme some chewin' gum, Red.' I kept handin' it to 'em, and first thang I knowed, I'd have to carry about three packs, because even givin' out one piece, it'd run out. And 'en it just got bigger 'n' bigger, and it started in out these big races, and the first thang

I knowed, I'as givin' the Goodyear people chewin' gum, I'as givin' the Union Oil people chewin' gum, and the first thang I knowed, I'as carryin' whole boxfuls.

"Speed week at Daytoner, I'll give out anywheres between fourteen hunderd and sixteen hunderd packs."

Tradition. Red's chewing gum has reached that point. Some racing people do not feel that they have been to a race if they miss getting their chewing gum from Red. It is said that there are drivers—a superstitious lot to begin with—who will not go onto the track until they get their chewing gum. One time Cale Yarborough—and Red loves to tell this story—missed Red somehow during the race preliminaries, and the word was given for the drivers to get into their cars—Red grins broadly at this point—and ol' Cale said, "Hell, we can't start this race, I ain't got my chewing gum yet. Where's Red?" And off he ran, looking for Red. When he finally found him, he said, "Red, if you don't start finding me earlier, I'm going to have to get somebody else to handle this job."

Red buys his chewing gum by the case lot down at C. B. Poole's Wholesale House in Gaffney. One of the hardest things is remembering how much of which kinds to buy, because it is difficult to remember who likes what. Not so hard with the big stars, though. Red remembers those. "Some of 'em likes Dentyne. Petty likes Dentyne. Pearson likes Spearmint. Cale likes Beechnut. Some of 'em, I give Teaberry to." He laughs. "I ask 'em if they want to drive funny today, I'll give 'em Teaberry.

"Then a lot of 'em want cotton for their ears. I got that. I got fried chicken, country ham biscuits, cold drinks, whatever they want." All free for the asking, of course. Just Red's way of showing his appreciation. "I keep everythang in my car from aspirin tablets to southern fried chicken."

That car, a red Ford XL, is parked on the back of pit row down by a Union 76 sign at the North Carolina Motor Speedway in the pine-green sandhills north of Rockingham. Beryl Brockman Robinson has just gotten himself a chicken leg and a canned soft drink from the trunk and he is sitting in his car with the windows rolled up, listening to the race on the radio as the cars whiz past on the track in front of him. He grins when he tells his full name.

"Nobody knows me by that except my bank and my lawyer," he says. "I was glad I was red-headed so they could just call me Red."

His hair isn't really red, sort of an orangeish blond, and now that he is pushing fifty, there isn't much left of it. He combs the few remaining strands across the top in a vain attempt to conceal the baldness. He is a big guy, tall, barrel-chested, with a considerable paunch. There is a big gap between his two center front teeth, and his face is splotchy red, with broken veins in the cheeks. He has the kind of skin that sunburns easily ("I blister real bad"), which is why he prefers to sit out the races in his car with the air conditioner on, listening to the race on the radio.

Something other than the race is on Red Robinson's mind, though. From his wallet, he takes a photograph and passes it around to the several people in the car. It's Linda Vaughn! Miss Hurst Golden Shifter! In a bikini! Red is beaming a big grin.

"She's forty-three inches by nineteen by thirty-seven. That's the truth."

The truth may well be that Red Robinson's avid interest in racing was brought about more by the racetrack beauty queens than by the race cars. Red collects beauty queens the way some people collect stamps or old bottles.

A quick scene change: Gaffney, South Carolina, 400 West Frederick Street. Red Robinson's Used Cars. The little white frame office building sits in the middle of the lot, under the big trees. The cars are lined up along the street under a single, sagging strand of naked light bulbs.

Red had worked in that finishing plant for twelve years, had risen to the position of foreman, and was still making only seventy-five dollars a week. But he'd been "messin' around some" with cars, buying one and fixing it up, selling it, and he finally decided that he could make more at that than he could at the finishing plant, so he left and got into the car business.

He has been well satisfied with his decision. He is not only a respected businessman and his own boss, but his work leaves him plenty of time to go to the races. Red has got the whole thing down to a system, and the secret is that he does his own financing.

"I keep about thirty-five or forty out financed all the time," he explains. "I just keep it snowballin'. I mean, a man that comes in here and pays off a '66, I put him in a '68, charge 'im five hunderd dollars' boot and a hunderd dollars in financin', see, and send 'im back out the door, twelve dollars a week, and that takes keer of him for another year. He pays the '68 off and I put 'im in a '69 or '70." It brings Red about three hundred or four hundred dollars a week, and he doesn't have to spend a lot of time at it. Everybody comes by to pay on Saturday, and he sees that there's always somebody there to collect.

On this particular afternoon, however, Red is in the office, even though there really isn't any need to be. But Red is going through his pictures—his beauty queen pictures.

"There's a purty good pichur of ol' Linder."

Linda again. Queen of the racetrack queens!

"Ol' big-chested Linder. I got 'er her first job. I met 'er in A'lanter, she'd just won a little beauty contest. She got married six weeks ago. I don't know what that char-act-ter does she married. He's some kinda joker out 'ere in Calerfornyer." He pulls out another picture of her. "That's what she looked like years ago, before she got so fancy."

They are all there, the Miss Firebirds, the Miss Southern 500s, the Miss World 600s, Miss Falstaffs, Miss Lemon Tree Inns, Miss Dixies, Miss Atlantas, Miss South Carolinas, Miss Sun Funs, the Union 76 Race Stoppers, Winston Cup girls, all of them posing with Red's arms around them, being kissed by Red, or giving him kisses. Some have inscriptions across a corner: "Red, To the most *lasting* love I'll ever know." "Love to you, Red, forever and a day." "Dearest Red, what a true *love* you are. I love you."

On the walls of the office, along with the racing posters, are the photographs and calendar pictures of the beauty queens

Red has known who have gone on to bigger things, to pose for soft-drink ads, or sing in nightclubs, to model in places like Atlanta and Charlotte and Birmingham. Red beams with pride as he thumbs through a box stuffed with pictures.

"There was Miss Southern 500 from last year. She's a airline hostess now. . . .

"See, I've knowed ever' Miss Southern 500 they is. . . .

"This'un here, she's over in Charlotte. She's made a couple movies. . . .

"There's a gal there I'da married if I hadn't been married. She was a Miss Apple Queen and ever'thang else in North Caroliner. . . ."

I ask Red what his wife thinks about all of this.

"Well, she just goes along with it, we been married so long. I been married twenty-five years. She don't encourage me to take 'em out, but she knows when I go to a race that I'm not goina be by myself. But she don't question me too much, and she knows that I git all this fan mail and that they call me and I do take 'em out and whatever. But she purty well goes along with it and accepts it because I give 'er—she's got a new home and diamonds and a new car and ever'thang else. . . ."

Back at the North Carolina Motor Speedway. Red takes another photograph from his wallet and passes it around.

"I been married to that beautiful woman right there for twenty-five years last Tuesday," he says. "I have a real good wife that puts up with me. She lets me go. She's kinda glad when the racin' season's over, though, when I'm there with 'er for a few weekends."

Jim McAllister, a newspaper columnist from Greenville, South Carolina, is sitting in the car taking notes, and he looks at the picture and says, "What does she think about this beauty queen business?" Red grins and says, "Aw, she just grins and goes on. You better put in there she knows they won't none of 'em have me and I'll be home right after the race."

Then Red looks out at the track and says, "Now Petty, they

fixin' to pit him. He'll come in and they'll throw two tires on 'im and fill 'im up with gas. After a while you git to where you can tell thangs like 'at. You got to kindly know what to watch for."

If proof is needed of how ardent a race fan Red Robinson is, it surely lies in the fact that he is at this race. On the day before, his brother had suffered a heart attack in another North Carolina town and was hospitalized in serious condition. That had not been enough to pull Red away from the racetrack. "Ain't nothin' I can do," he had said. "I called home last niat. I called home agin this mornin'. I figgered that was all I could do."

Red is talking now about racing, about how he thought ol' Fireball Roberts, or Farball, as he calls him, was the greatest driver who ever lived, and how he guessed he was the last person to talk to Fireball before the race that took his life. "I went over to the car, I give 'im his chewin' gum, I said, 'Farball, I'll see you in the winner's circle.' He said, 'No, not today, Red.' He just seemed to have a feelin' that sumpin' was goina happen and it did in the seventh lap." He tells about how he never got along so good with ol' Curtis Turner and his crowd, because Red has never taken a drink of likker or beer in his life. "Them folks, they got drunk and they started raisin' hell," he says. "It wasn't my kinda party." And he tells about the nerve that some of the drivers have. "If LeeRoy Yarbrough seen that he was goina run through that Winston sign yonder, they's no doubt that he wouldn't take his foot off that pedal. That boy ain't got no fear. I've seen 'im crash at Daytoner . . . didn't bother 'im at all. If it was a reg'lar driver, he'd be settin' over yonder with his head 'tween his laigs, shakin' all over.

"They really racin' 'ere now," Red says, turning his attention to the track. "See all them people standin' up. That's as good as it can git right there."

"Would you like to be out there?" I ask.

"Yes sir, if I'as thirty-two agin, I'd like to be out 'ere."

There is a sudden tapping on his window, some guy in a white racing jacket with red stripes who somehow had missed Red before the race started.

"Hey, how ye doin'?" Red says, rolling down his window. "I saved your'n for ye."

And through the window he passes a shiny eight-stick pack of Beechnut gum.

Preacher

The Racer's Prayer

Lord I pray as I race today,
Keep me safe along the way,
Not only me but others too
As they perform the jobs they do.
I know God that in a race
I, the driver, must set the pace.
But in this race of life I pray
Help me Lord along the way.
Although I know I am a sinner,
Help me to believe that with
GOD you're always a winner.

BROTHER BILL FRAZIER

EVIL. No doubt about that. In that great swath of the South where it began and now thrives, stock car racing simply was not countenanced by the fervent, fundamentalist, born-again Christians who made up the great bulk of the area's religious people.

Hard drinking. Gambling. Fighting. They knew what stock car racing was all about. And the language! Well, it wasn't exactly genteel. God only knew what went on out at those shabby dirt racetracks on the edge of town on Friday and Saturday nights. One thing was sure. It wasn't the work of the Lord. And those doings served as ammunition for many a preacher's hell-fire Sunday morning sermon.

"Oh, man, we was really low-rated," recalls old-time driver Louise Smith. "I'm telling you, we was *low-rated*."

Then as racing grew and became big business, the races were held on Sundays, when the crowds of working people would be able to come, and the crowds did come, ignoring church, flocking to those superspeedways. And the born-again Christians, who knew that God had set aside Sunday exclusively for preaching, praying, and gospel singing, would drive by those speedways and see all those people and . . . go to a race on Sunday? You might as well dance. It was the devil's doings. That whole stock car racing crowd was bound straight for hell.

And then the Lord sent Brother Bill.

Brother Bill Frazier knew what those guys who raced stock cars were like, knew that they could be rough and rowdy, and that they might drink and gamble and cuss and fight, chase wild women, and otherwise engage in sinful indulgences. But he knew, too, that that was all part of redemption—it made it so much sweeter—and that some day those wild ol' boys would be down on their knees praying to the Lord and crying about how their only regret was that they hadn't done better while Mama was alive.

Brother Bill knew because Brother Bill had been like them.

Wild? Bill Frazier was one of the wildest ol' boys in all of Alabama. He was born in Kentucky in 1941, but his parents separated when he was eighteen months old, and he was reared by his grandparents in Alabama. His grandfather was a foreman in a steel mill in Gadsden. The signs were there early that Bill Frazier was going to run wild. He quit school in the ninth grade and fell in with the "wrong crowd." The guys he ran with frequented the pool rooms, street corners, drive-ins, racetracks, and honky-tonks when they were old enough to get in them. They lived as if they had received a calling to raise hell.

Barbara Gunnells thought that she could change Bill Frazier. She was pretty and quiet and religious, a couple of years older than he. Her father was a deacon in the Baptist church. Bill Frazier married her when he was seventeen, and their first child, Lisa, was born the next year. Another child, John, was born four years later. Marriage tames some wild ol' boys, but not Bill Frazier. He tried. He got a job in the steel mill and kept promising that he was going to do better, but other, stronger forces had a hold on him. He continued to run with the same crowd and to the same places. He dreamed, of course. Even wild ol' boys dreamed. He had a friend who had an old race car that he drove at outlaw tracks. His friend dreamed of being a big-time stock car driver. Bill Frazier helped him with his car, but his dream lay in a different direction. He wanted to be a country music star, to go up to Nashville and be on the Grand Ol' Opry.

"I played in little ol' country bands in little ol' beer joints," he says. "I sang, was what I did, leaned on a gi-tar. I'as lead singer, and I'd just run a chord or two, you know, didn't have to play . . . but I never was any good at it, 'cause I drank so much. Got to where I couldn't hardly perform without bein' sloppy drunk."

The bottle had done him in. He was an alcoholic by the age of twenty-two. By the time he was twenty-six, he had long quit trying in his marriage, and people talked about how awful it was what he had done to that sweet girl and those two innocent children. But that didn't have much effect on Bill Frazier.

Then on an April night in 1967, after he'd been separated from his wife for six months, Bill Frazier was down on the coast, in Gulf Shores, Alabama, raising hell and having a big time, when a strange thing happened. He came out of a liquor store carrying a quart of Ancient Age under his arm—and he can remember every little detail of it now, the precise time, and all (it was five of seven)—when something told him to go home. Whatever it was that was leading him—and he wasn't sure then what it was exactly—it was a powerful force, and he obeyed.

"I just had an eerie feelin' when I walked out," he recalls. "I suddenly realized here I am twenty-six years old, my life's a bomb, you know. I said, 'Man, if I'm goin' to get all my stuff together . . .'"

He climbed into his '65 dark-blue Mustang and set out for Gadsden, three hundred miles to the north, sipping the Ancient Age as he drove.

It was almost three o'clock when he got there, and the first thing that he did was stop at a telephone booth to call his wife. He told her that he wanted to talk, and she told him to come on over. At three-thirty that morning, Bill Frazier knelt with his wife to pray for the first time in his life.

"Well, God," he remembers saying, "if you're really God, you can help me. I'm askin'."

Now Bill Frazier says: "I seen the need, well, that I needed to change my life, but I couldn't find nothin' to change it. You know. I tried to straighten up and do right and just couldn't. So I decided I'd, you know, try the religious part. I'd heard that it worked, but I'd never went to church or nothin'. I'd tried everything else and failed, you know; I mean, I'd tried friendship, confided in people, tried sex, women, drinkin'. . . . When I really made up my mind, I asked God to help me, I changed. Just like that. My life just changed. I got up the next day with a different outlook on life, started getting things back together."

He went back to work at the steel mill, started going to church, got baptized, began teaching a young people's Sunday school class, and started studying the Bible himself. Then he realized that the Lord was calling him to preach. He got himself ordained in 1968, and became associate pastor of a small country Baptist Church. But he was restless there. He didn't seem to be reaching out to the people who most needed to be reached. So he started going back to the racetracks and his other old hangouts, talking to his old buddies and telling them what he'd found. "They was very skeptical about it," he says, "because here's guys I'd raised hell with for ten years, all of a sudden I'd changed my tune." Most of them thought he was joking.

They soon realized that he wasn't. He started going out into the streets to talk with the young toughs, seeing himself ten years earlier, thinking about the pain he might have avoided and the pain he might not have caused if he'd had some direction at that age. He knew that his would not be a regular ministry. He had been reading about Bob Harrington, who was called the "chaplain of Bourbon Street" in New Orleans, and other such unorthodox ministries, and this had great appeal to him. He wanted to do something like that, and he had begun to think about racing.

He'd been to some of the big-time stock car races at Daytona, and now Bill France was building another superspeedway at Talladega, only a few miles from Gadsden. Bill Frazier began to read all that he could find about stock car racing, about the drivers, mechanics, crew members, and their families, particularly, and then it came to him that here were maybe four hundred or five hundred people riding this racing circuit every week, always racing on Sunday, never able to go to church—a whole congregation on the hoof, just waiting for some preacher to corral it.

Bill Frazier set out to do that. The Alabama International Speedway at Talladega opened in the fall of 1969, and when it held its second race the following spring, Bill Frazier was there with a pickup truck for a pulpit and a gospel quartet for accompaniment, ready to start his ministry. He still didn't know anybody in racing, so he figured he would have to start preaching in the infield and hope to attract attention. It rained, though, and he didn't even get to preach. On the Fourth of July, he tried again, this time at Daytona. He learned a lesson there. Nobody was going to pay attention to some nut getting up to preach on the back of a pickup truck in a speedway infield.

He pondered this problem on the way home, not knowing what to do about it. Then in Gadsden he rounded a corner and spotted, parked beside a church, a little chapel built on a trailer, and he knew immediately that he'd found his answer. He went to work with two-by-fours and plywood, building himself a church on a trailer bed, finishing it in time to make the race at Talladega in August of 1970. He painted the little church white, furnished it with a small pulpit and six two-man pews, and painted "THE CHAPEL" by the door. On the top, he affixed a bracket into which he could insert a wooden cross. He hooked the trailer to his '66 Chevy stationwagon and went off to the race.

He parked his chapel in the infield beside the garage fence. It had the desired effect: It attracted attention. A lot of people were curious about it. Bill Frazier chatted with some of the mechanics and crewmen through the garage fence, telling them of his plans to hold a service at eleven o'clock on race day, in-

viting them all to come, asking them to spread the word. The
sportswriters were attracted. They came and did interviews for
feature stories. The Chapel even got a little squib in *Sports Il-
lustrated*, which quoted Bill Frazier as saying: "You see Goodyear, Prestone, Grey-Rock, and just about everything else you
can think of at these races. I figured it was time the Lord got a
little representation. I'm going to promote God just like the
other guys promote STP." For racing people, Bill Frazier had
come up with a perfect angle.

At five minutes before eleven on that Sunday morning, however, he was standing in front of his little chapel looking at his
watch. Nobody had yet showed up for his service, and he was
beginning to think that he was going to have to preach to himself. A couple of minutes later, one man walked up. Bill Frazier
recognized him. When he had talked to the man earlier about
the service, the man had said: "I don't give a damn what you
do."

"Don't look like they goina have no service, do they?" the
man said. "They ain't nobody here."

"Yeah, we'll have it, if there ain't nobody but me and you
and the Lord."

"Well, let's git on with it. I got work to do."

The man, Bill Frazier would later learn, was Maurice Petty.
Just then Bill Frazier saw one of the drivers, Soapy Castles,
and three of his crewmen come out of the garage gate and head
for the chapel. Two teen-aged boys sitting nearby saw the men
going into the trailer and followed them. And Bill Frazier
preached his first racetrack sermon to seven people who had
come out of curiosity.

Later that day, he talked with some of the mechanics, who
told him that if he were really sincere his idea might go, but that
he would be watched closely. A lot of con men tried to attach
themselves to race people, who understandably had become
somewhat leery of newcomers. If he really meant business, Bill
Frazier was told, he would have to keep showing up at the races.

When he got back home, Bill Frazier talked it over with his
wife. He would quit his job and try to get into something that

would give him time to get this ministry started. She would have to take responsibility for providing for the family. She agreed.

So Bill Frazier hit the road, pulling his chapel to Darlington, Richmond, Martinsville, North Wilkesboro, Charlotte, and Rockingham, getting to know more people and more about racing, having a few more people turn out for services at each race. But the chapel broke down on Interstate 85 in North Carolina as Bill Frazier was headed home from Rockingham, and broke and unable to repair it, he abandoned it alongside the road. It was later hauled off as junk.

When he appeared at Daytona for the start of the new season in February 1971, Bill Frazier had a new red, white, and blue tent that he had bought at Sears. It would seat twice as many as the old trailer, and he would need the space.

For slowly, he was gaining the confidence of the racing people. His approach was low-key. He was never pushy with his religion. He was always around, always helpful if he could be. He tried to stay out of the way when he wasn't needed. He never showed disgust or dismay at the cussing he overheard or the drinking he saw. He was quiet, easy-going, a quite likable fellow, and his interest in racing and racing people seemed genuine. Beyond that, he never took up a collection or asked for donations. He was working, as he sometimes said, on faith. The racing people called him Preacher, and some of them began seeing to it that he got passes to the pits and garages at the various tracks.

It was not until the late spring that Bill Frazier knew that he'd been accepted. He was standing around at one of the drivers' meetings when a NASCAR official made note of his presence and asked the drivers if they'd mind if Brother Bill closed the meeting with a prayer. After that, Bill Frazier knew that he'd found his place, and the drivers' meeting prayer became standard procedure. By the summer of that year, his services had outgrown his tent, and he was invited by NASCAR officials to begin using the scoring stands near the garage areas, an advantage in that it made it possible for the racing people to escape the infield crowds and increased attendance even more. Many of the racers and their families began to attend.

The Chapel it was called now, an organization with a board of directors and an advisory committee that included two of the biggest names in stock car racing—Richard Petty and Bobby Allison—both of whom frequently attended services and sometimes made church appearances with Brother Bill, as he had come to be called almost exclusively. A sportswriter had dubbed Brother Bill the "chaplain of stock car racing," which he liked and now used on his stationery. The Chapel even had an emblem: racing's crossed flags, one of them the checkered, the other a Christian flag. There was a slogan too, taken from the racer's prayer that Brother Bill had written: "With God You're Always a Winner." Brother Bill had the emblem made into a shoulder patch, which he now wore on all of his shirts, jackets, and hats. The racer's prayer had been printed on decals and distributed to all the drivers, and there were few, if any, race cars that went onto a track without that decal affixed to the dashboard. Brother Bill distributed the patches and decals at cost. Still, he never asked for donations, although many would now come up after services and press a bill into his hand, and some donations had begun to come by mail from race fans. Richard Petty was offering deeds to tiny pieces of his Randolph County farmland for sale to fans to help finance the ministry. Then in 1972, at the May race at Talladega, for the first time the track opened its speakers so that all of the fans might hear the sermon that Brother Bill was delivering to his flock, and other tracks, not to be outdone, quickly followed suit. Brother Bill was now preaching to tens of thousands of people every Sunday. No other evangelist, except Billy Graham (who was opposed to racing on Sunday), could claim such multitudes, and not even Billy Graham with such regularity. Bill Frazier, at last, had become a star.

In 1972, the Chapel received more than fourteen thousand dollars in donations, and for the first time, Bill Frazier was able to take a small salary after expenses.

"We probably could solicit more money if we pressed the

idea," he said, "but I've avoided this for one reason. This is a young ministry, and we definitely want to prove to these people that we're sincere about the religious part, not the money part, and this is the biggest thing people holler about evangelists. A lot of 'em are professionals, spending an hour taking up the offering. . . . I've been to tent meetin's where they took up three or four collections. They's some professional hustlers. That's why I've never took a collection."

By 1973, Bill Frazier had begun thinking of expanding the ministry. He was talking about how all these millions of spectators attended stock car races throughout the country each year, only about a fifth of them at Grand National races, where he concentrated his attention. That left millions of racegoers to be reached by the gospel. His plan was to organize a group of associates to carry on the work at the small tracks of America. The trouble would be in finding the right people for the job.

"Our problem," he explained, "is goina be findin' somebody —it's not goina be that great a problem—but to find someone that's oriented enough with racin' to have a broad enough mind to know some of the things that goes on, see. First time he walks in and somebody says, 'Well, GD this,' he just jumps up and has a heart attack; see, he's just goina have to learn to live with it. We ain't in a church house. And you've got some radical religious people, I'm sorry to say, that they think if somebody says 'damn,' well, you know, the world falls apart, but that just ain't the way it works." He grins and says, "Plus we gotta find somebody who wants to do it for nothin'."

If racing has been good for Bill Frazier, he, too, has been good for it. He has done more than anybody to erase the idea that stock car racing is sinbound. And he never fails to promote racing as a clean, wholesome sport, which hasn't hurt him any with the promoters. Some call it luck that he came along at the right time to claim his success. He sees it differently.

"Racin' itself has took a different image in the past few years," he says. "It's the second-largest spectator sport. It's become a professional sport more than it ever was. In other words, it's a big business, it's not just git out here and run on the weekend, raise hell, drink likker, and like you used to read about. It's become very refined, and we just happened to come along at the same time. Any other time, it may not have worked, see.

"God knew when the right time would be. That's why he sent me at this time. You know. He knows what'll work. So that's why I purely go by faith and inside of what he impresses me to do. So on my part, I'm not amazed at what's happened because I let Him run the ball game. In other words, I didn't do it. I didn't set down and say, 'Now in six months, I'm goina do this, in a year, I'm goina do this,' I just said, you know, 'Well, Lord, I'm goina do what you tell me to do and leave the result to You,' so therefore, I'm not amazed a bit."

Some of the die-hard churchgoers criticize Brother Bill. They cling to the notion that anybody who goes to a racetrack on Sunday is going to hell in a seat harness, preachers included. Brother Bill tries to avoid dissension and controversy.

"The gospel can be preached anywhere," he says. "They's more folks out here at the racetrack than they are in a church house. If you ask any preacher, he'll tell you. . . .

"I try to avoid justifyin' or not justifyin' whether or not it's right to race on Sunday. You follow me? It's not for me to say, really. In other words, I don't preach against racin' on Sunday, or wearin' miniskirts, or long hair on kids. They's just as many bald-headed folks going to hell as they are long-hairs. I preach to a man's heart. The Bible says, 'Happy is the man doesn't condemn himself the thing that he allowed.' Now, you do somethin' in your life and it condemns you, you don't feel good, you better leave it alone. If you don't feel right goin' to a race on Sunday, you oughta stay at home, but that's not up to me."

Gimmick

THE LAST SEASON had to have been the worst. Wendell Scott couldn't remember a worse time in all of his years of racing, not even in those difficult first years.

He had run only a few races all season. He had taken his car to almost all of them, as usual, but the old car was about shot, and inevitably something would happen. He would have trouble of one kind or another and wouldn't even be able to get up enough speed to qualify. It went on like this week after week. Wendell Scott was always the first name on the scratch list.

Toward the end of the season, the car was handling so badly that he had to fight just to keep it on the track, and he couldn't seem to do much to correct it. It costs a lot of money to travel around to all of those racetracks, and drivers who fail to qualify collect nothing. As the end of the season neared, Wendell Scott figured that he had lost at least $17,000 for the year, and with the car in the shape that it was, he knew he couldn't go on. He took his car back home to Danville, Virginia, and parked it. He had almost reached the conclusion that it was all futile, that no matter how hard he tried, a black man just couldn't make it in this business.

Wendell Scott had to go to work in his garage fixing other people's cars to try to get money to pay some of his bills and get his family through the winter. His race car sat untouched through the winter.

The first race of the new season came in January, 1973, at Riverside in California, and Wendell Scott had felt the old, familiar tug. But he well remembered his last trip there. It had cost him nearly five hundred dollars just to buy fuel for his old gas-guzzling truck. Then he had blown his only engine sitting on pit row waiting to go onto the track. He figured that trip had cost him about four thousand dollars altogether. His income: zero. He had even let his car sit through the next race, the big one at Daytona, and that was really hard. It was the first time in eighteen years that he had let that race slip by without making a run for it. But by spring the old urge had come back full force, so strong that Wendell Scott could no longer resist.

The year before, when he was having his troubles, losing money on every race, he'd relaxed his pride and asked some of the tracks for help, for a little "deal" money. Most of the drivers got some deal money. The way he saw it, the tracks ought to at least assure him of enough money to meet expenses. He'd been in racing a long time, after all, and he'd never asked for help. And he *did* have a name, didn't he? Every race fan knew who Wendell Scott was. He figured the promoters owed him a little something—enough to keep him racing, anyway. The most he'd asked from any track was $250. But as soon as he had started asking, he'd started getting his entry blanks back, refused. Some promoters told him that he was welcome to enter their races, but they were sorry, they couldn't give him anything. It had embittered him. He couldn't help but think that if he had been a white man, it would have all been different.

"They think I want to race so damn bad that I'll do it for nothin'," he had said.

That was one of the things that had caused him to decide that he just wouldn't go back to a racetrack any more. He was through.

But when that old feeling had come back with the spring, Wendell Scott knew that he was helpless before it. There was only one thing that he could do.

"We goina give it one mo' try," he said, and set about to get his car ready.

He had sent off an entry blank for a Grand National East race at Hickory, North Carolina. It was midweek now, and the race was to be on Sunday, and Wendell Scott had been so busy that he hadn't had a chance to work on his car yet. He couldn't run it in the condition it was in, that was sure.

The car, a '71 Ford, painted pale blue, with a big "34" on the door and "Wendell Scott" painted over the driver's window, was rather sad-looking as race cars go. It lacked that sleek, glossy look that most of the cars had. It had been through too many wrecks and pieced back together with too many junkyard parts. The body showed where the dents had been beaten out, and the paint was flat and marked with brush strokes, obviously a poor man's car. It just didn't have the flashiness that the big-time promoters like; they wanted cars like polished jewels. This was an old plowhorse compared to the spirited thoroughbreds that Petty and Allison and Pearson rode, and now it was ailing.

Wendell Scott knew the problem. The car had been in one crash too many. The chassis was severely bent. That had been his trouble during the latter part of the past season. Two of the wheels, the right rear and left front, were barely touching the ground. The other two wheels bore all the weight.

He had spent the morning in his garage mulling over the situation. The garage was small, built of cinder block, and unbelievably cluttered. Wendell Scott spent a lot of his time there looking for parts and tools, and muttering about it. Outside were the rusting hulks of old trucks and race cars. The garage sat behind a little flat-top cinder block house with peeling paint in a black section on the north side of Danville. Wendell Scott had built the house, but he had moved out of it and into his mother's old house not far away, and one of his sons lived in the little house now. Wendell Scott was down on his haunches peering under the car.

"Now, if I jack dis right here and cut dat right dere. Naw, dat ain't goina do it. . . ."

After lunch he had decided to go get some advice. He had some errands he needed to run anyway, so he got into his old pickup truck, the back end loaded with old car parts, and set out across town.

"Here's where I run in my first race," he said, as the truck rattled down a new four-lane expressway. "Yeah, that was the first race I ran, right there. The Old Danville Fairgrounds." Only a trace of the old dirt track remained, off to the right, a ghostly junked car resting in the middle of it. "Now it's a highway and a shopping center."

That first race had been nearly twenty-four years earlier. Less than two years after Jackie Robinson made his heralded debut with the Brooklyn Dodgers, Wendell Scott was also moving into a white man's sport, a roughneck southern white man's sport, doing it in a time when no black child had ever set foot in a white southern school, when no black man would have dared sit in at a southern lunch counter, when black men were still being dragged from southern jail cells in the dead of night and lynched, when any black who didn't know his place was quickly shown it—and he was doing it unsung, without the help of a Branch Rickey or the protective glare of a national press. What was he trying to prove?

"I'd never really thought about it much in that respect," he said now. "I wasn't trying to break any barriers or anything. I was just doin' what I wanted to do, and I had the opportunity to do it, and I accepted it. I didn't go to them, they came to me. The promoter came to me and asked me to race."

A gimmick. Promoters were always coming up with gimmicks. And Wendell Scott happened to be one of them. Attendance had been lagging at the fairgrounds races, and somebody got the idea of putting a nigger out there to run against the white boys. That ought to pull 'em in. See the nigger run.

"It was through the po-leece department," Wendell Scott was saying. "That's really how it happened. They went to the po-leece to find out what colored boys had speedin' records. They thought they'd get ahold of some of those wild speeders in the streets, you know. The po-leece told 'em, 'You want somebody to drive a car, you want Wendell Scott,' so they came to me."

First he had to get a car to drive. He went to his brother-in-law. He'd just sold his brother-in-law a little car that he'd been using and he knew it would really run. Now he borrowed it back.

"Used to be a little likker car," he said, "and it got purty hot. You know, when it got hot, you'd get rid of 'em."

A likker car. Of course.

"That's what happened, see. That's the reason the po-leece recommended me. It was just something I did. I never made it. I just transpo'ted. The old drivers, most of 'em's retired now, practically all of them was bootleggers. You can't hardly think of a one that wasn't a bootlegger."

The offer had come at a good time for Wendell Scott. He had recently been caught with a load of moonshine, the only time that he had ever been caught, and put on three years' probation. He looked at this as a good opportunity to get into another line that was more fun, more exciting, possibly as profitable, and far less likely to stir the ire of the authorities. He knew little about the dirt track racing that was becoming so popular in the South after the war. It was exclusively the province of wild white country boys who knew how to make cars run fast and had the guts to drive them as fast as they could make them run. Wendell Scott was no different, except that his skin was a few shades darker. Not all that dark, really. His complexion was very light, and his eyes were blue, but he was dark enough to qualify him as black—and somewhat less than human in the eyes of most of the local whites. But the proposition sounded interesting, and he wanted to give it a try. He can no longer remember how he did in that first race, an amateur race. He didn't win. But he can remember the boos and catcalls, the derisive laughter. And he can also well remember what the race did to him: It set a fire in him to race.

The gimmick had worked too. The crowds came and took great delight in seeing those white drivers prove once again the natural superiority of the Caucasian race. And the gimmick also gave Wendell Scott the opportunity to race again. As soon as one promoter finds a successful gimmick, others rush to cash in on it, and Wendell Scott soon saw that he would be able to

continue racing. But there was one thing that he was determined not to continue. He was not going to let those white
boys keep beating him.

When he is asked about the problems that he had in those
days, Wendell Scott just laughs. "Startin' in a white man's sport
twenty-four years ago, you *know* I had problems. I had a lot of
problems. More problems I had, the more determined I got."

The other drivers reacted to him in different ways. Some ignored him. Some were openly hostile, making derogatory remarks and calling him "nigger" within his hearing. Some laughed
at him. A few would deliberately try to run him into the wall
on the track. If a white driver received such attentions from
another driver, he usually did not hesitate to express his displeasure in a very direct fashion: with fists or a tire tool. Wendell Scott, for practical reasons, could not allow himself the
pleasure of such indulgences. He knew what would happen if
he did, and he tried to avoid conflict.

"I've never really got involved in too many fights," he said.
"I've always tried to figure out a way not to have to do that,
'cause I knew one black with thousands of white people, I
wouldn't have too much chance. But I *have* been involved in
some right stiff arguments."

Not all of the other drivers were against him, though. "You'd
find one or two that was a nice guy. He'd try to associate with
you and make you feel good, keep your spirit up." These gave
him encouragement to continue, and hope that things would be
better.

And things did improve. In the early fifties, as late-model
stock car racing was just beginning to grow, Wendell Scott
was busy racing modified cars at dirt tracks in Virginia and
North Carolina, hitting several each week, Danville, Staunton,
Waynesville, South Hill, sleeping in his truck, coming back
home with a couple of hundred bucks in his pocket. He had
begun to win, too. In the late fifties, he moved into NASCAR
sportsman racing, became track champion at Richmond, and
won the Virginia championship in 1959. Two years later, he
moved into big-league racing, the only black ever to do so. He

ran his first Grand National race at Spartanburg, South Caro-lina. He'd never been in a two-ton race car before, and when he first took it onto the track, he said, "God, this ain't for me." But he stuck at it. He knew he was as good as any other driver, and he wanted to prove it. He would have wanted to prove it if he had been lily-white, but because he was the only black who had ever raced stock cars, he felt it was even more important to prove.

Wendell Scott found that things were not much different in the big league. He got much the same reactions from the drivers and the fans as he had at the smaller tracks. Although he had won genuine respect from some of the drivers who had raced against him, there were still some who could not stand to be passed by a black man, and they would put him into the wall to keep it from happening. And he still had to listen to the derisive and racist remarks and the laughter. The sportswriters and other drivers would stand around telling jokes about how ol' Wen-dell would pull into the pits in the heat of a race to get a slice of watermelon.

"Oh, I've been laughed at even lately," he says. "Lots of times I see guys where got plenty backin' standin' back laughing at my equipment and things like that. . . . Do it make me mad? No, I leave 'em to their ignorance. It makes me angry to a cer-tain extent, but I just leave 'em to their ignorance."

Despite the boos and catcalls, Wendell Scott began to build a following of fans, white fans, who weren't hostile, who gen-uinely pulled for him and applauded him. The old appeal of the underdog, no doubt.

For he was certainly that. He never was able to get any sup-port from the big automobile manufacturers, nor from anybody else. He bought his race cars second-hand, after other drivers had almost worn them out, worked on them himself, and got many of his parts from junkyards. It was always a struggle, but he managed to keep going, even to make a little money.

"I had some fair years," he says. "It got so one time I was making a decent livin' out of racin' and was takin' care of my family."

But that was before the cost of racing went so high and began to really put pressure on independent drivers like Wendell Scott.

Still something pushed him on, even when it got to the point that he was losing money. In all of his years, and more than eighty thousand miles of Grand National competition, Wendell Scott had managed to win only one race, at Jacksonville, Florida, in 1964. He kept racing despite it all. He loved it, for one thing. But he still wanted to prove something, too.

"I still think I'm as good a driver as any of 'em," he was saying. "I guess people hear me say that, say, 'That guy's crazy,' but give me the same car you give any other man and let me get used to that car, and I'll drive it just as good as he could."

The old truck pulled to a stop alongside Bobby Fleming's Body Shop, and Wendell Scott shut off the engine and sat talking for a few minutes. Bobby Fleming, a young, stocky white man who also drives race cars but at smaller tracks, came out of the building and over to the driver's side of the truck.

"What the hell you waitin' on," he said, grinning, "cuhrb serhvice?"

"We're just talkin'."

"You got yours ready to go?"

Wendell Scott grimaced slightly and shook his head. "You know, I just got that jack under that thing and I been thinkin' and tryin' to figger. That's what I came up here—to ast you somethin'. . . ."

He reached for a scrap of paper and began sketching on it. "I ain't did a thing but just been trying—okay, now dis wheel over here, dis is right rear. . . ."

He quickly sketched out rough drawings of the chassis and began to explain the problem, the conversation becoming quickly technical: "Don't it run a barh through your rocka panel?"

"See, it's squirrelly behind."

After a while, Bobby Fleming said, "You waited too late to start doin' shit like this."

"I know it," said Wendell Scott, his voice rising with despair, "but what can I do? I . . . I spent two days . . ."

"You shoulda brought that carh up here the other day like I told ya."

"I didn't want to bother y'all, I swear I didn't."

"We'da had that damn thing ready to race by now."

"You got your hands full."

"I know that, but I'd never stop you from racin'."

"I know, I know."

"Hell, we gotta race."

The conversation turned back to the problem with the car, and a course of action was decided upon.

"Cut them barhs aloose now," Bobby Fleming said. "If you don't cut them barhs aloose, you workin' against yourself."

"I know it."

"If you need any help, hollah."

Bobby Fleming said that he had four cars to paint before Friday. "But we can put some of them off."

Wendell Scott cranked the truck. "I'm goin' back," he said. "And if I don't get it right, I might not bother you 'til Sadidy."

As he pulled away, and Bobby Fleming walked back toward his body shop, Wendell Scott said, "He used to help me with my racer. I started him to racin'. He's a real nice boy. He's a lot better driver'n he gets credit for being."

Wendell Scott had several other stops to make. At a service station where he stopped to get kerosene for the garage heater, the white operator and another man in a business suit came up to talk racing. They asked if he were going to run any this year.

"I'll go when I can make some money," he told them. "If I can't make no money, I'll stay at home. These promoters has got so they givin' all the big names all the money and little guys like me . . ." He shook his head.

He had to go to the bus station to pick up some carburetor restrictor rings that had come in, and he wanted to stop someplace to find an *Ebony* magazine. Somebody had called and told him that there was a letter to the editor in the new issue of

Ebony wondering why no black company or rich black man had chosen to offer some assistance to the only black man in stock car racing. Wendell Scott had been wondering that, too, had been wondering why one of the automobile factories had not chosen to give him some help when they were into racing so big, had been wondering why he'd had to struggle on alone for all these years with little recognition, less money, and broken-down cars, always losing. He had been wondering even why he had done it.

"Well, I figger if I hadn't raced, financially, I think I'd have been better off. But it was something I liked, and I don't regret racin'. I just regret that I didn't get no factory help. By me bein' the only black racer, it seems like that would've had some bearin' on me gettin' some help. . . .

"The reason I think I didn't get no factory backin' was because I was a black man and the people that was over charge of the factory racin' business just wasn't goin' to help a black man in racin'. That's all. If I'd been demandin', if I'da went about it in a different way to where I could've prob'ly hurt different car manufacturers through talkin' or demonstratin', or somethin' like 'at, there is a possibility I would've got some factory help, but I didn't go about it the right way, I guess.

"Well, I don't really say I wish I had've, but if I had've done it, I don't think I would've regretted it, 'cause I know they was helpin' guys couldn't even drive a race car."

At the bus station, he went inside and came back carrying a small package and muttering about the high cost of racing. He opened the package, displayed three small metal rings, and said, "Sixty-five dollars for that. I tell you, ever'thing's just gone out of reach."

He made two stops, at a newsstand and a convenience food store, without finding the magazine he wanted, finally gave up the search, and headed back to his garage. On the way, I asked him why no other black had ever tried to get into stock car racing.

"It's an expensive sport, and the average black that like racin' don't have the money to get into it. They's a lot of blacks have interest and want to race, but they don't want to race bad enough to go through what I went through to race."

Among those blacks who would like to race are Wendell Scott's two sons (he also has four daughters), Wendell, Jr., and Frankie, both of whom finished college and became public school teachers. They had worked on their father's car and helped him at the racetracks since they were young, often the only crew he had, and they had always wanted to drive. But they wouldn't accept the conditions that he accepted, Wendell Scott was saying; they weren't willing to take any shit. He stopped the truck at the curb in front of his garage, and for a moment he sat looking into the distance.

"But *I* ain't takin' no more shit," he said.

Inside, he filled his heater with oil, lighted and adjusted it, then began rummaging through the great piles of tools and old parts, muttering as he searched for a lost tool. Finally, he hunkered down by the front wheel of his car, a little man, showing his age now at fifty-two. He ran a hand through his steel-gray hair as he pondered the situation, raised his bushy eyebrows, and twitched his mustache.

"Now, if I bend it right there . . . naw, that ain't goina work, he done tol' me wrong. I swear, I don't know what to do. . . ."

Stuffings, Part 4

Death at Daytona

Friday Hassler's
Last Race

IT WASN'T premonition exactly. You couldn't have called it that.
But Joanne Hassler sensed something—she wasn't sure what—
and she knew that her husband felt something too. He seemed
hesitant about going to Daytona. He'd even said something about
it.

"I might just stay at home and not go," he told her one night.

She thought it was just because he was running behind. He'd
decided to rebuild his car after the first race of the year at Riverside, and he wasn't finished yet. She knew, too, that he was a
little afraid of Daytona. Most of the drivers—and their wives
—were. Well, maybe not afraid, but apprehensive at least. They
might say that they respected the track.

Friday Hassler had seen a boy named Don McTavish killed in
a wreck during a sportsman race at Daytona, had been standing
very near the wreck so that he could see the terrible violence
of it, could see the boy when he hit, and when Joanne got to the
track that day to pick her husband up, she had found him wandering in the infield trying to shake the wreck from his mind.
He never really got over it, though, and it seemed to bother him
at times.

Despite all of this, some relentless force seemed to be pulling
him on to Daytona, and he was all but helpless to resist. But
he knew that it would be at least Sunday—only a week before

the running of the Daytona 500—before he could get his car finished and ready to leave, and he wasn't really sure about that.

On Thursday he worked all night on the car. His wife went to the garage that night to take him his supper, and for some reason he had started reminiscing about the "old days," going back over his whole racing career, laughing and talking easily. That wasn't like him. He wasn't a talkative person, not even at home. He seldom talked about himself, and his wife had never heard some of the things that he told her that night.

Raymond Hassler had gotten hooked on racing early, probably even before he built and raced his first Soap Box Derby car. As a teen-ager he got himself a job in a garage, and that was where he picked up the nickname that he would carry for the rest of his life. The mechanic had had so many boys come and go before he'd ever really learned their names that he decided he'd just call the next one Friday, as in My Man Friday. Raymond Hassler was the next one, and he stayed long enough for the name to stick. Only his family still called him Ray.

His family did not want him to get into racing. His mother and father were dead set against it. But Friday was determined to race, even with their opposition. He built his first race car at Juno's Service Station near his home and kept it secret from his parents. He had already been racing on dirt tracks around Chattanooga when he met Joanne. She was a waitress and she was cute and he was attracted to her immediately. He was a very shy and quiet person. Friends who knew him then say he'd probably never had a date until he met Joanne, and he was in his twenties then. He took her to a race. She'd never been to one before. "I just don't know beans about it," she told him. She didn't care much about it after she went either. It made her nervous.

A short time after they had married, Joanne Hassler could tell that her husband wanted to talk about his racing. He finally got around to it one day.

"Well, I guess I'll have to quit," he said.

"Why?"

"Because we're married."

"You don't have to give up anything because you married me," she told him. "Just be what you want to be."

She remembers how his face had brightened when she said that.

"You mean you wouldn't mind?" he said.

"I don't know that much about it, but I wouldn't tell you you had to quit."

He didn't drive much the first year that they were married, but the next year he built his first sportsman car and started racing on the Alabama circuit four nights a week. After that he never did anything but race. But that wasn't the end of the talk about quitting.

A couple of years after he had started on the Alabama circuit, his parents started putting the pressure on him, begging him to quit. They wanted him to work in his father's tractor business. He asked his wife's advice then.

"I cannot make that decision for you, and I will not make that decision for you," she told him.

He made the decision himself. He continued racing.

And he was doing quite well at it. He consistently beat the Allison brothers, who were real hot dogs, and one summer he won twenty-two feature races in a row at Birmingham. He was building a reputation as one of the top sportsman drivers in the country. But he was too good, really, to continue driving sportsman races, and he began thinking of moving on to bigger things.

When Friday Hassler went into Grand National racing in 1966, he did not go looking for a ride in somebody else's car. He was not the kind of person to ask anybody for anything. He did it the way he had always done. He built himself a car and went racing, knowing that it was risky and expensive. But he quickly established himself as a top independent driver. He could make a living racing, and he was very proud of that. He was also pleased with how he was doing. In the past season, he had finished sixteenth in the point standings, had won more than thirty thousand dollars, and he had taken great joy in winning his first Grand National race at Bristol when he had a chance to drive a car that Junior Johnson had built.

Through the years, Friday Hassler had been building himself a good collection of equipment, and he had a good car, although not good enough to run with the top runners, of course. He just didn't have big money to build a car like that and keep it running. Friday had hoped to get a good sponsor, but he knew the chances were slight. He knew race cars and he could drive them well, but although he was easy-going and well liked by the other drivers, he didn't have the looks and the outgoing personality that the big sponsors demanded to sell their products. He was just a quiet, stocky little man with a round face who loved to race. He was happy that he was able to do as well as he had. He had just moved his family into a new brick house beside his father's house on Mountain Creek Road in Chattanooga. The house wasn't even finished yet, in fact. He was planning to do some of the work himself. And a few months earlier, he'd bought a big Winnebago "motor home" so that he could take his family around to some of the racetracks. Yes, he was doing all right.

Joanne Hassler usually didn't go to Daytona. The race was in February, of course, and the kids were in school, so she usually stayed at home with them. But for some reason she decided that she wanted to go this time. She didn't know why. She just wanted to go.

It was funny. Friday decided that he wanted the children to go with them. He had never wanted to take the children to Daytona before. But she didn't want them to go. The two older boys, Matt, who was thirteen, and Bobby, who was ten, were in school, and she didn't think they ought to be kept out for a week. There were two more boys, Tommy, who was almost four, and the baby, Ray, Jr., who was not yet two.

Friday insisted at least on taking Tommy.

"I want Tommy with me," he told his wife. "You're going to let Tommy go with me."

"No."

"I want him with me."

"I . . . don't . . . want . . . him . . . to go."

She was surprised at herself. She never talked to her husband that way. She couldn't explain it.

"Why not?" he said.

"I don't know. I just don't want him with me."

The car was ready in time for them to leave on Sunday. Friday drove his truck with the race car on the back. His wife rode with him. Her brother was following in their Winnebago. They left three of their children with relatives, but they took Tommy, although Joanne was hoping that she would be able to leave him with her sister in Atlanta when they stopped there.

As they were reaching the outskirts of Atlanta, Tommy was bearing on Joanne's mind. She closed her eyes and said a little prayer: "God, I don't know why, but I don't want to take this baby with me. But if he insists, I can't argue with him."

They rode in silence for a while; then her husband looked at her and said, "You want to take Tommy?"

"No, I don't want to take Tommy, but if you want to, we will."

"No, if you don't want to, we'll leave him."

That was a great relief to her. They left Tommy in Atlanta and drove on to Daytona that day.

Any apprehension that Friday Hassler might have felt disappeared when he got to the racetrack. He worked at getting his car set up for the track, and at night he pulled the Winnebago into the camping area outside the track, where he parked beside some friends from Chattanooga.

Two 125-mile qualifying races are held on Thursday before the big Sunday race at Daytona. No other track holds such races, but they are popular at Daytona, where fans come from long distances to stay the whole week and need to be entertained. The races usually draw good crowds—and bring in extra money for the track, of course.

Thursday came with gray skies and chilly winds, but nearly forty thousand people were in the stands to see the qualifying races. Friday Hassler was to drive in the first one.

The Winnebago was parked in the infield in a special area behind the pits and garages. Joanne Hassler was cooking one of her husband's favorite meals, beef roast with gravy, for lunch, but it was late when he finally came over from the garage, and he was in a rush.

"We'll just eat after the race," he said. And he was gone.

Joanne climbed atop the Winnebago with her friend from Chattanooga to watch the race.

Richard Abercombie had grown up with Friday Hassler. He was a real-estate man in Chattanooga, and like Friday, he had an avid interest in racing. He sometimes helped Friday on his car, and he had helped him get a garage and a couple of local sponsors. He usually went to most of the races. He was late getting to Daytona, and by the time he got into the pits on Thursday, his friend was already pulling out to start the race. Friday spotted him, however, waved, and called, "See you later."

The first of the race went smoothly. But on the nineteenth lap, with the cars still bunched fairly closely, a tire blew on David Boggs' car as he was coming out of the second turn. Great chunks of rubber began flying through the air. The drivers behind him, not knowing what it was that was coming apart, began to dodge. After that—confusion.

A couple of cars started sliding. G. C. Spencer, one of the older drivers, a friend of Friday Hassler's from Tennessee, saw that one of the cars was Friday's No. 39 red Chevrolet. Spencer had cut down onto the grass behind Richard Petty to avoid the spinning cars when he saw Friday's car sideways on the track. A sitting duck, he thought. But he didn't see the crash because somebody hit him, destroying his car.

Jimmy Crawford's Plymouth hit Friday's car full in the right side. Raymond Williams, another driver, said the crash sounded like a bomb going off.

G. C. Spencer's car slid to a stop, and for a moment he just sat there. He wasn't hurt, and it was always safer to stay in the car. But then he saw Friday's car, and he couldn't remember having ever seen a race car damaged any worse. The car was bent like a horseshoe. Spencer cut loose his belts, climbed out of his car, and ran toward his friend. He saw him slumped in his seat, and he knew that it was bad. He started waving frantically for an ambulance and motioning the oncoming cars to keep to the outside.

The wreck was finished, cars and parts of cars strewn all over the track, when Don Tarr, a physician who drove race cars for the fun of it, came out of the turn at 170 miles per hour. He couldn't stop and he couldn't help but hit somebody. He remembered hitting a yellow Dodge. When it was all over at last, twelve cars lay in wreckage, and Friday Hassler was dead.

Joanne Hassler had lost her husband's car on the track. There were so many red cars out there, and she couldn't read their numbers until they got into the fourth turn. She thought that maybe he had come into the pits, which she could not see, but it would be unusual for him to have trouble so early in a race.

"He's okay, he's okay," her friend kept saying. "There he goes, there he goes. That's him."

"No it's not, that's Coo Coo."

She had just turned toward the backstretch when she saw the commotion, far across the infield in the second turn. Cars were going every which way in the smoke and dust, then a big puff of smoke billowed up and spread out lazily. Then she saw Don Tarr's car come out of the turn, and the whole thing seemed to be starting over again.

"Oh, my gosh! Oh, my gosh!" she could hear herself saying.

She was searching frantically for her husband's car now. Still she couldn't spot him. She was growing scared. The race had been stopped—it takes an awfully bad wreck to stop a race, she knew—and she didn't know whether her husband was in the wreck, or if his car was stopped with the others near the pits. She decided to make her way over to the garage area to try to find him. She was so excited that she almost went off the wrong end of the Winnebago. Then she saw the wrecker pulling in the red car.

"Oh, my God!"

"That's not his car," her friend said.

"Yes, *it is*," she cried, "and it looks like a doodlebug, it's so smashed!"

She was frantic now. She had to find Ray. She hurried, almost running, to the garage gate. She had it in her mind that she would sneak past the guard and find her husband. She heard a loudspeaker saying, "Don't touch those cars, don't touch those cars, you know it's illegal." This to the drivers who had stopped.

By the time she got to the gate, she realized that she would never be able to get by the guard. She had calmed somewhat. She had almost convinced herself that her husband was in the garage. "That's where he is," she kept telling herself. All she had to do was to find somebody to find him for her. Then she saw Bobby Allison standing inside the fence talking to some other men. He was one of Friday's closest friends, one of a very few people that he would talk to openly. She called to him, and he came over, and she didn't have to say anything. Her face told what she wanted.

"Friday's not out there, is he?" he said.

"Y*es*, he *is*."

"I didn't know. Let me go see if I can find out something."

When he returned, she could tell by his face that something was wrong.

"How bad?" she said.

"Real bad."

She started to cry. Bobby Allison was going to take her to the track dispensary where the ambulance had taken Friday, but a car pulled up and somebody inside told Joanne Hassler to get in.

"We're going over here," Bobby Allison said.

"Get in."

"No, I'm taking her over here."

"Just get in here. We'll take you," said the voice inside the car.

The car had been sent by the track officials, and inside was a Baptist preacher, a close friend of Bill France, who served as a sort of track chaplain. Joanne Hassler finally got into the car, not certain exactly where it was going to take her. By the time she realized where the car was headed, it was already outside the track. She knew now what they were doing: They were trying to keep her from getting to her husband!

"You've brought me plumb outside the track!" she said. The car had stopped at the main NASCAR office building at the front of the track. "I'm going back over there," she said emphatically. "If you don't take me, I'm going to walk!"

"Go in here with me," she remembers the preacher saying gently. "We've got some things to talk about."

All she wanted was the truth. Why couldn't they just tell her the truth and take her to Ray? That was all she wanted.

"I'm not going anywhere with you. I want to go to Ray. I . . . want . . . to . . . go . . . to . . . Ray."

She found herself being guided toward the building by strong hands and soothing words.

"Come up here and talk with me. . . . Let me call and see if he is still over there. . . ."

"I know he's over there! I know he hasn't left this track!"

"Well, let me just call, and if he's over there, I'll take you."

She was in the building now. They went up the stairs to Bill France, Jr.'s, office. The preacher made his call.

"Please sit down," he said softly, when he had hung up the receiver.

"No, I'm going back over there. I *would* like to know the truth. I know it's bad or you wouldn't be acting like this, but it doesn't matter how bad, I want to know the truth."

"He's gone. . . ."

All that she could think as his words came out was: "I've got to get to him, I've got to get to him."

Suddenly she was running, out the door, through the hall, running down the stairs into the glass-enclosed lobby, heading for the glass doors when she saw the two burly state cops with pistols on their hips guarding the doors, and she knew that she would never get past them—but wait! They were stepping back, smiling. They were going to open the door for her.

"Grab her!"

It was the preacher on the staircase. The cops caught her and pulled her back into the lobby. She was afraid now that she would get hysterical. Yes, she knew she would. Why wouldn't they let her get to Ray?

She realized that all of the people in the lobby were looking at her. Were they all moving on her? Yes, they were. Encircling her, moving closer, like beasts of prey. Now their heads were growing bigger, their faces becoming grotesquely distorted, all of them moving on her, grinning, eyes bulging, leering, like something she'd seen in a strange movie one time. She closed her eyes.

"Oh, my gosh," she said to herself. "I'm having a nightmare. Not any of this is happening. I'm going to wake up."

She opened her eyes and Richard Abercombie, her husband's boyhood friend, was standing there.

"Please help me get to Ray," she begged him. But one look at his stunned face convinced her that he would be no help.

"Get a shot in her," she heard somebody say. "Get her to a hospital. She needs a doctor."

She didn't want any shots, and she knew that if they got a chance to knock her out, they would. Then she would never get to Ray. She closed her eyes again, and this time she said a little prayer: "God, you gotta help me get out of here. I gotta convince them I'm not in shock, I'm not going to get hysterical."

She pulled herself together and looked the preacher straight in the eye.

"Look, I don't want a shot. I don't want a doctor. I don't want to go to any hospital. I want to go to Ray. I've got to go to him, and if you don't take me to him, I'm going to *die* on you, right here." She thought she would too.

"You're not goin' nowhere," one of the cops said.

"I think she knows what she's saying," the preacher said. "I think that's going to be the only thing to help her. Okay."

She kept her eyes on his.

"Right now!" she said, and wheeled and was out the door.

Brother Bill Frazier was in the pits when the wreck happened, and when he heard that somebody was hurt, he went immediately to the dispensary. He saw one of the NASCAR officials outside the door. The official had a walkie-talkie and he had already received word from the men on the track that somebody was seriously hurt. "Looks like it's bad," he said to Brother Bill, "better stick around." It was quickly obvious how bad as soon as Friday Hassler was brought in.

Brother Bill was still waiting outside the dispensary when Joanne Hassler was finally brought over. She spotted him and ran to him.

"Brother Bill, is Ray really dead?"

"Joanne, he is."

She braced herself before she went inside. She had guessed that the reason they were so intent on keeping her from her husband was because he was so badly mangled, maybe unrecognizable, or in several pieces. It could be anything, she knew, but she had to see for herself.

"I've got to keep top-notch control," she told herself, "or they're going to take me right out of here."

Inside, a nurse was waiting for her with a needle. She might have gotten her, too, if she hadn't been wearing a raincoat.

"I don't want any shots!" she said emphatically. "I don't want any needles. I just want to see Ray."

She was led into the room where his body lay, still dressed in the driver's suit. Something happened to her as soon as she walked into the room. Her whole body suddenly went weak. She felt drained, limp. It was . . . relief! It had to be that. Relief. He wasn't mutilated at all. He seemed to be sleeping. There was only one mark on his whole body, as far as she could see. A small bruise on his cheek. Probably made by his goggles.

She walked over to him and touched his hand. She was struck by how cold it was, like something she might have just taken from the refrigerator. But the moment she touched him, she felt something very strange inside. She didn't really hear voices, or anything, but she knew that he was talking to her.

"It's okay, it's okay," he was saying. "I'm all right. We'll all be together again soon."

He was reassuring her. Yes. He was. There was no doubt. She

knew then that he was in a better place, and that indeed they all would be together again soon. And suddenly everything was all right.

"I know," she whispered to him. "I know. . . ."

Joanne Hassler sat now in the yard beside her house watching her two youngest children play in the gravel driveway. She was wearing a simple red dress and no makeup, and her long brown hair was pulled back to one side. It had been more than a year since her husband had been buried on the day of the Daytona 500. Those intervening months had not been easy ones for her.

What was it that Bobby Allison had said? "She was just a country girl and Friday was all she had." Yes, that was it.

"He was just my whole life," she said softly.

While she talked about her husband and her life since his death, her youngest son, Ray, Jr., hurt his finger and Tommy brought him to her for a Band-Aid. "He thinks a Band-Aid heals everything," she said with a laugh. Then Tommy fell on the gravel as he started to run back to play and came up squawling. "Oh, my," his mother said, going to his aid, "now *you* need a Band-Aid. Bless his heart."

Matt, the oldest boy, tall and handsome with a serious demeanor, arrived home from school. "Here comes my baby," his mother said. Then Bobby, now eleven, came up on the back of a friend's motorcycle. "Here comes the baby that's just like Ray. And talk about mechanics—that kid, I can't keep a wrench out of his hand. And he's motorcycle crazy. He is the racing bug. It seems like he just likes to get his hands on something he can take apart and put back together. Hey," she called to him, "did you get the parts?"

Bobby went into the basement to work on an old motorcycle engine, while his older brother rode his friend's motorcycle around the yard.

"Roll up your britches leg," Bobby's friend told Matt as he mounted the motorcycle.

"And please, please be careful," his mother added.

Joanne Hassler began to talk of her husband's death again, about the suddenness of it in particular. Her eyes would close halfway when she paused, then flutter as the words started coming again. They'd never thought about dying, she was saying. They had both assumed that they would die of old age. People grew old and then they died. That was the way it had always been in their families.

"But you don't just die of old age every time," she said. "For me it's taken away my fear of death. It made me realize it's not dying we should fear but whether or not we're ready to go."

If somebody had asked her before her husband's death what her reaction to it would have been, she was saying, "I'd have said I couldn't've taken it. I'd just throw up my hands and scream and never stop screaming.

"We just have to give the good Lord credit for the way we've accepted it. I couldn't've explained it before I experienced it, and I have a hard time explaining it now. I just have to say—I just have to give credit to the good Lord.

"He not only gave us the strength to bear up under it, He just gave us such a tremendous understanding that we should've had, really should've had before, and should've been teaching the children.

"Now I have a tremendous understanding. . . . It doesn't have anything to do with the fact that I want Ray here and I miss him and I wouldn't want him to be gone. It's not that at all. Some people have confused the two, and it's made me look bad, but it doesn't have anything to do with the fact that we love him and we miss him and we ache to see him again. It doesn't have anything to do with that. Except that helps you to accept it. But the good Lord was so gracious to us in letting us know that he was okay, and I said since it had happened we just had to feel beautiful about that. I mean, since it was out of our control, we were just thankful to the good Lord for letting us feel that way and just—oh, I don't know—just incident after incident after incident has just let us know that he was okay.

"So many of the things he wanted, he had said he wanted,

just happened. Every day something would happen that he had wanted, just, you know, the things you want for your children, things you want for your family. They just kept taking place.

"It's made me feel better and better, and just made me feel bigger and bigger, and I am, I hope, a better person and a much bigger person, and I have just such a tremendous understanding of really what death is all about. Whereas before, we just dreaded it."

And Now, Ladies and Gentlemen (at Last), The Southern 500!!!!

A Night in the Infield

THE SCENE was somewhat reminiscent of one of those old land-rush movies with the covered wagons racing through the dust, Paw madly beating the team, Maw clinging frantically to the young'uns. The pickup trucks and cars were streaming through both tunnels, while the bigger vehicles, the "motor homes" and rental trucks and trailers, were pouring across the banked first turn, racing to claim favorite spots in the Darlington infield, the most favored being in the turns, where the wrecks usually happened. Some of the people had occupied the same spots every year, for which privilege they were willing to pay the price of waiting a day or so outside the gates.

Feverish activity. A great unloading: tables, chairs, cots, cook stoves, gas lanterns, charcoal grills, ice chests. Tents set up. Tarpaulins unfurled. Generators cranked. Minibikes rolled out. Portable radios, tape players, TVs turned on. On the backs of pickup trucks men hammered together viewing stands of steel bars, two-by-fours, and plywood. Then the final touches. Signs tacked up: "RICHARD PETTY FOR PRESIDENT!" Flags sent flying, some of them bearing the numbers of favorite cars, but mostly . . . the proud stars and bars of the Confederacy!

So many Confederate flags fluttered over this instant city that it might easily have been mistaken for some gigantic assembly of the Sons and Daughters of the Confederacy, which, in a sense, it was. Through the years, the Southern 500, the big race at Darlington, had evolved into a celebration of being southern, redneck southern, and all that that meant.

Redneck. They were never quite sure just what the term meant, certain only that it was condescending. High-toned folks used the word, writers, psychologists, sociologists, intellectuals, liberals, and other such pointy-headed, carpetbagging riffraff. Maybe they were right. Maybe they *were* rednecks. What was that country song they were always playing? "Red Necks, White Socks, and Blue Ribbon Beer." Damn straight! Redneck and proud of it! None of those high-falutin', condescending intellectual sonsabitches could ever know what it was to work in those cotton mills day in and day out, or to prime tobacco in the broiling sun. They didn't know what it was to be constantly prodded and pushed, to have to fight the bastards at every turn. And they would never know the joyous release of the "rebel yell"—WHOOOOOOOOOOOOEEEE-EEEEEEEEEEE!!!!!! So let 'er rip. Us rednecks going to have a high ol' time. Oh, yes, boys, they's going to be some hell raised tonight!

By dusk a haze of dust and charcoal smoke hung over the encampment. Hamburgers, hot dogs, T-bone steaks sizzled on charcoal grills. Children chased about, playing. Dogs yapped. Older kids buzzed around on minibikes. Teen-agers wandered in groups. The roadways that had been left open remained clogged, with cars going in mindless circles, cruising, just the way they did at the drive-ins back at home. Front bumpers sported license plates bearing pictures of Confederate flags, cranky old Confederate soldiers saying, "Fergit Hell!" or "Put Your [picture of heart] in Dixie" or "Get Your [picture of south end of northbound mule] Out." A purple Dodge filled with beer-swilling boys paraded, bedecked with banners for STP, Royal Triton, and other automotive products, wearing a crown of empty beer cans fastened to the top with gray tape. One of the boys was hanging out a window of the car, beer can held aloft, chanting, "Pearson! Pearson! Pearson!"

"Who's 'at?" somebody yelled.

"Who's David Pearson? You'll see who he is tomorrow, god-damnit, he's goina blow that fuckin' Chevy off the track!"

"Sheeit, man. When he does, I wanta see it."

"You wanta put five on it?"

"Hell, make it ten."

Nightfall brought only slight relief from the oppressive heat, but a marked increase in the air of tension hanging over the track. People were looking for some of those wild stories they had heard to materialize: sex, violence . . . something. Groups of young men prowled in search of girls, trouble, or both. Two lank-haired girls, barefoot, belly buttons showing above low-slung jeans, breasts jiggling provocatively under thin tops, padded past one group of boys.

"God-a-mighty damn!" said one of the boys. "Look at that. Whoo-eee. Hey, come 'ere, honey, where you goin'?"

The girls hurried on toward the rest rooms, giggling.

"Hey, boys," cried another boy in the group, "come on, they's a lot of pussy over yonder."

I made a complete turn through the infield at about ten o'clock. The night was riven by drunken yells, the regular popping of firecrackers, the mournful sound of a Merle Haggard song playing somewhere in the distance. Occasionally a sky-rocket sputtered into the air to explode with a flash and a mighty bang. Here and there, TV sets, powered by batteries and gasoline generators, flickered. Quite a few boisterous poker games were under way. Some craps. A lot of beer and bourbon was being consumed. At one spot a group of Bluegrass musicians had drawn a crowd with guitars, banjos, and nasal singing. Several entrepreneurs were selling beer illegally. One worked out of the back of an old bread truck that had cases of cheap beer stacked to the ceiling. No whore hearses in sight.

"Wanna buy some beer?" the beer man called to a passerby. "Ten dollars a case."

"They're selling it over yonder for seven."

The guy shrugged. "That's all right. Don't get it tonight, I'll get it tomorrow."

The cops prowled in pairs, or larger groups. They wore pistols and handcuffs on their hips and carried flashlights and big sticks. A fight down between the first and second turns had brought a dozen or more cops on the run. A lot of people had apparently been involved. They stood in little groups glowering at one another across a barrier of cops. The cops talked to the leaders, trying to cool things.

One guy was staggering drunk. "That motherfucker comes over here agin, I'll cut his fuckin' balls off," he shouted, and repeated, muttering.

"You ain't cuttin' nobody," a big cop said, pushing him back. "Get over there and shut up before you get in trouble."

I went back to my van and sat beside it in a lawn chair, drinking a beer kept nice and cold in my new Styrofoam beer-can holder. How many beers had that been today? I'd lost count. I was tired and my feet hurt. A little after midnight, I made another round of the infield and was disappointed to find things so peaceful and dull. I had another beer and lay in my van to rest for a while. I was on the verge of dozing when I was disturbed by the whap-whap of a flashing red light atop a rescue squad ambulance rushing past. The ambulance stopped at the little track hospital near the garage area. I got up to investigate and saw that a man was being taken inside. A group of kids had gathered around the hospital door when I got there. When the ambulance driver came out, a kid said, "Hey mister, did he get shot?"

The driver said nothing, brushed past the kids, and climbed back into the ambulance.

A couple of kids standing back from the group heard the kid's question and ran off shouting, "Somebody got shot, somebody got shot!"

A man approached the driver's window.

"What happened to him?"

"Cut. Laid his face open."

I got another beer and wandered over to the press gate across the track. I was supposed to meet a friend there at two o'clock. I sat to wait on a grassy bank leading up to the main grandstands and soon fell asleep. I was awakened by shouts.

"What in the goddamn hell!"

A couple of startled drunks stood below me.

"It's a fuckin' 'possum, ain't it?" one said incredulously.

It surely was. A fat 'possum was waddling across the track toward the infield, presumably without a ticket.

"Shit, let's catch 'im," one drunk was saying.

"What for?"

"Hell, we'll eat the sonofabitch."

The Week Before

THE ACTIVITIES at the Darlington Raceway had begun on Wednesday, when most of the drivers and their crews had arrived, towing their race cars on trailers or the backs of big trucks. The drivers were eager to try the track, because it had received a new coat of asphalt since they had last raced on it in the spring. They wanted to see if the new pavement would help, or if the track would remain as hard to drive as it had always been.

Darlington had always been the most difficult track on the circuit. Some drivers hated it and dreaded driving it.

"It's a sonofabitch," one driver had growled when I asked him about it. "*Goddamn*, it's a tricky bastard."

Since it was the first track of its kind, nobody had really known how it should be built. And nobody had guessed when it was built that stock cars would one day be going nearly three times as fast as they were then.

It was originally a mile-and-a-quarter track, with short straightaways and turns banked at sixteen degrees. Then it was enlarged to a mile and three eighths by pushing out the first and second turns and banking them another ten degrees in 1953. The third and fourth turns were banked higher in 1969. Still, it was essentially a one-groove track with little space for passing. A groove is a driver's chosen route around a racetrack, usually for the better drivers the route that would get them around the fastest. Once into a groove, a driver seldom varies from it. On some tracks, there are several high-speed grooves, but at Darlington, only one. If you wanted to run fast enough to win, you had to stay in that groove.

If racetracks had personalities, Darlington's would likely be the crankiest and most cantankerous of all. At other speedways, a driver could "set up" his car to give him the best possible handling in negotiating all of the turns. Darlington demanded a different setup for every turn, and a driver had to do the best he could. The high-speed groove carried the cars within six inches of the wall on the third and fourth turns. The good drivers could give the railing a gentle slap on each lap, leaving a distinctive stripe of courage on the right sides of their cars. That left little room for error, or course. The slightest miscalculation could send a car into the wall or careening wildly down the frontstretch. Some of the best drivers had made these mistakes and suffered their most spectacular crashes at Darlington. The track had put fear in many drivers, and it had taken the lives of two. Each year, the sportswriters wrote dramatic pieces referring to the track as "the lady in black."

"At Darlington," Richard Petty has said, "you don't race the other drivers, you run against the track."

The drivers found out what the new pavement had done for the track when they went out for their first practice runs on Wednesday.

"Same ol' Darlington," said David Pearson. "They made it smoother, but the grooves are the same, and you still drive the same number of inches off the walls."

Thursday was the first day for qualifying. Sixty-one drivers had submitted entries for the race. Only forty would be able to run. The first day of qualifying always belongs to the "hot dogs." The first five or six starting spots inevitably go to the same drivers—those with the best cars. There is a great scramble among the second-echelon drivers to grab the next few spots, because the top ten qualifiers get free tires from Goodyear, and that means a savings of hundreds of dollars. Only twelve cars would be qualified on the first day.

The hot cars all took to the track for practice on Thursday morning. When they were not driving or making adjustments to their cars, the drivers were clocking the competition. Even before the qualifying runs, they all knew about how the others would do. And the word was already out around the pits that this one looked like a two-car race, the cars being Bobby Allison's Chevrolet and David Pearson's Mercury. Those cars were expected to take first and second starting positions, although it would have been hard to say in which order.

But late Thursday morning, as David Pearson was making a last-minute practice lap, a puff of white smoke came from beneath his engine, and he coasted back into the pits with a look of resignation on his face. The engine had blown, and it would not be possible to get the car ready to run again for at least a day. He would have to qualify later and start the race farther back in the pack than usual. It didn't seem to bother him. He laughed and wandered off to the locker room to change his clothes.

Richard Petty got a cold drink and a stopwatch and clambered onto the back of a tow truck on the backside of the garage. He climbed onto the tire rack above the cab of the truck and perched himself on a racing tire, from where he could see the other cars as they qualified. He had already qualified his red-and-blue Dodge (he had switched from Plymouth at mid-season), as had Buddy Baker, who was driving a white Dodge owned by Petty. Their positions had been first and second, Petty having qualified at 149.072 miles per hour, Baker at 148.069.

Now Petty's lanky frame sat hunched against the sky as he squinted behind his sunglasses at the stopwatch in his hand. He shook his head when Bobby Allison made his run. Both Allison and Fred Lorenzen had flashed across the starting line with speeds better than his. Allison had beaten him around the track by almost a half second.

"How about that Allison?" Petty said. "He was faster than we were going into qualifying, and then he picks up even more speed on his qualifying run. I qualified about the same speed that I've been running all along."

It only confirmed what Richard Petty had believed all year. He had suffered a slump of sorts, having won only a few races all season, none in the past four months, although as usual he had finished consistently close to the top and had remained high in the point standings. He was convinced that the problem wasn't entirely his fault. He, like a lot of other drivers, thought he was being discriminated against.

When speeds of stock cars had gone over two hundred miles per hour, raising a hue about the growing danger of stock car racing, NASCAR had moved to cut the speeds and "equalize" the competition by requiring carburetor restrictor devices. The devices limited the amount of fuel-and-air mixture allowed to the engines. The trouble, as Petty saw it, was that some cars were allowed larger holes in the restrictors. Bobby Allison's Chevrolet, for example, could have an opening of an inch and three eighths, while Richard Petty's Plymouth was allowed only an inch and one eighth, the difference due to the size of the engines. Richard Petty did not think that this equalized the competition.

"NASCAR's twisted the rules to favor the Chevy and the Mercury," he said.

Allison's Chevrolet and David Pearson's Mercury had, indeed, been running away from their competitors all year. Petty would run his car as hard as it would go during the first part of a race just to stay even, but Allison and Pearson would always seem to find some extra power as the end loomed, and he would watch with a feeling of helplessness as they scooted away from him.

Petty was convinced that NASCAR was giving the Chevrolets more power for one reason: to draw bigger crowds to the races. When General Motors had pulled out of stock car racing in the early sixties, Chevrolets had almost disappeared from racing. There had been no competitive Chevrolets for years.

This had caused a lot of Chevrolet-driving race fans to stay away. And now Petty, and a lot of other drivers, felt that they were being penalized in order to bring them back.

"They're more in show business than the business of equalizing competition," Petty said of NASCAR. "They can flat control who wins and loses."

Bobby Allison guided his red-and-gold No. 12 Chevrolet down the pit road to cheering from the small crowd in the grandstands. The car was sponsored by Coca-Cola, and the track announcer always called it the "Coke machine." Allison brought the car into the garage area and drove the length of the garage, revving the engine a couple of times before he brought the car to a stop. Mechanics and crew members immediately swarmed around the car, and a small crowd gathered as Allison climbed out the window and began unbuckling his helmet. He had made one of his qualifying laps in 32.304 seconds, a speed of 152.228 miles per hour, almost 2.5 miles per hour faster than anybody else had run that day. Clearly, he had won the pole position, the first time that a Chevrolet had done so at Darlington in fourteen years.

Several sportswriters with poised pencils and pads squeezed in close to Allison.

"Pearson was right," one of them said. "You were sandbaggin'."

Allison grinned.

"I guess I was."

A crew member handed him a frosty can of Coke and winked in victory.

"If he'da run I don't know that I'da beat him," Allison was saying of Pearson.

Allison was wearing white socks and brown patent-leather loafers decorated with gold clasps with his driver's suit. The track's loudspeakers crackled with the news that his speed had put him in first place, and he winced when the crowd cheered. Engines roared nearby, causing long pauses in his talk with the sportswriters. Dave Marcis went out to qualify in his stubby red, white, and blue American Motors Matador, the only car in stock car racing with factory support.

"That's going to be the sleeper there today, boys," Allison said, as they paused to watch the start of his run. A sportswriter stepped out of the circle to aim a squirt of tobacco spit at a grease mark a few feet away.

Somebody said, "Bobby, you feel more comfortable in a Chevrolet?"

"Well, you know . . ."

It was like old times. The sportswriters and radio announcers kept saying that as they crowded around Fred Lorenzen. "Like old times, ain't it, Freddy?"

He was smiling, actually beaming as he told them, "Man, you can't imagine how good it feels . . . that ol'-time feelin'."

He would be the feature of many newspaper stories the next day, and they would all say that it was like old times. They would be calling him the Golden Boy again.

He had been on edge when he took his bright yellow Chevrolet onto the track for his qualifying run. He knew what people had been saying about him, and he knew that they would be watching him closely. But he seemed more intent on proving something to himself than to everybody else.

Hoss Ellington, a former driver who owned the car Lorenzen was driving, had been very pleased after his driver's run. Lorenzen was not as pleased.

"I should've run quicker," he was telling the sportswriters. "I messed up on my first lap and got the tires hot."

Still, he had run at just a fraction under 150 miles an hour, second fastest of the day. He would be starting on the front row again, and people were saying, well, maybe the old boy hadn't lost his nerve after all. Maybe it *was* like old times. Maybe this would be the race that would show he *could* make a comeback.

Certainly, nobody wanted to win this race more than Fred Lorenzen, and he had been talking as if he might do it. The car, while not among the best, was a good one. Hoss Ellington had bought it from Junior Johnson, and it had seemed to give back some of Lorenzen's old confidence, even a touch of his former cockiness and brashness, and some of his old intensity. Hoss Ellington had seen it in recent days, as he watched Lorenzen fretting around the pits and garage, trying to get everything perfect, the way he used to do. Hoss Ellington was happy about it. "That means he thinks he's got a chance to win," he said with a grin.

There was more than one reason that Lorenzen wanted so badly to win this race. Darlington held special memories for him. "The reason I started racing was to race here and win here," he said. "The first race I ever heard on the radio was the Southern 500. I was mowing my father's lawn and I had a radio in my tent and I heard the words Southern 500 and Curtis Turner and Fireball Roberts and Joe Weatherly and I said to myself, 'What's this?' And I decided that day that I wanted to race and win the Southern 500." That was in his hometown of Elmhurst, Illinois, a suburb of Chicago.

In 1961, at the age of twenty-seven, after having worked his way through the ranks of stock car racing in the Midwest, Fred Lorenzen finally found himself doing battle at Darlington with Curtis and Fireball and all the rest, and he went on that day to outduel Turner and win the race. But it had been the spring race, the Rebel 300, and not the Southern 500, which he wanted to win. Still, it was the race that started him to stardom.

Lorenzen became one of the biggest stars of the midsixties. He drove for the Ford factory team, and the sportswriters called him Fearless Freddy. His style was to hold back in the first half of a race, but it didn't pay to get in his way in the second half. He won a lot of races, placed high in many more, and made himself a lot of money. He was young, blond, good-looking, and popular with the fans, especially the girls, and when he wasn't racing, he was usually making personal appearances somewhere, taking in all of the money that he could while it lasted. He was not so popular with some of his fellow drivers and some of the sportswriters, who didn't like his cockiness, aloofness, abruptness. They said he was "high-strung" and had "the big head." It wasn't that at all, he was telling the sportswriters now. Nerves, he said. That was all. He was so intense, and he demanded perfection. Nerves.

"I'd just get so wrapped up in the car and the race," he said. "It wasn't the speeds we were hitting. . . . It was all the personal appearances. I never had time for myself."

Finally, the nerves, the pressure of it all got to him. In 1967, suffering from ulcers, he quit racing and took his money back home to play the stock market. He had won twenty-one major races, but he had not won the one he set out to win, the Southern 500.

As many other drivers have discovered, Lorenzen found retirement to be not all that easy. Racing has a way of pulling at men who are attracted to it, and they find it hard to resist. In May of 1970, his ulcers healed, Lorenzen quit resisting and returned. But things were different now. The factories had left racing. He no longer was able to command the best equipment available. His comeback was something less than spectacular. He drove a second-rate Plymouth and kept having mechanical problems. He couldn't seem to get his luck back.

Then in the fall of 1971, his luck changed. He landed the ride in the Wood Brothers Mercury, one of the best cars in racing. He got the car just before the Southern 500, and he knew that with this car he could finally win it—and make good his comeback at the same time. At ten-thirty on the gray Thursday morning before the race, he took the car out for a practice run to check its handling before the afternoon time trials. The car was running exceptionally well, and after a few laps at top speed, Glen Wood, the car owner, waved Lorenzen in, but Lorenzen continued on for another lap. As he came into the fourth turn, still at speed, something happened. He couldn't remember later what it was, but the car went into a slide and slammed into the outside wall, both right wheels actually climbing the wall before the car bounded back onto the asphalt, crossing the track at an angle to hit the inside wall a tremendous blow that sent chunks of concrete spewing through the pits, leaving a gaping hole. The car took flight then, knocking down two metal light poles and shearing a thick wood utility pole six feet from the ground before it slammed back onto the track, did a roll, and landed on its wheels, immobile at last, spewing smoke and steam, a total wreck. Some who watched the wreck figured Lorenzen had had it. Several drivers and pit workers ran to the car, put out a small engine fire, and unstrapped Lorenzen, who was slumped unconscious in his seat, his face bloodied. An ambulance took him straight to the hospital in nearby Florence, where he was found to have a concussion, a broken ankle, cuts, and bruises. Considering the terrible wreck, the extent of his injuries was almost miraculous.

The sportswriters were all asking Lorenzen about the wreck.

"Well, I just hung it out too far," he told them. "My foot's a lot lighter now. I could be pretty reckless at times, but not any more. . . . Yeah, that wreck knocked a lot of the cockiness out of me."

So the sportswriters would write that it was like old times, and maybe it was. Fred Lorenzen, at least, knew that he had the old feeling back now. His spirit was high. He smiled. And laughed. He stopped to chat with people in the pits and garage. Other drivers and crew members came by to congratulate him.

"Atta boy, Freddy," called driver James Hylton. "You said you'd do it."

And if all of that weren't enough to make it like old times . . . well, there were the two chicks in the stands. They were young and attractive with long hair, flat brown tummies shining above hip-hugging jeans, breasts unfettered except for wispy wrap-around tops, and they had kept binoculars trained on Fred Lorenzen all day. When he was in the garage, they would come down to the front of the grandstands, cling to the wire fence, and gaze wistfully in his direction. He had taken a ribbing about them all day, and late in the afternoon some of his crew members started kidding him again, laughing loud, and one of them picked up the chalkboard and blocked out some big letters on it in yellow chalk.

"Hey, Freddy," he called, "get over there by the wall and hold this sign up."

Lorenzen read it, laughed, and declined.

With everybody laughing, the crew member carried the sign out and held it aloft.

"Fred," it said. "Holiday Inn."

The car was not handling particularly well, but the engine was running smoothly, and Larry Smith thought he might have a chance. He had wanted very badly to grab one of the first twelve starting spots. That would look good. This race, more than ever, he had to make a good impression.

Larry Smith's car, a white Ford that he had built from a kit, bore the yellow bumper stripe of a rookie. Across the stripe he had lettered, "Run Rookie Run." Larry Smith wanted to be named Rookie of the Year. He had worked hard for it, but the competition was keen, and now he was worried that he might not get it. A good showing at Darlington would surely help. But now there was another reason why he had to do well in this race.

Larry Smith had accomplished in his first year what many other drivers had never been able to do. He got a sponsor. The deal had been worked out just a few days earlier. He'd heard that the Carling beer company was thinking of getting into stock car racing in some fashion, so he'd gone to talk with them earlier in the year. They turned him down at first. But they'd had a change of mind and called him about a week before Darlington. He was tall and good-looking, with modishly long, dark, wavy hair, and he handled himself well before people, and the company had decided that he would present an acceptable image. Beyond that, the company knew that he had a good chance of making Rookie of the Year, and that would draw a lot of attention to him, and to his sponsor, if he had one. So the contracts were signed, and Larry Smith's car was taken off to be decorated with advertisements for Carling Black Label Beer. It wasn't a big deal, but it would certainly help Smith. He would be getting three hundred dollars a week from the company, an extra hundred for any race in which he finished in the top ten. The sponsorship was on a trial basis for the few remaining races of the season. But Smith had been told that if he did well, and the company executives were impressed, it might result in a far more lucrative contract for the next season. That had given Smith hope because he knew if he didn't get Rookie of the Year, and didn't get that contract, he probably wouldn't be racing next year.

Cars had been a big part of Larry Smith's life for as long as he could remember. He was reared from the age of six at a crossroads near Lenoir in the hills of western North Carolina, where his father owned a garage. He spent most of his out-of-school hours at the garage, and his knowledge of cars seemed to grow naturally. He was building his own cars from junkyard parts and driving them on back roads long before he could legally drive at the age of sixteen. As a teen-ager he was interested in drag racing, but by the time he finished high school, his interest had turned to stock car racing, and he began building a car to drive in amateur races at dirt tracks near his home. He drove his first race the year he married, at the age of nineteen. Within a few years, he was making good money running at outlaw tracks, much more money than some of his schoolmates who had gone to work in the furniture factories in Lenoir. He knew cars and how to handle them, and he was good at it. He knew, too, how dangerous they could be. His body showed that.

Larry Smith had no kneecap on his right leg. Several of his bones were held together by steel pins, and there was a plate in his head. Plastic surgery had obscured the worst scars. He had been in so many wrecks, both on the track and off, that he could no longer remember them all, only the worst ones. At age eight, he was hit by a car near his daddy's garage and almost killed. Both legs were broken and his skull was fractured, along with other injuries. One day in 1963 he was driving his new 407 Ford back home from a lake, pulling a boat down a straight stretch at 130 miles per hour, when the car left the road and slammed into a creek bank. He wasn't sure later what happened. "Went to sleep, I guess," he recalls, "I'd been drinkin' a little that day." The boat was flipped on top of the car, and he was pinned beneath the car's engine, which had been shoved into the passenger compartment. His head rested on the spare tire from the trunk. His skull was fractured again, his ankle mangled, kidneys damaged, face partially torn away, and his kneecap gone. He spent six months in the hospital and returned to racing when he got out—only to wreck in a race at Columbia, South Carolina, and break his back. But he didn't let such things stand in the way of his ambition. He had always returned to racing.

His ambition was to get into big-league racing, and the year before, he had sat down and counted his money. He had twenty-eight thousand dollars that he had accumulated from racing, working on cars, running a service station, swapping cars, guns, coin collections—money that he and his wife had been saving to build a new house. They had been living in a trailer behind his daddy's garage. Now he had a new plan for the money. He wanted to use it to make a stab at Grand National racing. His wife Patricia, who ran her own beauty shop, wasn't particularly enthusiastic about the plan. She didn't care much for racing, and she worried that her husband was going to kill himself at it. But he had already made his decision.

"I told her I was goina do it," he recalled later, "and she said, 'Well, you got it in your blood, they ain't but one way to get it out.'"

It would be a one-shot, go-for-broke venture. Larry Smith knew how costly it would be, knew that it would take all of his money to run for a year, even if he did well. He promised his wife they would get the new house later. "There's always a way to make money as long as you're ambitious enough to work for it," he told her.

He was ambitious, but he had no illusions. He knew that rookie drivers didn't win races or become overnight sensations. He knew it would be a struggle. He knew, too, that he worked better if he set himself a goal. His goal was to make Rookie of the Year. That would be his only chance, he thought, to continue racing. The Rookie of the Year commanded five hundred dollars a race appearance money the following season. That would give him a chance to get to the point that he could do well enough to turn a profit. His plan for the year was to make all of the races and run "balls out." The car took most of his money, but he had it finished in time to make his debut at the Daytona 500 in February.

He got off to a bad start. He blew an engine in practice, another one in the qualifying race, and he loaded up and returned home without even making the race. He figured the week had cost him about five thousand dollars, and had damaged his chances of being Rookie of the Year. He got his car ready to run again in time for the spring race at Rockingham, where he finished a respectable eleventh. On his first run at Darlington in the spring, he'd been embarrassed. Because Darlington is such a difficult track, rookies are required to pass a driving test judged by veteran drivers before they can run it. On his test run, he got out of the groove and spun out, ruining four new tires. "That skeered the shit out of me," he recalled later. "I said, 'Goddamn, I have fucked up now. I have had the licks.'" But he had been allowed to come in, put on new tires, and try again. This time he passed. At Atlanta he had wrecked and torn up his car, which further hurt his chances. Still, he was fairly well pleased with his performance so far, and he knew that he still had a chance at achieving his goal, although he was far from confident of it. The money had been going fast. He was spending about twice as much as he was winning, and it looked as if he would have to borrow to finish the season. That was why the beer contract had been so welcome. It had given him more incentive.

Now he was hoping to prove himself by qualifying in the top twelve. That would be an achievement worthy of note. He ran well, and it looked for a while as if he might have made it. His speed was 145.633, almost 7 miles per hour slower than Allison's, but still a good run, and for a while he was in the top twelve. But when qualifying had ended, he had been pushed into thirteenth. He would have to run again the next day.

It was about four o'clock when he took the car out for a few practice laps to try to improve the handling. Suddenly, coming out of the second turn, the engine blew, spewing oil onto the track and white smoke into the air. Smith lost control, and the car went into a spin and slammed into the backstretch wall.

"Action on the backstretch!" cried the track loudspeakers. "That's Larry Smith of Lenoir, North Carolina, in that Carling Black Label Special number ninety-two. He's all right."

In the garage, Larry Smith's mechanic, Kenny Barlow, ran to see what had happened. Somebody called out to the wrecker driver who was laughing with a group of mechanics, "Hey, Henry, git on the ball, boy, you got a customer on the backstretch."

Larry Smith was grim-faced when the wrecker pulled his car in and deposited it in the garage. He walked around the car, examining it, wiping his hands on a grease rag. He said nothing. His mechanic came running up from the other side of the garage.

"Bud Moore's got an engine for us," he said.

Smith nodded grimly, and the two of them began an intense inspection of the car, Smith crawling under the back, then burrowing under the hood. A small crowd had gathered to check the damage.

"Kinked ever'where, ain't it?" said a fat mechanic in a dirty T-shirt.

"Yeah, boy, she's sprung all over," said another.

"That's too bad," somebody added. "He just got him a nice sponsor."

The inspection showed that the car was more heavily damaged than it had first appeared. In addition to the blown engine, the chassis was bent, the rear end out, springs broken, and wheels damaged, not to mention the crumpled body.

"No way I can get it ready in time," Smith said, shaking his head.

By that he meant that he wouldn't be able to make another qualifying run, but he was going to try to get the car fixed in time to make the race. He *had* to do that, or it would all be over, all of his hopes blown. He would have to stand on the speed of his earlier qualifying run. That, he knew, would be enough to get him in the race, but he would have to start far at the back. When he went off to the tower to tell the NASCAR officials, Kenny Barlow was already breaking down the car.

When the results of the first day's qualifying were posted, the following drivers were listed in the top twelve positions: Bobby Allison in a Chevrolet, Fred Lorenzen in a Chevrolet, Richard Petty in a Dodge, Buddy Baker in a Dodge, Dave Marcis in a Matador, Dick Brooks in a Mercury, Bobby Isaac in a Dodge, Benny Parsons in a Mercury, James Hylton in a Mercury, Lee-Roy Yarbrough in a Ford, Donnie Allison in a Ford, and Cecil Gordon in a Mercury.

David Pearson made his qualifying run Friday afternoon at a speed of 152.342. He had beaten Allison, but he seemed unconcerned about it.

"It didn't really matter whether we topped Allison or not," he said afterward, then grinned, "but still it gives all of us a good feelin'."

He would be starting at the top of the second day's qualifying group, putting him in thirteenth position, a definite drawback at Darlington because of the difficulty in passing on the track.

"Sure, it creates a problem to start that far back," he told the sportswriters. "It means I'll have a little more traffic to go through, but my speed proves I've got the fastest car."

Leonard Wood, a thin, bespectacled young man, who with his older brother Glen, owners of the car, had worked to get it ready after their problems the day before, had his head under the hood, checking the engine after the run.

"We've been having trouble with valves spottin' recently," he said.

He said that he was glad the engine blew when it did. "That was the engine we had planned on using in the race, and if it hadn't blown Thursday, you can imagine what might have happened Monday." He wiped his hands on a pink rag. "I just hope this engine doesn't have any bugs."

The race seemed to be shaping up according to prediction.

If they could avoid mechanical problems and keep out of trouble, it would clearly be a two-car race: Allison and Pearson. But everybody knew that in racing anything could happen.

The parade was held, as always, on Saturday morning. It was the biggest and grandest ever. Thirteen bands and 145 floats and decorated convertibles circled the courthouse square in Darlington. The parade was always the same. The Shriners on their funny cars and bicycles, the Miss Southern 500 beauty contestants smiling on the backs of convertibles, Senator Strom Thurmond, tanned and ramrod straight on his convertible. This year Donna Douglas, the TV star, rode in the official pace car, and the grand marshal was Admiral Kent Lee, a local boy who had gone off to the Navy and made good. The police estimated that eighty thousand people turned out to watch the parade, a good many of them blacks, because blacks make up a large part of the area's population. But few blacks would make their way out to the racetrack.

Business was booming at Goldie's Drive-In and Strickland's Lunch out by the track. By Saturday afternoon a great crush of people had fallen on the area surrounding the racetrack. The big fields around the track were now filled with vehicles and people, and the roads were jammed. Highway patrolmen, red-faced and sweating under campaign hats, worked to keep the traffic moving.

A lot of the people bought two-dollar tickets to get into the grandstands to watch the final qualifying, although there wasn't a great deal of enthusiasm for it. The last day was for strokers, those drivers who couldn't or wouldn't ever go fast enough to win a race unless all of the other cars dropped out. They didn't generate a lot of excitement. But there *would* be a race, the consolation, a losers' race. And to race fans with nothing to do, any race is better than no race at all. Besides, they would get to see the hot cars take their final practice.

The final sixteen starting spots were to be filled on this afternoon. Eight drivers had stood on earlier runs. At least four of those looked safe. Three others might make it. If that proved true, twenty-two drivers would be vying to snag those other nine spots. These cars would qualify at speeds almost ten miles per hour slower than the front runners.

As the cars made their runs, some of the drivers gathered in anxious clumps around a chalkboard in front of the tower on pit row, waiting to see who would be bumped. The speeds were chalked on the board as each car made its laps.

A young crewman came up and whispered into the ear of one driver, who reacted angrily.

"I ain't got no passes to give them fuckin' whores!"

The crewman retreated.

One of the most anxious drivers was a young man named Harry Schelling. He had taken his last eight thousand dollars and come to the South to race after he had lost his California business in a flood a few months earlier. More than half of his money was now gone, and he had not yet gotten into a race. But he still had a chance to make this one. He had qualified at 141.395, and he was now in the hot seat. Qualifying was almost over, and he was the next driver to be bumped. Then Ron Keselowski, a driver from a Midwest racing circuit, drove his Dodge around the track at a little over a tenth of a mile per hour faster than Harry Schelling's speed, and it was all over. Harry Schelling shook his head and walked away.

A short time later, the drivers brought their cars onto line for the start of the consolation race. Harry Schelling would start in first position. There were thirteen other cars. The drivers stood in little groups alongside their cars as they waited for the usual brief drivers' meeting.

"I got a rear end leaking real bad," rookie Doc Faustina was telling several drivers. "I'm only goina make a couple of laps. The rear end is bent like this."

Bill Shirey, a lanky veteran driver, stood with one foot propped against the side of his car, his helmet in hand. "All right," he said, "let's get this thing over with so I can load up."

The drivers' meeting was held by the pit wall. John Bruner, the NASCAR steward, went through his usual recitation. "Now, in the event of a yellow flag . . ."

Finally the track announcer, a guy with a melodious voice who tried to wring the maximum drama out of every word, began the introductions. When he got to the last one, he said, "And star-ting in the scratch po-si-tion, the un-o-ffic-al mayor of Dan-ville, Virginia—Wen-dell Scott!"

It was the only introduction to draw any real response from the crowd, but the response included a lot of jeering and mocking laughter. Then somewhere up in the stands, some guy boomed out: "GI'EM HELL, WEN-DELL!" And the crowd laughed.

That obviously irritated Wendell Scott's sons, who had come to help him. It showed in their faces. This had been another in a long string of bad weeks for Wendell Scott. On the way to Darlington on Wednesday he had stopped for a meal at a truck stop. The food must have been bad, he figured, for that night in a little out-of-the-way motel that catered to blacks he became awfully sick. He was so sick that he had been unable even to come to the track to attempt to qualify until today. He hadn't been able to work on his car either, and it was in bad shape, handling and running poorly. He could coax no speed from it at all, and of all the cars that had been brought to the track this week, his battered old Ford was the slowest.

The cars took one lap behind the pace car, and the race was on. It wasn't much of a race, fifteen laps, and Harry Schelling stayed in front all the way. His car was hissing and steaming when he pulled back into the pits after taking the checkered flag, and he was smiling.

"I'm pretty happy," he told a reporter. "I won a race at Darlington the first time here, and not many drivers can make that claim."

His victory was worth two hundred dollars.

After a couple of laps of the race, one of Wendell Scott's sons had walked over to the pit wall and waved his father to come in. A driver needed only start the race to claim the hundred-dollar guaranteed minimum award; one hundred dollars would barely pay for the entry fee and pit passes. No need to burn up gas, wear out tires, and risk wrecking or ruining an engine. Make a lap or two, bring the car in, and load it up. But Wendell Scott had not responded to his son's wave. His son waved for the next couple of laps, and he didn't respond then either. His son finally gave up in disgust.

Wendell Scott had run the entire race, and he had finished in the same position in which he had started: last. When I asked him later why he hadn't brought the car in after a couple of laps, he said, "I don't race like 'at."

For him it had been a matter of dignity.

After the race, when the faster cars took to the track for final practice, Larry Smith's car was among them. He and Kenny Barlow had worked frantically on the car all day Friday and for the biggest part of this day. His father had driven down from Lenoir bringing needed parts. His earlier qualifying time had been good enough to put him at the top of the last day's efforts, which meant that he would be starting in twenty-fifth position, right beside David Boggs, another young driver who was his chief rival for the Rookie of the Year award. Fortunately for Smith, Boggs had been having his problems, too. When Smith brought his car back in after a few laps, it was immediately obvious from his face that he was pleased. "Runs better'n it did before I wrecked it," he said.

Saturday night. For Red Robinson, this was the highlight of the week. The Miss Southern 500 pageant was being held right on the track. A makeshift stage had been erected on the starting line, the backdrop decorated with lots of big sparkling yellow smiley faces in keeping with this year's pageant theme: "A Smile for Every Mile."

An electric organ had been hauled out and set up in front of the stage, and a great many lights on spindly stands kept the stage illuminated. Folding chairs had been lined up on the track in front of the stage for the special guests, and beyond the track wall and the high wire fence that topped it, several hundred race fans had bought tickets to sit in the grandstand to watch this spectacle.

The contestants were twenty-six girls from towns all over South Carolina. The master of ceremonies was a dapper young TV "personality" from a local station, who tried to fill little voids in the proceedings with corny jokes. The girls paraded in swimsuits, evening gowns, and huge brown paper sacks when the judges were picking the girl with the prettiest legs. They wore numbers on paper triangles attached to their wrists. Backstage they engaged in nervous chitchat.

"My feet hurt."

"I thought I was *going to die!*"

"I just wanted to sleep so-o bad."

Miss Columbia, hiding her face behind a smiley face paper plate on a stick, stuck out her tongue petulantly as she waited in line to parade onstage.

Red Robinson was everywhere backstage. He didn't miss a girl. Usually he had his arms around two at the same time, copping a feel here and a kiss there. The girls smiled gamely and never protested. They seemed to think that Red was a track official, or some other racing big shot, an impression he did nothing to allay. He certainly looked the part, decked out in a sky blue double-knit suit, set off with a bright pink tie and blue suede boots. None of the girls wanted to risk the possibility of not becoming Miss Southern 500 by telling Red to get lost.

"Y'all done good, all of ye," Red kept telling the girls as they traipsed offstage.

The pageant was fraught with minor catastrophes. The lights had attracted a goodly part of the insect population of Darlington County. They almost totally distracted the organist, a great cloud of them buzzing constantly around her head, and finally a guy was stationed beside her, and he kept jumping up with an aerosol can and wafting clouds of insecticide around her head. The girls onstage had a rough time of it, too. Bugs would fly into their mouths when they smiled, and they had to pretend that nothing happened. Mosquitoes would perch on their legs and draw blood unmolested, because no girl would dare ruin her poise and slap.

Then the lights went out. Technicians scurried about, trying to find the trouble. The pageant marched on, considerably dimmed. Five finalists were chosen. To help the judges determine which of these could best serve as a racetrack queen, the TV announcer asked questions to test their intelligence.

What thoughts passed through Miss Greenwood's head when she looked into the mirror this morning?

"Oh no! What am I going to do? All these girls are so-o beautiful!"

What would Miss Easley most look forward to if she were chosen to reign?

"Meeting people," she gushed. "I'd just love traveling around the state. It would be the most wonderful thing that could happen!"

With this, the judges retreated to mull over the possibilities, and Donna Douglas was brought on to fill the time. She was wearing a frilly, country-looking dress, and she took the microphone and frisked to the edge of the stage. Up in the grandstand a lot of ol' boys were whooping and hollering and whistling, and she went into her dopey-country-girl Ellie Mae voice to tell them all what a thrill it was to be there.

"Where's Jethro?" some guy yelled to great laughter.

"He's still in the woodshed. We don't let him out."

The crowd roared with mirth.

She'd never been to a race before, she was saying now, and she was really looking forward to this one because she just knew that it was going to be such a thrill.

"Some feller tol' me he'd give me a ride in his car," she said.

Up in the stands some ol' boy suffering from the heat and the beer rose unsteadily to his feet, cupped his hands around his mouth, and roared, "HELL, I'LL GIVE YOU MY CAR!"

The judges had decided. The new Miss Southern 500 was contestant No. 22, Miss Easley, a tall, long-necked girl named Fran Jean Riggins, who was wearing a clinging pink swimsuit and had her long hair teased so that it stood out wide on the sides of her head. She was twenty years old, a student at Clemson University. She had listed her hobbies as "reading, all sports, and singing." She had blue-gray eyes, long, shapely legs, and nice tits.

"I just can't believe it," she kept repeating, her eyes moistening, as the previous year's queen, Lynn Hollis, placed the crown atop her head.

Race Day

MISERY. My head throbbed. My stomach was in rebellion. Somehow I thought that I was suffocating. I was sweating. My skin felt clammy. All that beer. Not enough sleep. God, it was hot.

I pulled myself up and rousted my friend Bill Lee. He had been sick when he arrived a few hours earlier. A virus, he suspected. Fever. Churning stomach. Diarrhea. "Man, this is no place to be with the runs," I had told him. "You ain't seen those filthy toilets." But he had stayed.

"How you feeling?" I said.

"I'll make it, I guess."

"I'm not sure I will. You want a beer? That might help."

I got the beers from the ice chest and washed down some aspirin and vitamin pills. The beer supply had dwindled drastically, and I was afraid that I might be forced into dealing with one of those profiteering infield bootleggers after all. I felt obligated to eat something, so I made a peanut butter sandwich and sliced a banana on it. My friend declined breakfast.

I could smell bacon frying on campstoves nearby. The infield activity had quickened with the excitement of race day. Across the way I could see people already filing into the grandstands, although it was still nearly four hours until race time. I could hear race car engines roaring to life as mechanics made final adjustments and moved the cars through inspection and onto line down by the fourth turn.

When I got over to the pits, I ran into Brother Bill Frazier. He was wearing black jeans, boots, and a white Banlon shirt with his "With God You're Always a Winner" emblem on the pocket. It was almost time for his service.

"I got to go set up my bell," he said. "Looks like we're goina be late."

A small group of drivers' and mechanics' wives and children were waiting in the scorers' stand by the fourth turn when Brother Bill hoisted his heavy black bell onto the back of his pickup truck and started ringing it. He greeted arrivals as a village pastor might: "Hey, how ya doin' this mornin'? Glad to see ya." A handful of drivers and mechanics joined the congregation before Brother Bill climbed onto the scorers' stand and took up his microphone to begin the service.

After some introductory remarks, he turned the pages in his Bible.

"This mornin' I want to take my scripture readin's from the fourth chapter of the Book of Matthew beginnin' with the first verse. . . ."

He preached a quiet sermon about possession, obsession, and temptation, talking about how the devil gets into people. Out on the track, cars were still being moved into line, their noise occasionally interrupting Brother Bill.

When he got to temptation, Brother Bill fell into personal confession.

"Man, you talk about temptations, I had 'em and I took advantage of 'em, too, and I'm here to tell you I did. I'm not proud of it, but I did. I give in to it. Ever' temptation that befell me, man, I just jumped on it and just took advantage of it. I'd cheat and lie and do anything else to try to git ahead in this world. And I tried to live right, tried to do better, tried to join a church two or three times. Y'all've heard me tell it before. I'as baptized so many times that ever' tadpole in Alabama knows my first name. I'd go to the creek and they say, 'Here he comes.'

They *know* me. They all knew me. Because I didn't mean it. . . ."

Marty Robbins sat in the drivers' lounge, his feet propped on a table. Thin, tanned, his blond hair curling at his ears and the base of his neck, he would in three weeks be forty-seven years old. He looked younger.

Marty Robbins was a country music superstar. Born in Arizona, he had started performing in the Navy during World War II. He began recording in 1952, moved to Nashville, and joined the Grand Ole Opry the following year. His first big hit, "Singing the Blues," came out in 1956. He'd had one or more almost every year since.

Less than three years before, Robbins had suffered a massive heart attack. Two of the arteries to his heart were totally blocked, the other 80 per cent closed. He underwent surgery to bypass all three arteries, only the fifteenth person in history to have such an operation. Four months later he was plowing on his farm near Nashville—and driving race cars again.

"I been doin' well," he said. "I feel fine."

Robbins had raced stock cars for years. He used to drive at the Nashville Fairgrounds on Saturday, then rush to the Grand Ole Opry to sing. He laughed.

"If I'm racing I like it better," he said. "If I'm singing, I like it better. It's just that I get a kick out of two different things in life."

He got into big-time racing in 1966, but for several years he only ran once a year and didn't do very well at it. The year before, however, he had run in five races, all big ones, and he'd finished seventh in one, the Southern 500. It was his first race at Darlington, and he had been named Rookie of the Race.

I asked him what his wife of twenty-four years, Marizona, thought about his racing.

"She doesn't like it," he said. "Neither does anybody else, really, connected with the business I'm in. But I enjoy it, and that's life, you know. If you can't enjoy life, what can you do? Be mighty boring."

He grinned.

"Who knows, I might luck up and win one. If everything's right, I mean, on a given day, I could win a race, same as anybody else. So I fool around, just take a chance on finishing good, see. I don't really have the equipment or the experience to win a race. But James Hylton won at Talladega a few weeks ago. Who knows? I'm just waitin' around."

The prerace show had begun. Omar's Imps, Shriners dressed as clowns, cavorted on funny bouncing bicycles and in an old car that backfired loudly. Down by the starting line, the St. John Junior High School band was playing.

In front of the drivers' lounge a couple of drivers stood in a small group that was talking about the infield crowd.

"Boy, it was *wild* out there last night," somebody said.

"Boy got killed, didn't he?" said one of the drivers.

"Got stabbed."

A rescue squad volunteer joined in to fill in the details. "Stabbed 'im right here. Right beneath the heart. Eighteen-year-old boy. Killed 'im deader'n hell."

"I tell you, I wouldn't want to be out there," one of the drivers said.

"Nosiree, I wouldn't spend a night out there for a thousand dollars," somebody added.

The story of the death of the boy had made its way in various forms throughout the track. Some said it was a hippie. Others said it was just a nigger trying to fool with a white girl. No doubt, everybody at the track who was not passed out drunk had heard the story, and it was believed to be true.

No such thing had happened. Nobody had been killed. Such stories got around every year, though, and nobody knew how they started. It was not difficult to see why they were believed. The legend of the infield demanded it. A death, a sacrifice to the speed god, was needed to make it *really* wild, and everybody knew that the Darlington infield was the wildest infield there was.

At a little after ten-thirty, as a WAF drill team was beginning to perform on the frontstretch, the drivers crowded into their small lounge for the drivers' meeting. Some sat on the few chairs and sofas, but most hunkered on the floor or leaned against the wall. The room was filled with talking, laughter, and cigarette smoke.

A whistle blew.

"Everybody in the pool," somebody shouted.

"Goddamn, Pearson, make some noise!"

"Did Pearson fart again?"

In one corner somebody kidded Dale Inman, Richard Petty's crew chief, about his role in the movie that had just been made about Richard's life.

"Dale's goina git a 'Cademy Award."

"I'll git one 'fore you do, 'cause you didn't even git in the movie."

John Bruner, sixty-seven years old, short, pudgy, bald, NASCAR's chief steward, started calling roll in his gravelly voice.

"Number twelve."

"Here."

"Twenty-six . . . uh, twenty-eight."

"Here."

"Don't call the numbers, call the names!" somebody yelled. "Shit, I can't remember my number."

"Forty-three."

"Heuh."

"Eleven."

Buddy Baker, six feet, five inches tall, two hundred and fifteen pounds, driver of Richard Petty's number eleven car, was just slipping into the room, grinning sheepishly.

"Here," he whispered.

"Down Buddy!"

He flopped to the floor. The roll call proceeded as most of the drivers continued to talk and laugh among themselves. They continued when John Bruner went into his ritual spiel about the rules. Most had heard it so many times before that they no longer listened.

"You fellas all know how to start. I want to see those cars all pass in line just the way they're lined up down there now. . . ."

"No passing 'til after the checkered," somebody said, mockingly.

"We got a lot of new drivers that haven't driven competition here before. You fellas goin' down the straightaways, this is for the new drivers that hadn't been here and don't know what it's all about; comin' down the straightaway, you see a car behind you, you know it's goina pass you before you get through the two turns, through the third and fourth or the first and second turns, don't go into the turn up high. Drop down to the second groove so a man can go on around the top of you, 'cause you can't pull it down off the wall when you're already halfway through the turn."

"John, tell us where that second groove is," a driver called. "I been here a week and ain't found it."

Bruner ignored the remark. The drivers continued to talk and laugh.

"Now the other thing is, comin' out of the pits, you must stay on the bottom lane . . . until you get to the backstretch!"

"What you talkin' about, the bottom lane?"

"The bottom lane on the bank, there's four lanes . . ."

"Hell, that's the groove," laughed another driver.

A few drivers engaged in a debate about how they usually came out of the pits, and the meeting broke into chaos.

"Listen!" Bruner finally shouted, "if you want to talk to somebody, take 'em outside."

The room quieted for a minute, but the disorder resumed shortly.

"Come on, let's go, John," somebody called over the din, and Bruner struggled on, finally saying, after much more discussion and confusion, "Everybody clear now?"

Lin Kuchler, a top NASCAR official, interrupted to say a few words, and after that the meeting drew mercifully to an end.

"Is Brother Bill here?" John Bruner said.

Brother Bill stepped into the center of the crowded room as the drivers all rose noisily to their feet.

"Hold it!" Bruner shouted. The room quieted. "All right, Brother Bill."

"Take your hats off, gentlemen," Brother Bill said. He began to pray. "Our Father God, we thank you, Lord, for your love and your blessings and we bow our heads today to ask you to overshadow this track and give us a safe race. Help us all, God, we pray, to know that no matter how we place today, with God you're always a winner. Let every man say, 'Amen.'"

"Amen."

"God bless."

Drivers' meetings bored David Pearson. "They're all the same," he said. "The same drivers ask the same questions every race. I think they just like to hear themselves. I got things to do."

No matter what he is wearing, David Pearson always looks as if he had just come in from plowing. He has that country boy look. A powerful, rugged-looking man, almost six feet tall, one hundred and eighty-five pounds, his face full, with high cheekbones and quick, dark eyes, his dark, curly hair flecked with white, he claims Cherokee Indian blood. He grew up in Spartanburg, South Carolina, hanging around service stations, garages, and dirt racetracks. He could tear down an engine and put it back together by the time he was sixteen, and he started driving in dirt track races not long afterward.

Pearson had been a top modified and sportsman driver before he moved into Grand National racing in 1960 and became Rookie of the Year. He won three superspeedway races his second year, driving a Ray Fox Pontiac, and the sportswriters started calling him "David, the Giant Killer." His career had its ups and downs after that, but mostly ups. He won three national driving championships.

In 1967, Pearson had begun driving a Ford for Holman-Moody, one of the biggest organizations in racing at the time.

Three years later, when Ford pulled out of racing, Holman-Moody asked him to take a cut in his percentage. He quit instead. He returned driving a Pontiac, but it was not a competitive car, and talk began to circulate that he was washed up. It had continued into this year, but he knew better.

Five months earlier, the Wood Brothers had asked him to drive their Mercury, and he was suddenly back on top again. He had won five superspeedway races and more than a hundred thousand dollars since then. That had brought his number of career wins to sixty-six, second only to Richard Petty, and his winnings to more than eight hundred thousand dollars. He had invested his money carefully in real estate and businesses in Spartanburg, and he was doing very well. He wouldn't have to race any more if he didn't want to, but he did, although it wasn't the same as it had once been.

"I don't enjoy it nothin' like I used to," he had said earlier, while changing into his driving uniform. "I can remember when I'd race for nothin'. That day has long since passed."

As Pearson made his way out of the drivers' meeting, he was intercepted by a PR man from Purolator, the oil filter company that sponsors the Wood Brothers car.

"I'll do that tape as soon as I git wired up," Pearson said. He went next door to the small track hospital, where seven drivers were being wired to miniature EKG machines that they would carry in their cars during the race. They had agreed to assist in a research project that would enable doctors to study stress on their hearts during critical parts of the race.

Two doctors were taping sensors to the drivers' chests, three for each driver: one red, one white, one green.

"I don't want no green on me," Pearson told the doctors.

Like many race drivers, Pearson is superstitious. Green has always been considered an unlucky color around racetracks.

The doctors thought that he was kidding at first, but he quickly made it plain that he was not. So they put two reds and a white on him, marking one of the reds to show that it should be green.

Outside, Pearson was joined again by the PR man. "Let's do this quick," he said. "I'm starvin'."

"You eat this close to a race?" said the PR man.

Pearson laughed. "You don't want me to starve, do you?"

The PR man led him off to make the brief advertising tape. He was back shortly, and Leonard Wood handed him a ham-and-cheese sandwich. He gobbled down the sandwich with a soft drink, then sat on a bottle crate chatting with people who stopped by to wish him well.

A sportswriter said, "You get nervous before a race, David?"

"Ain't no need to git nervous. You git nervous when you go to work in the mornin'? If I got too nervous I'd say I was in the wrong business."

The track loudspeakers prattled incessantly. "Everything shapes up for the greatest of all Southern 500s with this, the twenty-third edition. . . ." It was still an hour before the start. The prerace entertainment was just finishing up. The "Grey Rock Brakers," a chorus line of long-legged, bosomy girls in flared hip huggers and little halter tops, had just finished their last dance and climbed into a white trailer that was being pulled around the track by the Grey Rock Brake Lining motor home, on top of which sat a small rock combo. Most of the drivers had now gathered on the grassy area near their cars at the fourth turn.

"All drivers, down to your cars immediately," said the loud-speakers. "The introductions are about to start."

Darlington introduces the drivers differently from other tracks. Most tracks begin by introducing the driver starting in last position, then working toward the front, thus building drama for the introductions of the most popular drivers, who always start at front. Usually the drivers are called onto a little platform of some sort, where they wave at the crowd and get a kiss from a race queen. Darlington uses a little more flair. The drivers get into their cars down at the fourth turn, and as their names are called, they roar toward the starting line from a cloud of tire smoke.

"La-dies and gentle-men! May we intro-duce to you the world's finest race drivers! . . ."

Bobby Allison cranked his red-and-gold Chevrolet.

"Starting in the pole po-sition, from Huey-town, Alabama, driving the num-ber twelve Co-ca-Cola Chev-ro-let: BOBBY ALLISON!"

With smoking tires, Allison raced for the starting line, as his fans rose to cheer.

While the drivers were being introduced, the scorers' stand began to fill. A lot of drivers bring their wives and families to the tracks, and there is usually a special place set aside for them. At Darlington, it is the area around the scorers' stand. Drivers who haul their race cars on trailers, park the trailers in that area to keep them out of the way of the garage, and when the families have squeezed their cars in around the trailers, it is a very crowded area.

The drivers' wives have an auxiliary that tries to help new families adjust to the racing life style and make them feel welcome, and most of the families know each other well. "It's just like one big family," they are fond of saying. Some of the families were visiting now between cars before the race started and drowned out conversation. Others were eating picnic lunches out of car trunks. Kids played between the crowded cars.

Many wives serve as scorers for their husbands. It gives them something to do and makes them feel a part of things. It isn't a difficult job. A big digital clock stands in front of the scorers' stand. It marks off every second of the race. When a scorer's car passes, the scorer enters the exact time in a little block on the score sheet. Every five laps, the scorer holds up the score sheet, which is marked with the driver's name and number, and it is noted by a NASCAR official. Many of the wives were already at their places in the stands, seeking respite from the sun.

Margaret Baker rested her heavy arms on one of the scoring tables and looked out at the track. Her face showed the wear of the years now, and her hair was mostly gray. She had been around racing longer than any of the other wives, and she had scored a lot of races. It was about 1950 when she first started going to the races with her husband. Buck Baker was in this race today. He would be, at fifty-three, the oldest driver on the track. He had been racing since the earliest days, and he had been very good, having won forty-six races and two national championships. He had won three Southern 500s, and only one other driver could boast that. He only raced a little now, but he almost always ran at Darlington, where he had known his greatest glory, although his car—which some drivers laughingly called a tank—certainly posed no threat to victory. Margaret and Buck Baker were no longer married, however. He would be scored today by his second wife, a younger woman, who was seated nearby. Margaret Baker was scoring for her son, Buddy. She was talking now about her son.

"He got started by following his daddy," she said. "That's his hero. Personally, I never thought he'd become a driver. He didn't like to come to the races, but a lot of times we had to make him come 'cause we didn't have nobody for him to stay with.

"When he was about fourteen, he started changin'. His daddy give him a car and I think that's what started him off. I believe he was nineteen when he started racin'. He wasn't really old enough, but his daddy signed for 'im."

Margaret Baker was there for one main reason, she said. She likes the races. It didn't worry her when her husband was racing, and she doesn't worry about her son.

"I think they're a lot safer on the track than they are out on the highway," she said.

Patricia Smith couldn't go along with that.

"I think it's dangerous," she said. "It scares me. It's nerve-racking."

Because her husband, Larry, was a rookie, she sat apart from the other wives, away from the scoring stand. She didn't know any of the other wives, and they didn't know her. She had only been to a few races. She was a tall, pretty, dark-haired girl, and she was wearing a simple white-dotted brown dress. She didn't like racing, she was saying, not only because it was dangerous, but because it also took up so much of her husband's time.

"Even when he's home, he's always workin' on the car," she said. But he had been racing when they married, and she had had to accept it. "I knew he would be a racer. It's what he wants to do. He wouldn't be happy doin' anything else."

She had driven from their home in Lenoir that morning with her sister-in-law, who sat with her. When she was asked if she was going to be a scorer, she said, "Lord, no! I tried that once, but it made me a nervous wreck." She laughed. "If I messed up, he'd kill me."

The drivers had been introduced now and were out of their cars again, milling on the grass in front of the grandstands with crew members, track and NASCAR officials, beauty queens, PR men, special guests, sportswriters, photographers, and assorted others whose reasons for being there were not immediately clear. The crowd—it now numbered more than seventy-two thousand, and it would later be touted as "the biggest crowd ever gathered for an event in South Carolina"—was growing restless now, eager for action.

A photographer with a half-dozen cameras strung around his neck started to snap a picture of Richard Brooks, a young driver from California.

"Say cheese," said the photographer.

"Puss-eee," said Brooks, grinning broadly.

Red Robinson circulated importantly through the crowd passing out his chewing gum, pausing in his work to have his picture taken with his arms around two Union 76 Race Stoppers.

The preliminaries were not yet over. Checks had to be presented to drivers placing high in the third leg of the Winston Cup point competition. Visiting pace cars had to make their lap of the track bearing the names and dates of future races. Special guests had to be introduced. Barney Wallace, the track president, a totally colorless man, had remarks to make. Senator Strom Thurmond, lean, tanned, stern-faced, came on to say that he was "delighted on this auspicious occasion . . ." and so on, speaking for a couple of minutes without saying anything, as politicians are wont to do. The place was crawling with politicians, running for everything from county coroner on up. Finally, a local preacher prayed, the junior high band squeaked out the National Anthem, and the crowd roared with anticipation.

The drivers climbed into their cars, crew chiefs helping to strap them in, the hot dogs testing the radios inside their helmets. Doctors hurried to connect the heart test drivers to their equipment.

Along the pit rows—one on each side of the track—all was in readiness. Air wrenches were laid out, Goodyear Blue Streak Stock Car Racing Specials were stacked neatly. Tool chests and ice chests loaded with soft drinks and ice water stood ready. Special fast-emptying gas cans lined the pit walls. Crew members waited in fresh, clean uniforms, gaudy things, most of them, decorated with sponsors' advertisements, their own names stitched over their shirt pockets.

Brother Bill walked the pit row carrying a cane with a camp stool taped to it. "It gits to be a long day," he said. "Man, you git tired."

"Gentle-men," blared the loudspeakers dramatically. "Start . . . your . . . engines!"

A great cheer went up.

I climbed atop a truck at the back of the garage with Brother Bill to watch the start of the race.

"The start is the most dangerous time," he said, as the pace car began to lead the cars toward the first turn. "Starts and restarts. Far as danger to the driver, that's the worst time."

Starts, he might have added, are terrifically exciting.

Everybody was standing now, craning to see. The cars were making the parade laps, bunched tightly, two by two, behind the pace car, moving slowly, easily, steadily, building tension. Suddenly, in the third turn, the pace car quickened, pulled away, darted toward the pit road. The cars seemed to pull back, gracefully, as if in slow motion, crouching like a big cat closing on its prey.

"They comin' now," Brother Bill said.

The green flag fell. The cars sprang forth in a great cloud of blue smoke, a tremendous surge of noise and power— GRRRRRRRRRRRRRRRAAAAAAAAAAAAGGGGGG- HHHHHHHHH!!!!!!!!

The great American orgasm!

Beautiful!

The excitement being felt at the track wasn't confined there. Out across the country, in areas as far-flung as Maine and Oregon, California and Iowa, millions of people would be clinging to every turn on radio. The race would be echoing through a thousand service station bays, blaring over transistors at beaches, wafting across backyards. The Darlington Raceway has its own radio network of more than three hundred stations in twenty-four states. Not as big as some. The Daytona 500, for example, is carried by more than eight hundred stations.

Most of the people inside the track had their ears pressed against transistor radios, as well. They were hearing an excited announcer telling them that Bobby Allison had gone into the first turn first, and they were watching him now as he pulled away from the pack.

Bobby Allison, thirty-four, a trim man, not quite six feet tall, with clean-cut good looks and modest sideburns, was having the best season of his career.

He had been reared in Miami, a city boy, but he moved to Alabama to race. He ran modified and sportsman cars on the Alabama circuit, running as many races as he could, and he had become a real hot-shot driver in those divisions. He had come to Grand National racing in 1961, entering four races, finishing far back in all of them, and winning only $650 for the season. He went back to the small tracks.

He was ready to try the big league again in 1965, entering eight races and not doing much better than he had the first time. But things improved in the following years. He sought success like a driven man, and he finally found it in a Chevrolet that he built himself and raced against the factory-backed cars. He won three races in 1966, six in '67, two in '68, and five in '69, but he was finishing in the top ten in almost every race—and making money. He was also making a reputation as a fierce and ruthless competitor, and some of the drivers disliked him intensely.

Allison had not given up small-track racing. He still ran as many as he could. Just a year and a half earlier, in fact, after the spring race at Darlington, he had found himself in trouble, almost broke, and talking of having to return to the small tracks full time. A few days later, however, he was offered the Holman-Moody Ford that David Pearson had abandoned. He took it and won eight races and more than $236,000 in the last half of that season. Then Holman and Moody split, and he found himself looking for a ride again. He didn't have to look far. Richard Howard and Junior Johnson asked him to drive their Chevrolet. So far this season, he had won seven races and nearly $180,000, and he was leading the Winston Cup point standings for the national championship.

Now, as he sped around the track far ahead of the other cars, he looked a good bet to chalk up another win—if, of course, he could keep out of trouble.

By the second lap, Richard Petty had moved ahead of Fred Lorenzen, but he couldn't catch Allison. David Pearson, meanwhile, was moving up fast. Deeper in the pack, Larry Smith, the rookie, eager to impress his new sponsor, was moving up too.

It takes about ten laps for a race to pick up a rhythm and for the crowd to settle down from the excitement of the start and get adjusted to the noise. The noise is incessant and overwhelming once the cars get strung out around the track. It is impossible to carry on conversation. In the pits, almost everybody stuffs his ears with cotton, as do the drivers. Drivers who have been racing for a long time almost always suffer some hearing damage. Richard Petty, for example, who has started more races than any other driver, has only half hearing in one ear, 75 per cent in the other. The drone of the engines drowns out the track loudspeakers, and in the infield and pits, where it is difficult to see more than one section of track, it is almost necessary to keep a transistor radio affixed to the ear to know what is going on. Some of the regulars in the pits wear headsets specially made for racing that not only muffle the noise but also have transistor radios built in.

At the end of ten laps, Allison still had a comfortable lead. His average speed: 149.471. Petty was a slower second, and Pearson had now moved from thirteenth to third. Buddy Baker was fourth, and Fred Lorenzen had fallen to fifth. Lorenzen was running much slower than the top runners. He was holding to the fast groove, nevertheless, and faster cars were beginning to back up behind him.

Larry Smith was pushing his car hard to gain position. It was running well, but he was worried about it anyhow. He always worried about the car. He was always tense, listening for some little thing to go wrong. He never worried about the danger. Just the car. Suddenly, the engine began to splutter and lose power, and he said, "Oh, shit!" and headed for the pits.

Lap thirteen. In the third turn, Tommy Gale's Mercury, a slower car, edged into the high groove and clipped the fender of Donnie Allison's Ford. Both cars started spinning. And cars were suddenly going everywhere, sliding and spinning in clouds of smoke and dust. Debris flew as cars crashed into each other and the wall. Other drivers attempted to shoot blindly through the confusion.

People in the grandstands rose to their feet as one, many of them using binoculars to try to see what was happening. Wreckers and ambulances headed toward the area. The caution flag went out.

"It could be a rough one here this afternoon," the loudspeakers could be heard saying, as the noise abated somewhat under the caution flag.

Eight cars had been involved in the wreck, including Tommy Gale's, which was relatively undamaged. Three cars sat demolished on the track, their drivers climbing out one by one. Nobody was hurt. Other cars limped into the pits badly damaged.

The cars of Joe Frasson, James Hylton, Dave Marcis, and

Benny Parsons, all of them in the second echelon of almost-competitive cars, were heavily damaged but able to continue after repairs—at least for a few more laps.

The three drivers knocked out of the race were among the best, however.

LeeRoy Yarbrough had been driving Grand National races for more than ten years, and in 1969, he'd had a phenomenal year, winning a record seven superspeedway races (including the Southern 500) and more than $188,000. He was named the Martini & Rossi American Driver of the Year for that, the first stock car driver to be so honored. He had driven less frequently after that, and just a year before, he had almost died from Rocky Mountain spotted fever. He had come back this season driving second-rate cars but making a creditable showing, nevertheless. In this race he was driving Junie Donlavey's No. 90 Ford, a car that had finished second at Talladega a month earlier after all of the top runners had fallen out.

This time he had been caught in the pack that was backing up behind Lorenzen.

"I could see there was goina be trouble," he told the sportswriters back in the pits, "so I backed off, but I couldn't avoid the pile-up."

Donnie Allison, Bobby's younger brother, had been driving Grand National races regularly since 1967, winning three races and more than $92,000 in his best year, 1970. Like his brother, he drove a lot of small-track races, and he had even ventured into championship racing at Indianapolis, where in 1970 he was named Rookie of the Race. He had been driving Bud Moore's small-engine Ford this year, and it had not been a particularly good year. In ten starts, he had finished in the top five only twice.

He was angry about this wreck, and he didn't hesitate to say so. It was Lorenzen's fault, he told reporters.

"He was hogging the groove," he fumed. "He wouldn't move over and let anybody else around. . . . If you can't drive a car fast enough to ride the high-speed groove, you ought to move over and let the others go ahead and race. . . . If Lorenzen

wanted to stroke, why didn't he move over and let the pack
pass?"

Bobby Isaac was angry, too. He stormed away from his demolished car, his face flushed, refusing to talk to anybody. He
was quick-tempered and moody. His friends said that he was
not really moody, that he was only shy and insecure because
of a hard upbringing. He had been reared near Catawba, North
Carolina, in the hill country. As a kid, he'd had to drop out of
school and go to work in a sawmill. As a teen-ager, he was working swing shifts in a cotton mill and dreaming of racing. He
started racing sportsman cars at nearby Hickory in 1955, and
he was a fearless, hard-charging driver. He raced whenever
there was a race, and it took him only three years to win the
state championship. He began driving in the big time in 1963
and won his first race the next year. He didn't really find success, however, until he teamed up with car builder Harry Hyde
to drive a Dodge owned by insurance millionaire Nord Krauskopf. He had driven that car since, and won thirty-six races
and more than $400,000. He won the national championship
in 1970. In his early years of big-time racing, Isaac had picked
up the nickname Hard Luck. Nobody had called him that for
a long time, but this year it seemed it might apply again. He
had won the pole position for eight races, but something always
seemed to go wrong. He had won only one race for the season,
and the frustration was beginning to show on him. People
who knew him kept their distance when he was angry, and he
stalked off to the locker room alone.

All of the front-runners had made pit stops under the yellow
flag, and Richard Brooks led the race for one lap in Bill Seifert's
Mercury before he, too, came into the pits. H. B. Bailey took
the lead then in a Pontiac and kept it until the green flag fell
again. He was quickly passed by Coo Coo Marlin in a Chevrolet, who held the lead for two laps, until Allison moved back
in front. Pearson had now taken second place, clinging to Allison's bumper, and on the thirty-seventh lap, he passed him for
the first time. The Pearson fans leaped to their feet, yelling,

waving him on, but their exuberance lasted only briefly, for four laps later, Allison slipped back around him.

Joe Frasson became the fourth driver to leave the race. His red No. 18 Dodge had received extensive damage in the wreck, but he had managed to keep it on the track for more than twenty laps, fighting it all the way, before he brought it in and parked it under one end of the garage. A doctor in a white suit hurried to the car to disconnect him from the heart test device. Frasson squeezed out of the car window, the top of his suit unzipped. He removed his red helmet, which had a big star on one side along with his name. A bull-like man, six-foot-one, 233 pounds, broad-shouldered, thick-necked, with a crooked, oft-battered nose, he looked more like a heavyweight boxer than a race driver. He was wearing a big mustache curled at the ends. A loud, gregarious person, Frasson was always clowning in the pits. He usually wore a floppy black hat and carried one of those gigantic cigars that are sold in joke shops. He lived in Minnesota, where he ran a concrete company that his father, Mario, had founded. He had raced on a Midwest circuit before coming South in 1970 to show those hillbilly boys how to drive a race car. Thus far, he had mainly shown them how to spend a lot of money and tear up a lot of equipment. His best finish had come earlier in the year at Darlington, when he had come in third. Since then, he had returned to his regular routine of engine failures and wrecks. The night before, he had sat at a country club cookout in the South Carolina woods eating thick hamburgers and thinking aloud about the upcoming race. "I think I'll hold back tomorrow," he had said, "just set back and take it easy." He took a sip of a soft drink, looked into the distance and laughed. "No I won't either. I'll get in there and run like hell. I'd run over my own grandmother to win a race."

"What happened, Joe?" somebody was asking.

Frasson shook his head. His face was streaked with grime, and beads of sweat glistened on his hairy chest.

"Just wouldn't handle any more."

A few sportswriters clustered around, leaning close to ask their questions over the noise.

"I was just settin' back, ridin' easy," he was telling them. "I'm just awful disappointed. I mean, here I am settin' here, tryin' to hold back, and—WHAM!"

In the area where the drivers' families were gathered, Bobby Isaac's wife, a young woman with a thin, pretty, country face and long, black hair, the mother of young twins, sat in her black Lincoln Continental talking about her husband's streak of bad luck.

"Here of late it's happened quite a lot," she said. "He hasn't been able to finish many races this year. . . . Well, he's been racing about twenty years now altogether and he's used to it, he handles it purty well."

Her husband came up to the car on the other side. He was wearing a sport shirt and tight slacks. His hair was wet from his recent shower, and his lean face was red and stony, with a cold, hard look in his eyes. He was carrying his helmet and a handbag containing other gear. He jerked open the car door and slammed the gear into the back. His wife leaned across the seat and said something in his ear. He nodded, his expression unchanged. His wife looked mildly surprised. He closed the car door, walked around to the front, and stood looking out at the track. A brochure advertising an upcoming race in Delaware protruded from his hip pocket. He took it out, looked at it, crumpled it in both hands, and flung it to the ground. A reporter approached him and asked a question. He looked away, shook his head no, and the reporter retreated.

Lap forty-six. Coming down the frontstretch, Benny Parsons' Mercury, damaged earlier in the wreck, spurted flames from beneath the engine, and trailing a great cloud of white smoke, it coasted around the track powerless, the engine blown, spilling oil as it went. Parsons steered the car down the pit road and straight behind the wall. The yellow flag came out again. Crews of shirtless young men in pickup trucks took to the track to dump fifty-pound sacks of Sta-Dri on the oil. Drivers started coming in for another pit stop.

During a regular pit stop, a driver gets two right-side tires, twenty-two gallons of gas, a cold drink, and has his windshield cleaned—all in about twenty seconds (the record is less than fifteen seconds). A pit stop by a fast, experienced crew is a sight to behold. The men tense as they wait to leap over the wall as soon as their car comes to a stop. Two men hold air wrenches, testing them in the air, the lugs held in their mouths. The jack man and gas man bend over their equipment. The tire man crouches, one huge wheel under each arm. They are over the wall the moment the car screeches to a halt. As the right side of the car lurches into the air on the jack, the gas man is already emptying his first can into the tank. From the other side of the wall, men clean the windshield with long-handled squeegees and pass the driver a drink in a cup set in a metal ring attached to a pole. The old tires come off, fresh ones are slapped on. One man on each wheel applies the lugs, the wrench man tightening them close behind his fingers. The gas man finishes his second can, the jack man yanks the jack from beneath the car. Wrench men rush to the wall, whipping air hoses out of the way. The gas cap goes on, and the driver spins away, tires burning, gas spewing from the overflow. A pit stop can, and often does, mean the difference between winning and losing, and there is keen competition among the crews. Each spring at Rockingham, the pit crews have their own races.

Larry Smith was not concerned now about the speed of his pit stops. He was hoping only to get back in the race. His car had been pulled behind the wall, and he and his mechanic, Kenny Barlow, were working desperately over the engine.

The race was going according to prediction thus far. It was still a two-man race, Pearson and Allison, with Allison seeming to have a slight advantage. Petty was running well back in third, and his car was handling poorly.

Once a race gets well under way, as this one now was, the drivers having found their grooves and set their paces, it takes on a certain droning monotony. Beyond the first five positions, it is difficult to know who is running where. The lead changes that take place are not necessarily significant. For the drivers it becomes a matter of endurance: Stay as close to the front as possible without putting unnecessary stress on the car, hope that the car holds together and that nobody gets in the way. Some of the fans still hang on every turn and position change, but many lose interest, especially in the infield.

Where the drivers' families waited, only a few were now watching the race. Some sat in air-conditioned cars with windows rolled up and engines running. One wife was curled on the front seat of her car, taking a nap.

A lot of people in the infield were sleeping, too. Many had given up on the race for the time being and returned to other pursuits. Cars still cruised. Motorcycles and minibikes buzzed about. A Frisbee drifted through the air. High on a platform on the back of a pickup truck, a poker game had resumed. A fight broke out at the entrance to the women's toilet down by the third turn.

"Look at 'at!" somebody yelled. "Goddamn fight! Hell of a fight!"

A dirty, scraggly-haired, washed-out blonde was scuffling with a younger, dark-haired girl. The two of them fell against a nearby car, the blonde on top. The blonde's left arm was in a cast, and she was using it as a club to beat her opponent on the head. She had trouble aiming her blows, however, because the younger girl was distracting her by pulling her head back with two handsful of bleached blond hair.

A dumpy, gray-haired woman waddled up on heavy legs, yelling, trying to separate the two, pulling at the blonde, giving the younger girl an opportunity to land a couple of quick blows.

"Come on, Kay!" the old woman said, pulling now at the dark-haired girl. "Stop it! Come on, Kay!"

"I didn't start it," the girl was screaming.

The old lady was between them now, pushing the younger girl toward the toilet door. The blonde followed yelling, "Ain't no goddamn bitch goina accuse me of that!"

A young man ran up. He was barefoot and barechested, wearing bluejeans with no belt, his dark hair oily, a snake and dagger tattooed on his left biceps. He held a can of beer and a cigarette in his right hand. His arrival temporarily distracted the combatants, the old woman seizing the opportunity to push the younger girl into the toilet.

The young man turned to the blonde.

"Git up to the car," he said forcefully.

The blonde made a move toward the toilet.

"She ain't goina crawl my goddamn ass!"

He grabbed her shoulder.

"You go on git the goddamn hell up to the car, I told you! I'll slap the fuckin' shit out of ye!"

"You ain't slappin' nobody!"

"Shut your fuckin' mouth and git on back up to the car!" He gave her a shove in the proper direction.

The blonde began to slink away, catlike, turning, snarling, but leaving.

A big crowd had been attracted by this diversion, and the young man now turned on them.

"What the fuck you lookin' at? Git out of here! This ain't no goddamn sightseein' attraction!"

"What started that?" somebody asked as the crowd began to break up.

"Prob'ly the heat."

The sun was unrelenting, and a lot of people had sought shelter from it. The temperature was now at 95 degrees, and the heat of the asphalt on pit row could be felt through shoe soles. Junior Johnson soaked a clean grease rag in ice water and draped it over his head as he stood with one foot on the pit rail watching his car on the track. He always worked as chief of the pit crew. In the cars on the track, the temperature was now at least 150 degrees, and it was beginning to take its toll.

On the frontstretch, Richard Brooks reached for a water bottle that he kept in the car, and as he took a drink, he let his car get out of shape and drift into the high-speed groove—just as Buddy Baker was about to pass at 150 miles per hour. Baker was running fourth. He caught Brooks' right front, flipped him around, and pushed him at full power along the wall, the nose of his car hard in Brooks' side. Halfway through the turn, the

cars finally untangled and dropped down off the high bank.
Brooks' car was destroyed. He was unhurt.

Baker made it around the track and back into the pits. His
crew, led by Maurice Petty, vaulted over the wall to inspect the
damage, which seemed confined to the left front. The front left
tire was chewed to shreds.

"Over here, over here!" Petty was yelling to his other crewmen.

Richard Brooks walked into the pits and was immediately
hustled off to the tower by a radio network spotter to tell
the listeners what had happened. The sportswriters gathered
around him when he had finished his brief performance on the
air.

"It was my fault," he said. "Where Buddy came from I'll
never know. I was five or six car lengths in front of him on the
backstretch, and I didn't have any idea he'd pulled up on me.
I had just taken a drink of water from a jug I keep in the car. I
was messin' with the jug and I didn't look in the mirror goin'
into number one. I should have, but I didn't."

He slumped against his wrecked car.

"Man, it pisses me off to make a mistake like that. I'm sorry
Buddy got messed up, but I 'specially hate it for Bill."

Bill Seifert was an independent driver who owned the car.
He had three race cars, and he'd advertised all of them for sale
a week earlier, hoping to get enough money to build one good
car.

Maurice Petty got Buddy Baker's car back on the track, but
Baker made only a few laps and brought it in. It was hopeless,
and he pulled the car behind the wall and climbed out angrily.
The sportswriters and radio spotters didn't bother him immediately. They knew that he always needed a little time to cool
off after something like that. It never took him long. It was
quite a thing to see, in fact. The most frustrating and disap-
pointing things possible could happen to him—and often did—
and he would stamp off furiously, flinging things and cursing
under his breath, seeking a place to be alone. A few minutes
later he would return to face the reporters completely com-

posed, relaxed, laughing, cracking jokes about his bad luck. When he had calmed himself, he came into the drivers' lounge where it was cool and flopped into a chair. Nobody said anything at first, then a sportswriter said, "Buddy . . . does it hurt?"

"Man, you know it hurts. Especially when you got a chance to win." He sighed. "I can't feel *too* bad about it, 'cause we're probably both lucky to be alive. Man, I tagged 'im, and I kept the power on. I cocked the wheels so he wouldn't start flippin' and stood on it 'til both of us got out of the groove. If we'd stopped in the groove, it could've been a ba-a-d scene."

People are often surprised the first time they hear Baker speak. He is such a big man that it seems he should have a deep and booming voice. It is just the opposite, a shy, quiet voice. He laughed now.

"Usually I got time to cuss a little 'fore I wreck," he said, "but this one happened so fast I didn't have time to say a word."

All week there had been rumors around the track that Baker was going to quit Petty and start driving for Harry Hyde in one of Nord Krauskopf's Dodges. The newspapers had carried stories about it already, but Baker himself had said nothing. When the sportswriters asked him about it now, he grinned.

"Man, let's just talk about this race today."

Larry Smith was back on the track. He had lost eighty laps before he got the car running right again. He'd put on a new carburetor and a distributor, and the engine seemed okay now. When the race started again after the Brooks-Baker wreck, Smith came out strong, pushing hard to make up some of the lost time. He found himself running close behind Cecil Gordon. He was faster than Gordon, but Gordon wouldn't let him pass.

It was understandable that Gordon might not want to be passed by a rookie like Larry Smith. It would be understandable, too, if he were envious of Smith. Some of the top-running independent drivers couldn't understand why a company like Carling would choose to sponsor an untested driver like Smith over one of them. Many of them had struggled along for years trying to latch onto a sponsor without any luck, making good showings for the equipment they had, knowing that they could do better if only they had more money, and here was this rookie, Smith, with a sponsor his first year.

At thirty-one, Gordon was a year older than Smith. He was born and still lived in a small community called Horseshoe in the North Carolina mountains. After high school, where he had been a catcher on the baseball team, he'd gone to work as a boiler tender at the chemical plant where his father worked. He had sacrificed and worked hard to be able to race, and he was just now beginning to get together the equipment that he needed, although he was still doing the work on his car in the basement of his house. The year before, he had finished third in the point standings and had turned a nice profit for the first time. It had taken him nearly five years to get the small sponsorship that he had finally picked up this year from Collins and Aikman, a textile company that had developed a fire-resistant fabric from which the uniforms of Gordon and his crew members were made.

Gordon, who had been nicknamed "Flash" and had that painted atop his car, didn't drive to win races. He drove for points. Points were given for the number of races entered and the number of laps run, as well as for the position finished (the system was changed for the 1974 season). Some of the top drivers, such as David Pearson, didn't do particularly well in the point standings because they entered only the big races and ignored the smaller ones. Gordon drove every race. He tried to stay out of trouble and finish as high as he could, and he had been doing very well at it.

Larry Smith had made four or five laps riding the bumper of Gordon's bright yellow Mercury, holding back, looking for a chance to get around on the outside, growing increasingly impatient. Coming off the fourth turn, he decided to hell with it. He was going to get around one way or another. He saw an opening on the inside and shot for it. At the same time, Gordon had begun to pull to the inside, motioning for Smith to pass outside. It was too late. Smith smacked Gordon's fender, sending

Gordon careening across the track and into the outside wall. Smith continued around the track, his car only slightly damaged.

Cecil Gordon's car was pulled behind the pit wall by a wrecker. His crew swarmed over the car to inspect the damage even before it had been lowered to the ground. A small crowd gathered around the car. The right front wheel was gone, and the fender, hood, and grill were twisted, bent, and torn. Gordon was smoldering, his eyes intense slits. He walked around the front of the car and stood staring at the damage with his hands on his hips. A short, stocky man, his hair carefully styled and combed over his ears, muttonchop sideburns sprouting from his jaws, he wore tennis shoes that were decorated with a blue star and red stripes. His anger was justified. He had been running fifth in points this season, and this wreck could set him back considerably, possibly costing him several thousand dollars in earnings in addition to the damage.

"Right in the fuckin' ass end of me," he muttered.

He squatted to look beneath the car, where crew members were crawling, assaying the damage. It looked bad, too bad to get back into the race.

"Fix it!" he snapped.

A crew member looked up helplessly.

"I just want it good enough to roll," Gordon said, "and that motherfucker can look out, good buddy."

Crew members ran for tools. Gordon stood, whirled, walked over, and stepped across the steel rail onto the pit road, and stalked over to the concrete inside track wall, where he sat holding his helmet in one hand. The caution flag was still out, and when Gordon saw Larry Smith coming, he stepped over the wall and walked out onto the track. A NASCAR official blew his whistle and hollered, but Gordon didn't stop. As Smith rode past, Gordon violently shook his fist at him. Smith looked startled, and turned his head to look back as he passed.

"Go to the truck and git me a tire wrench," Gordon told one of his crew members when he had come back to his car. "I'm goin' back out and trounce his ass." He looked at his damaged car again. "I might as well finish wipin' it out with his ass."

Kenny Barlow, Smith's mechanic, hurried across the infield from his pit on the back side of the track. Smith had sent him to apologize to Gordon.

As soon as Gordon saw Barlow, he charged at him, grabbing him by the front of his new Carling Black Label uniform shirt, pushing him back, screaming into his face.

"What do you mean he can't see! He run right into the back of me! You tell him you don't let me see him after this goddamn race! Don't let me see him after this fuckin' race, see. . . ."

Gordon's older brother and chief mechanic, Lee, intervened, pulling his brother away.

"You better git the fuck out of here!" Lee Gordon shouted to Barlow.

He pulled his brother off to the side.

"We'll git him in a back alley," he was saying. "We'll git 'im."

But Cecil Gordon would not be content with getting Smith in any alley. He wanted to do it in front of seventy-two thousand people and the cameras of "Wide World of Sports." After a while the crew got his car able to roll again, but barely. He limped back onto the track, moving very slowly, like an old lady on a Sunday drive, keeping on the apron. He made three laps before he got a shot at Smith. On the fourth, as Smith came around, Gordon pulled high, but Smith had been watching him, and darted quickly beneath him. NASCAR officials gave Gordon the black flag on that lap, and he came back into the pits. Lin Kuchler, the top NASCAR official present, took him aside for a talk, and Gordon seemed to calm somewhat after that. Then Joe Frasson came up smiling, put his arm around Gordon's shoulders, and they walked off down pit row talking.

After 184 laps, the halfway point in the race, only 24 cars were still running. Six were out because of wrecks. Mechanical problems had claimed the rest. Bobby Allison was leading. Pearson was second. Petty was falling farther back in third. And Fred Lorenzen was even farther back in fourth, with little hope of bettering his position unless the top three cars fell out. On the next lap, Pearson passed Allison again. He held the lead for eleven laps before Allison squeezed back around him.

Some of the drivers were suffering badly from the heat now. G. C. Spencer had been as high as sixth position, but he had fallen to eighth when he pulled into the pits and told his crew that he had to have relief. Spencer crawled from his car and collapsed on a table in the shade of the garage. Somebody brought a cold towel and put it across his face.

In the late forties and early fifties, Grover Cleveland Spencer was a real flash on the dirt tracks of Tennessee, Kentucky, Indiana, and Ohio. He was working in a car plant in Evansville, Indiana, when he first started racing modifieds. They were soon calling him the "King of the Modifieds," and his '34 Chevy coupe was widely known as the *Flying Saucer*. By 1958, he was ready to move to the big time. He came to the Southern 500 that year and drove a Chevrolet owned by Buck Baker. He finished 16th and won $315. He was 33 years old at the time. He had been running Grand National races since, and now at 47 he was one of the older drivers. This was the 375th Grand National race that he had entered, and he had never won even one of them. In all those years, he had won only $180,000, less than a top driver would take in a single season. His best year had been in 1966, when he won $25,000. This had not been a good year at all. It had gotten off to a bad start at Daytona, when his good friend Friday Hassler was killed and his own car was wiped out in the same wreck. He sat in the garage and cried openly that day. "I'm gittin' too damn old for this," he had said. And he had begun to talk of quitting. He didn't quit, but he did cut back some. This was only his tenth race for the season, and his winnings had amounted to less than $7,000, barely enough to buy tires.

Now the heat had him. Joe Frasson had volunteered to drive relief and was now gunning his Dodge around the track. Spencer sat slump-shouldered and exhausted on a tool box in the garage, drinking a soft drink, the wet towel draped around his neck, a lonely figure, gaunt, with a high forehead, thin hair, and leathery skin, his face deeply lined because he had only two teeth (the rest were all knocked out in wrecks; he had false teeth, he said, but only wore them for chewing steak, which wasn't often).

"ACTION!" the loudspeakers were screaming. "ACTION IN THE SECOND TURN!"

Lap 276. Somehow Larry Smith and Joe Frasson had tangled, and suddenly it was a repeat of the earlier big wreck, cars spinning and darting all over the place.

Patricia Smith saw the crowd in the grandstands come to its feet, and then she saw all the smoke and dust rising over the far end of the track. She jumped up with fear in her eyes and began scanning the track for her husband's car. When he didn't come back around, she stood looking in the direction of the wreck, biting her lower lip, a transistor radio pressed to her ear. Moments later, she slumped to her seat, relief on her face.

"He's okay," she yelled to her sister-in-law. "He's out of the race, but he's okay."

Eight cars had been involved in this one. Pearson and Allison were almost caught by it. Allison had shot low on the grass to avoid it, while Pearson had gone high. It was the worst wreck of the day. Of the eight cars involved, five were left strewn around the track. Jabe Thomas, Elmo Langley, Dean Dalton, Joe Frasson, and Larry Smith were out. Frank Warren, Ed Negre, and Jim Vandiver had gone to the pits and were able to continue with repairs. An ambulance backed up to the door of the track hospital carrying Jabe Thomas. The attendants helped him out on his feet. He had taken a nasty blow on his head, and he was rubbing his forehead. Somebody handed him a Dr. Pepper, his favorite drink, before he was led inside, followed by Brother Bill, who always stood by at the hospital after a wreck.

Dean Dalton's car was towed into the pits by a wrecker. He was hanging out of the window, a lean, blond young man from Asheville, North Carolina, looking tired and excited.

"Frasson caused that one," he was saying. "Joe Frasson pulled right straight up on Smith down here. Wudn't nothin' for Smith to do but hit 'im. Frasson caused it all."

Frasson came up pit row with big strides, and Cecil Gordon walked down to greet him, both of them smiling broadly.

"He got into it that time, didn't he?" Gordon said gleefully. "Run right into the ass end of me."

"I believe I'll go have a beer on that one," Gordon said.

Frasson told the reporters that the wreck was caused by Smith. "He drove right down into me," he said.

On the opposite side of the track, one of Larry Smith's crew members came up to him and said, "Frasson's on the radio over yonder blaming that on you."

That irritated Smith. "He pulled up on *me!* I was following Petty through the traffic, about five lengths behind. Frasson pulled over to let Petty pass, and he cut right back up into me. Shit, I was runnin' thirty miles an hour faster. I smacked 'im. I couldn't stop. I just dead-centered his ass."

His hair was slick with sweat, and his white uniform was smeared with grease. He opened a can of his sponsor's beer and took a long drink.

"I got out of the car and went over to where Joe was standin', I said, 'Joe, what'n hell happened?' He said, 'I didn't see you.'" He shook his head. "Shit, I plowed right into his ass."

I asked if he thought Frasson might have wrecked him deliberately because of the earlier business with Gordon. It had looked to me as if there had been a little game of get-the-rookie going on.

"Man, you don't wreck these cars intentionally. You just don't do it in this business. It's too risky and too expensive."

He walked over and looked at his car, which was battered from every side. It would take a lot of work and a lot of money to get it running again.

"Tore all to hell," he said morosely.

He took his beer over and sat on the back of his truck.

"Damn, what a day!" he said. "What a *week!*"

G. C. Spencer stood in the garage looking at the wreck of his car that had been dumped before him, a twenty-thousand-dollar machine reduced to worthless junk. The second time this year. He looked in despair, and nobody approached him until Joe Frasson came striding up. Then his expression changed, and he forced a smile.

"Smith wiped it out," Frasson said. "He had the whole fuckin' top end of the racetrack. He come down, run right into the ass end of me. I started to run into the back of Elmo. . . . I'm sorry."

Spencer grinned. "That's okay," he said.

When Frasson had gone, Spencer stood, a haggard, dejected, slump-shouldered figure, staring blankly at his car, his mind obviously on other things. His car was gone. He had lost more money this year than most workingmen make. He'd seen a friend killed. And his body was reminding him that he could no longer stand up to the stresses of racing 500 miles in 150-degree heat. Twenty-five years of racing lay behind him, and now he was going to give it up, quit, haul this pile of junk back home to the hills of Tennessee and help his wife run her little antique shop.

Jabe Thomas sat in the drivers' lounge nursing a big raw spot on his forehead. A big country boy, forty-two years old, a service station operator from the Blue Ridge Mountains of Virginia, Thomas was agitated and still a little stunned from the blow he'd received in the wreck. When Little Joe Weatherly was killed in 1964, leaving open the position of Clown Prince of Stock Car Racing, the sportswriters had bestowed the title on Thomas. He was always telling corny jokes and "carrying on," making people laugh.

One time when a high-powered Yankee psychologist came down to do a study on stock car drivers—as they often do, trying to learn what makes them do what they do—some of the other drivers sent him over to talk to Jabe, as the story goes. Ol' Jabe, they knew, would send the guy back with something to work with. The first thing that Jabe did was to slip off his watch when the psychologist wasn't looking, then bend over pretending to pick it up off the ground.

"Oh, dropped my watch," he said, examining it closely, then holding it to his ear.

"Did you break it?" asked the psychologist.

"Naw," said Jabe, "it landed on its hands."

The other drivers break up telling that.

Thomas was rubbing the red spot on his forehead.

"How you feel, Jabe?" somebody asked.

"I don't feel like the Lone Ranger, I tell you that. Boys, that thang 'bout knocked the doo-doo outta me. I tell you what. Wolcott couldn't've give me a lick like that. I might take up boxin'."

"What happened?" a sportswriter asked.

"I tore my car up, that's what happened."

"Tear up Elmo's too?"

"It wiped mine out, got all the way into the motor of Elmo's. I know I hit him a hell of a lick, I know that. . . . How come it started?"

Frasson was there, and he started loudly telling his story again of how "Larry Smith had the whole goddamn half the race-track" and came down on him.

The press box called, and Thomas told a questioner what had happened.

"Let me go back and find Betty [his wife]," he said, jumping up suddenly. "I bet she's havin' a fit."

Somebody asked what he was going to do about the rest of the season now that his car was torn up.

"I don't know what I'm goina do," he said. "I tore up one last week and one this week."

"How'd you like to be me?" said Frasson. "I tore up two today."

"Hell, Joe," said Buddy Baker. "You wrecked everything but the pace car."

"I sure hope I got a lot of good race fans to send me a little money," Thomas said, "or I won't be back racin' anytime soon. 'Cause I ain't got no car. I ain't got nothin'."

He recalled then that he'd once let Richard Petty borrow a car when he needed one.

"I'm goina go see if I can borrow me a car," he said, brightening.

The last part of the race was a two-man race for certain: Allison-Pearson, then Pearson-Allison. Petty was far back in third. He'd been blistering tires frequently in the last half and having to stop to change them. With 20 laps to go, Allison, in the lead, whipped into the pits and took on 10 gallons of gas in 12 seconds. Pearson came in on the next lap, got his gas in 7 seconds, and roared back onto the track with a lead of 3.8 seconds. But Allison was whittling away the lead with every lap. At lap 352, Pearson's lead was down to 3 seconds, 2.7 seconds at lap 354, 1.2 seconds 3 laps later, and by lap 359, Allison was hugging Pearson's bumper. Pearson began maneuvering to keep him there. The crowd was standing, waving and cheering wildly. It promised to be a close and terrifically exciting finish.

Five laps from the end, Pearson pushed into the fourth turn just a tiny bit too hard and drifted high toward the wall, his burning tires sending up little puffs of blue smoke as he fought to regain position. It was too late. Allison dropped low and shot around him. Pearson didn't have a chance after that. Allison took the checkered flag flashing across the finish line two lengths ahead of Pearson. Allison's crew threw up their arms and leaped into the air. It was the second year in a row that Allison had won the Southern 500. For Pearson, who had never won the race, it was the fourth time in five years that he had finished second.

Allison coasted around the track and was met on the front-stretch by his jubilant crew members, who piled onto the car, sitting on the hood and trunk and clinging to the windows, as he steered it toward the small fence-enclosed victory lane, where waited champagne, Coca-Cola, race queens, a gallery of photographers, track officials, and a garland of plastic red roses.

"I've never had a tougher race," he told the radio network reporter who squeezed in and thrust a microphone in his face.

In the press box, Bill Kizer, the track PR man, began compiling the final statistics for the sportswriters. The race had lasted 3 hours, 54 minutes, and 46 seconds, and only 18 of the 40 starting cars were still running at the end. Allison's average speed was 128.124 miles per hour. There had been 30 lead changes among 7 drivers. Allison had led 13 times for 229 laps, Pearson 11 times for 123 laps. The other drivers had led only under caution flags. There had been 5 of those for 43 laps.

Bobby Allison had won $21,040. David Pearson got $11,190. Richard Petty had finished several laps back in third and won $6,890. Fred Lorenzen finished fourth for $4,940. LeeRoy Yarbrough, driving in relief for H. B. Bailey, took fifth place and $4,830. The other top 10 finishers were Buddy Arrington, Dave Marcis, Jim Vandiver, Marty Robbins, and Coo Coo Marlin, in that order. Bobby Isaac got last-place money of $760.

The grandstands were emptying. Cars and trucks jammed the infield roads, rushing to be among the first out. But thousands of people were now streaming across the track and through the pit gates to mingle with the drivers, the crews, and the cars— especially the cars. They stood stroking the cars, caressing them as one might a loved horse that had been run hard. Those cars that did not lie in destruction now sat with their once-gleaming finishes chipped and scratched, flecked with asphalt, filmed with oil and dirt. Crew members moved about purposefully, backing trucks and trailers into position to load race cars, gathering up equipment, eager to bring the long, hot day to an end.

A man approached Maurice Petty and asked him to pose for a photograph with his attractive wife, and Petty did, grinning, squinting into the sun, his hat cocked to one side, his arm around the woman's waist.

"Hey," called one of his brother's crew members, "tell 'er she can get one with Petty's oil man right here."

A group of men stood looking under the hood of one of the race cars. "'Nother words," one of them was saying, "the cam lifts so high that you got to have a spacer. That's what I was thinkin'."

At a concession stand in the infield, two men, pot-bellied, shirtless, sunburned, bleary-eyed, and sweating, had realized that it was all over now for another year and they hadn't scored again. They were swilling beer and trying to put the make on a middle-aged woman in the concession stand.

"Come on, honey," one was saying. "We'll show you what a good time is."

She was laughing at them.

A long-haired young man came up for a pack of cigarettes. The men eyed him suspiciously.

"You hear about that knifin' last night?" one of them asked him.

"Yeah, I heard about it," he said uneasily, picking up his cigarettes and moving warily away. He looked back over his shoulder as he went, but the men had already returned their attentions to the woman.

"Come on now, what time you git off? . . ."

David Pearson was sprawled on a bench in the locker room, his face crimson from the heat and smudged with track film. Richard Petty sat on a bench in a corner, his uniform unzipped, a big cup of ice water hanging limply in his hand, resting his head against a bank of lockers. Other drivers, equally exhausted, occupied other benches. A few were showering or toweling down. Sportswriters had crowded into the little room and gathered in clumps around Pearson and Petty.

"I can't remember a rougher race," Pearson was telling them. "I'm sure I drove harder than I ever have before. I *know* it's the hottest I ever been in a race car. I'd almost bet you that the bottoms of my feet are blistered."

The sportswriters wanted to know what had happened there at the end.

"I just flat got my fanny outrun," he said. "That's what happened. It's that simple. . . . I thought for a while I could outrun 'im, but when he caught up with me so quick after that last pit stop, I knew it was over. Man, it was a helpless feelin' watchin' 'im come up on me in my rear-view mirror. When he caught me so quick, I knew I didn't have a chance. He was flyin'. I done ever'thing I could, but it wudn't enough. I just had one problem—Bobby was faster'n I was. It would've took a miracle to beat 'im. . . ."

Petty was still complaining about the curburetor rules.

"We've had to run flat out from the start just to keep up with the Chevy," he was saying, talking about the problems he'd been having all season. "Heck, if we could loaf like the Chevy does, then our chances of havin' problems would decrease, understand?

" 'Nother words, if the Chevy had the same size restrictor plate as the rest, things would be just the opposite. The Fords and Chrysler products would be outrunnin' the Chevy like it's outrunnin' us now. Why not experiment until we find a size that would make the Chevy equal instead of so much faster?

"I had trouble today, but it wouldn't've mattered. Speedwise, there was three classes out there today—Allison in a class by himself, Pearson in another one, and then me and all the others. You see what I mean? 'Nother words, if everybody couldn't see that the Chevy and the Mercury was the fastest and had the advantage, everybody was blind!" He laughed.

Pearson stood and began to take off his sweat-dampened uniform. It was hard to imagine that it had once been white. As he was stepping out of it, a photographer snapped a picture.

"Hey, Pearson's goina be in one of them centerfolds, like Burt Reynolds," somebody said to laughter.

Pearson chuckled and went off to the shower.

Bobby Allison was escorted through the mob of fans and taken to the big steel tower on the outside of the first turn, where he climbed wearily to the press box and sat on a table by the windows to face the reporters. He was tired but exhilarated, and he handled the questions easily.

"We definitely had the best car out there," he said in response to one question. "I believe it's the best ride in NASCAR. We *have* been beat a few times, but . . .

"The Wood car is always regarded as the top car, or one of the top cars, on the circuit, and David has done a good job with it, but I really feel like we beat 'em both today.

"A lot of people claim that once the Wood car gets out front late, it can't be beat. Well, we did it today."

Allison said that he had been quicker through the turns, particularly the third and fourth, and that had worked to his advantage, especially at the end.

"I knew I had to make my move there. I think David pretty well knew I was going to pass him there."

Allison went on to talk about the wrecks and how he had gotten through them, and how the new asphalt had made perception difficult in the first and second turns, and how Darlington is a hard track to drive anyway. Finally, a sportswriter said, "Bobby, why is it you're so hard to find when you *lose* one?"

He smiled. "I like to win, and any good winner is a bad loser. And I *am* only human. Like at Charlotte when I run over something and it cost me the race, I know myself well enough and I felt like I would be better off not to say anything. I have said the wrong things before, and I don't want to do it again."

Later, when he'd gone back to the locker room, one of the sportswriters told him about the complaints that some of the drivers had been making about the rules allowing the Chevrolet to be faster. He laughed.

"I've gotten used to that," he said. "Look, I've won eight major races this year, Ford's won eight, and the Chrysler products have won eight. Sounds pretty equal to me."

This time, Fred Lorenzen was the driver who was hard to find after the race, and none of the sportswriters would be able to write his response to the angry charges that had been made about his driving.

A crowd had gathered outside the locker room.

"I'm waitin' on David," said a girl with dark, flashing eyes who was standing on the fringe of the crowd. I might have guessed. She had "DAVID" written on her blue T-shirt in big Magic Marker letters that swelled across her enormous breasts. She had rolled up the T-shirt and tucked it under her breasts to lend them emphasis. She was pretty, twenty-three years old, with the features of the mixed-blood Indians who live along the eastern area of the North Carolina-South Carolina line. She was wearing blue jeans cut very short, the beltline low enough to expose her navel, and on her hair, which lay in curls on her shoulders, she wore a hat decorated with stars and red, white, and blue stripes.

I asked why she liked David Pearson.

"He's good-lookin'," she said. "And he's got a good personality. He's got a lot better personality than Bobby. Bobby don't have a good personality."

Had she met David Pearson?

"I've danced with 'im I don't know how many times. He's got such big arms. They wrap all the way around you—how come you askin' these questions anyhow?"

"For a book maybe."

"Well, you can put in there that I'd like to be Miss Purolator."

"You would? Why?"

"Then I could pull that much harder for the car. I've always been pullin' for the Mercury, ever since Cale drove it." She smiled. "And I could travel with 'em to all the races for nothin'."

She said that she usually went to several races a year, but always to Darlington, because she lived so close, and that her sister-in-law went with her. Her sister-in-law was standing nearby with two other girls. They were all in their twenties, and they were talking about what a good time they'd had at a race up at Bristol. The sister-in-law had "GO DAVIED" misspelled across the front of her sweatshirt.

"She was so-o-o polluted when she come down to that motel," one of the girls was saying, laughing.

"Well, you know how I slept, don't you?" asked another. "On the floor!"

"No, you didn't, Preston did."

"She didn't say she didn't sleep with Preston!" They all broke up over that.

David Pearson appeared at the locker room door now, smiling, looking somewhat refreshed after a long rest, his curly hair still wet from the shower. He was wearing a short-sleeved sport shirt and dark slacks. The crowd closed quickly around him.

"David Pearson! Git yo'self over this way!" cried the girl in the misspelled sweatshirt. "Don't y'all hang 'im up around the door! Push 'im this way!"

But Pearson was trapped, and it would be a long time before he could get away. He was signing autographs, posing for photographs, passing out postcards, chatting with the people who crushed in around him.

"David, wouldn't that dern Mercury run, son?" said an old man.

"We wouldn't've gone fifteen minutes more. I had a blowed head gasket."

"You done real good, David."

"David, you met my wife?"

"Fixin' to."

"Hey, David, how 'bouta kiss?"

"Where's your old man?"

"Oh, he's over'n the pits."

"Okay then," pecking her on the cheek.

There in the middle of the crowd, standing on tiptoes, eagerly awaiting her turn was a beautician with teased hair from Tabor City with her two friends (one a strange-looking girl wearing—could it possibly be?—pedal pushers). They were in their late twenties or early thirties, all unmarried, obviously women who had spent their whole lives trying earnestly to believe that it *really* wasn't good looks but what a person was on the *inside* that counted, while the evidence daily mounted to the contrary. And so they made do with fantasies, with fleeting moments of contact with men they dreamed about. Men like David Pearson. For several years, they had been going to five or six races a year, always fanning out through the pits after the race, chasing frantically after drivers to get autographs and pictures. They always made certain to find David Pearson. The beautician had sixty-five David Pearson autographs, and almost as many pictures of herself posing with him.

What was it about Pearson? I later asked her. Sex appeal?

"No, now Buddy Baker's got more sex appeal. David's good-lookin' now, but he's just a real nice person. He's got a good personality. He's got the best personality of all the drivers, I think. Now, you take Bobby Allison, he don't have a good personality. That's just the way he is. But David . . ."

She was in ecstasy now, posing with Pearson's arm around her, as one of her friends snapped their picture. Then she took the camera to take her friends' pictures. "She hollered herself hoarse for you, David," she said of the girl in pedal pushers, who was now posing beside him, smiling. The girl wore thick glasses that magnified her eyes grotesquely.

One of the girls noticed a St. Christopher medal that Pearson was wearing and asked to look at it.

"David," asked the beautician warily, "are you Catholic?"

"Naw, somebody gimme that."

"Can I have it, David?" asked the girl who had it. "I always wanted something of yours."

"What's it for?" somebody asked.

"'Sposed to be good luck."

"If it's your good-luck charm, I don't want it," said the girl.

Pearson told her it was all right, she could have it.

"No, David! Let me have it!" cried the beautician, trying to snatch it away from her friend.

"David!" cried the girl, clinging to the gift. "That's mine," she said to her friend. "He give it to me!"

"You got to give me somethin', too, David," said the beautician, plaintively. "I got to have somethin' of yours."

Pearson laughed. "I ain't got nothin' else."

"Gimme this curl then," she said, running her fingers into his hair.

He pulled back, laughing. "No, don't you . . ."

"David, don't you have *somethin*'? Surely you've got somethin'. A penny! Gimme a penny!"

He dug into his pocket.

The party girls had been watching this demonstration with disgust, waiting for their turn.

"For heaven's sakes," said one of them. "Why don't they leave 'im alone. I bet he's give out. I know I would be give *completely* out." In the South, that means very tired.

Finally, after the crowd had thinned to only a few people,

one of the girls went over and extricated Pearson and he walked over to where the others stood smiling.

"Whew!" he said. "I'm give out. Got anything to drink?"

"My Rambler's over here in the first turn," said the girl who had spelled "David" with an *e*. But Pearson decided not to go to her car. His son brought him a soft drink, and he stood chatting about the race and laughing with the party girls. Then the beautician was back.

"David, I hate to bother you again, but the camera messed up."

They did this a lot so that they could pose with his arm around them twice. He posed again, while the party girls looked on sullenly.

"I 'preciate it so-o-o much, David," the beautician gushed, and she and her friends were off to their dull little town to await the next race and dream about having a big, strong, good-looking, curly-haired race-driving man like David Pearson to cook and care for.

The crowds in the pits had almost dissipated now, and David Pearson's son had driven his black Lincoln Continental over near the drivers' lounge and parked it. Pearson broke away from the party girls saying, "Y'all be good."

"If we can't be good, we'll be keerful," one of them said, giggling.

Pearson walked over to his car and began rummaging through some food baskets in the trunk for a sandwich.

"He told me I could write his name all over my Rambler!" the girl in the sweatshirt was telling her friends as they left. "He said to be sure and spell it right."

While Pearson had been trapped in that mob of fans, Bobby Allison had come out of the locker room almost unnoticed. Nobody accosted him, and he slipped around the edge of the crowd and walked over toward the pits where his young son was waiting for him. Together, they walked toward his race car, which was already loaded onto its trailer, ready to leave for the next race.

So it was over. Two kids ran through the empty grandstands kicking beer cans down through the concrete seats, setting up a clatter that could be heard in the infield. The race cars and big trucks were gone from the pits and garages. The lights of the press box shone in the gathering twilight as the sportswriters drank free beer and finished their stories. Only a few stragglers remained in the infield.

The infield was a mess, a great sea of garbage. The toilets stank unbearably, the commodes all plugged and overflowing, the walls shit-smeared, cigarette butts asail in ankle-deep urine on the floors.

I walked across the infield with my friend, Bill Lee, picking my way through the beer cans, liquor bottles, food wrappers, chicken bones, watermelon rinds, cardboard boxes, newspapers, broken lawn furniture, shards of Styrofoam ice chests, food remains, discarded clothing and shoes, and all the rest. A few people were scavenging through the trash for lost coins and other valuables.

"You know," I was telling my friend, "it was all here! Everything. The whole works encapsulated in this racetrack this weekend. America, man! This is what it's all about. If this ain't America, what is? I mean, if a foreigner wanted to know what this country was all about, all he'd have to do is come to Darlington and spend a weekend in the infield at the Southern 500. This is it, man!"

"You need a beer," he said.

We headed for the press box to see if the sportswriters had drunk up all the free stuff yet. As we passed through the press gate, I remembered something.

"I wonder what happened to that 'possum?" I said.

Epilogue

The Next Season

AFTER THE RACE at Darlington, Bobby Allison continued his streak, winning big races at Charlotte and Rockingham, giving him the best season of his career. He won ten races for the year, and more money—$284,000—than any other driver. At the end of the season, he quit his ride with the Richard Howard-Junior Johnson Chevrolet, and with his share of the winnings, he went into business for himself, building his own cars to run the next season. He took his sponsor, Coca-Cola, with him. But in his own car, he did not fare nearly as well, winning only two races and $100,000 in the following season.

David Pearson won only one of the season's seven remaining races after Darlington—at Dover, Delaware. When he returned the following season, however, his Mercury was the hottest car on the circuit, seemingly unbeatable. He won eleven of the eighteen races that he started and nearly $214,000. At the end of the year, he was named the Martini & Rossi American Driver of the Year.

Richard Petty won three of the remaining races after Darlington, all of them on short tracks, but they helped him edge out Bobby Allison in the points race, and he won his fourth national championship, the first driver to do so. He started the following season by winning the Daytona 500, the biggest race of the year, but after that he won only five more races, all at small tracks, and he finished the season with less than $160,-000 in winnings, a poor year for Petty. But he returned to start the 1974 season by winning the Daytona 500 for the fifth time.

Bobby Isaac quit his ride in the Nord Krauskopf-Harry Hyde Dodge shortly after the Darlington race. He had driven for the team for eight years and had set twenty-eight speed records in the Dodge. He gave no public reason for quitting. He finished the season driving a small-engine Ford for Bud Moore, and came back in the car the following season. But his bad luck continued, and he finished only six races in the top ten. Then during the August race at Talladega, Isaac suddenly brought his car into the pits in midrace, got out, and walked away, waving people away. He was leaving racing.

"Something told me to quit," he told a reporter the next day. "I don't know anything else to do but abide by it. I had no thoughts of quitting before the race. Nothing happened on the track to influence me."

Isaac didn't stay retired long, however. He was soon driving again at a couple of small tracks in lower divisions, and when the 1974 season began, he was back.

As rumored, Buddy Baker quit driving for Richard Petty after the Darlington race. He took over the Dodge that Bobby Isaac had deserted. He won only two races the next year, however, and as the season neared an end, Nord Krauskopf, the millionaire insurance man who owned the car, pulled it out of racing because of NASCAR rules and threatened to keep it out unless the rules were changed. Baker quit the team in mid-1974 to drive for yet another car owner.

The Darlington race ended Fred Lorenzen's comeback. He went home to Illinois, got married, and missed the next few races. He returned for the Charlotte race a few weeks later, had a dispute with his car owner, Hoss Ellington, and left abruptly. He did not return. Track gossip had it that his new wife didn't want him to race any more.

G. C. Spencer took his wrecked car home to Tennessee from Darlington, planning never to race again. But after missing the rest of the season, it began to get to him. "When there's a race and I'm not there, I get nervous," he once told a reporter. "I'll turn all the radios on in the house and start walking the floors. It's something I can't really get away from." Spencer built a new car and took it to Daytona for the first race of the new season. He had decided to stick with his decision to quit driving, however, and he gave one of his crewmen a chance to break into big-time racing in the car. In the next race at Rockingham, Spencer stood on pit road watching as the young man sped away in the car. He put his hands on his hips and shook his head. "These fuckin' young boys, you can't tell 'em a goddamn thing!" he said. He was soon driving the car again himself.

"These hot dogs gotta have somebody to pass," he said in explanation.

Not having made the Darlington race, just one of many that he hadn't made, Wendell Scott, the black driver, left feeling discouraged and thinking of quitting. But, like Spencer, he had been around racing too long to quit easily. He started trying to get his old Ford ready to run again the next spring. He made one small-track race, and saw that if he were going to do any good, he'd have to get a new car. He went into debt twelve thousand dollars to buy a second-hand racer, a Mercury, and things began looking up. He thought that with the new car he might have a fairly decent season, certainly better than the year before, when he had trouble even getting into a race. The first race to which he took the car was at Talladega in May. He made the race. But Bill France had decided to increase the size of the field for the race from forty to sixty cars, despite complaints from some drivers who said that so many cars on such a fast track would be dangerous. Shortly after the race started, the biggest pile-up in NASCAR history occurred on the back-stretch. More than twenty cars were involved, and many of them were destroyed, the damage mounting to hundreds of thousands of dollars. Several drivers were hurt, and three were taken to a hospital in nearby Anniston. The most severely injured was Wendell Scott. His pelvis was crushed, his left leg broken in four places, the right leg in three. He had broken ribs, a damaged kidney, and more than seventy stitches were required to close a wound on his left arm. He remained in the hospital for more than a month before returning home to Virginia to recuperate. His new car was damaged beyond repair, and he was left with a twelve-thousand-dollar debt to pay and no car to race. "Tore it all to pieces before I made the first payment," he told me with resignation. "I got a long row to hoe. . . . This been my worst year, but it's been my best, too. I could've got killed. I'm just lucky to be livin', not goina let it worry me."

By fall, Wendell Scott had recovered enough to drive in a couple of sportsman races at small tracks near his home—and his son, Wendell, Jr., had also started to drive his father's old Ford in a few small-track races. Scott finally returned to big-time racing in the fall race at Charlotte, driving a car provided by another driver, Doc Faustina.

As yet another season started, I asked Scott if he intended to race.

"I don't plan to retire," he said. "I still plan to race, but I really don't know what my plans are. I'm hopin' somethin'll happen, but so far it don't look too good. I can't get in no more debts on no more cars, that's for sure."

Nothing good did happen for Wendell Scott, however, and big-time racing lost its only black driver.

Larry Smith left Darlington thinking that he probably had blown his chances for becoming Rookie of the Year, and with it, his new sponsorship and his future in racing. He was wrong.

At the NASCAR awards banquet in Daytona Beach the next February, Larry Smith stood at the podium smiling broadly, holding aloft the Rookie of the Year trophy.

"I set out to get it," he told the crowd, "I worked hard for it, and I got it!"

His sponsor had come through with a nice new contract, much better than he had hoped. He had a sleek new car to race, and a huge, impressive new van—a rolling billboard for Black Label beer—to haul it in. He wore red blazers now, with little company emblems on the pocket, and he attended a lot of cocktail parties and other social functions as the company's representative. He posed for magazine ads and did a TV commercial. And he was away from home even more. Later in the season, he hooked up with John Green, one of the best young mechanics in racing, who began looking after the car, giving Smith more time to handle matters more suited to a big-time stock car racing driver. He had not dreamed, he said, that things would work out so well so fast. He began to talk of becoming a big name, a superstar, within three years. His future looked bright indeed.

As his success had grown, however, his marriage had suffered, and he and his wife, Patricia, had separated.

Larry Smith was one of the first drivers I had talked with when I went to Darlington that first time. I had picked him out early to play a role in the book. I felt a rapport with him. We were the same age. We both had grown up in similar circumstances, among the same kind of people, in small towns only a hundred miles apart. I can't really say that I understood him, even after I got to know him better, but I liked him.

In August of 1973, the second race of the year at Talladega was held. I didn't go. I had started writing the book then, and I stayed home to work on it. As it happened, I was listening to a tape of a conversation I'd had with Larry Smith when I remembered that the race had started. I turned on the radio and tuned it to the race. At that moment there was a crash. A car had hit the wall in the first turn and slid off the high bank to the grass at the bottom. Larry Smith.

"Those safety crewmen were right there," Ken Squier, the announcer, was saying.

No other cars had been involved. With the yellow flag out, the other cars were making their pit stops. Ken Squier was describing all of this. There was no particular concern for Larry Smith. Just another racing wreck. He did mention that Smith had been taken to the track dispensary. Nothing unusual in that. Drivers were often shaken up after such a wreck.

Nevertheless, I suddenly had a very bad feeling. I thought it was probably the sheer coincidence of having been listening to Larry Smith's voice, then turning on the radio at the precise moment he hit the wall. I'd never had such a feeling. It was more than dread. I was almost certain that Larry Smith was dead.

Ken Squier had promised a report from the dispensary shortly. When it didn't come, I went outside and walked around, trying to shake the feeling.

As I was opening the door to come back inside a few minutes later, I heard Ken Squier's voice, hushed and somber . . .

"Larry Smith, a fine young driver, killed in that crash on the first turn . . ."

I stood for a minute listening as Ken Squier said, "It just didn't look that bad." He said it several times.

I went back out and sat on the steps in the hot sun. I thought about Larry Smith's wife. She hadn't wanted him to race. She was scared for him. Now her fears had proved justified. I wondered where she was and what she was feeling. I wondered the same thing about his father, who had helped instill in him the love of cars and speed, had helped him race. I wondered, too, about the validity of this sport in which the possibility of death is such a prime element. Was the glory, the money, the thrill of speed and competition worth this terrible risk?

Obviously, Larry Smith had thought so. To race was the most important thing in his life, he had once told me. Something he *had* to do. I never really had been able to understand that. That had been the difference between us. I could never understand it, and he could never explain it.

To me it had seemed almost predestined that he would die this way. I looked at all of the crashes, the fractures, the ruptures and cuts and bruises of his past and saw a pattern of doom. He considered the same evidence and thought himself invincible to cars. I had talked to him about this. It was on the tape. I went inside and got it and came back out to play it. I remembered him smiling when I asked if he didn't think he ought to get as far away from cars as he could and never go near another one.

"They are dangerous as hell," his voice was saying from the recorder. "I realize that now more than I used to. When you get out there racing, though, you don't think about things like that. You worry about the car holding together. You worried about that car, every little thing on it."

"No fear at all?"

"Anybody's scared a little bit, you know. You have that little feeling. It always bothers me most right before the race starts. But if I ever get scared, I'll quit. And if I ever feel like I'm endangering anybody else, I'll quit."

I was wishing that something had happened to scare him, but I knew it never could have. Then I remembered something that Ken Squier had told me a couple of months before.

"The stock car driver is the new American cowboy," he had said. "There aren't any new frontiers, not even the moon any more. The only thing left for these guys is to go a little deeper into that first turn."

Perhaps that was it. Even I had wanted to be a cowboy at one time, but I got over it. Maybe Larry Smith just never did.